Captain Clark, Chaboneau, Sacágawea, and Papoose in the Cloud-burst near the Great Falls, on June 29, 1805.

DAKOTA EDITION

THE
WINNING OF THE WEST

An Account of the Exploration and Settlement
of Our Country from the Alle-
ghanies to the Pacific

BY

THEODORE ROOSEVELT

IN SIX VOLUMES

VOLUME III

G. P. PUTNAM'S SONS
NEW YORK AND LONDON
The Knickerbocker Press
1908

CONTENTS

CHAPTER I

PAGE

THE MORAVIAN MASSACRE, 1779–1782   I

CHAPTER II

THE ADMINISTRATION OF THE CONQUERED FRENCH SET-
TLEMENTS, 1779–1783   32

CHAPTER III

KENTUCKY UNTIL THE END OF THE REVOLUTION, 1782–
1783   53

CHAPTER IV

THE HOLSTON SETTLEMENTS, 1777–1779   87

CHAPTER V

KING'S MOUNTAIN, 1780   119

CHAPTER VI

THE HOLSTON SETTLEMENTS TO THE END OF THE REVO-
LUTION, 1781–1783   186

CHAPTER VII

ROBERTSON FOUNDS THE CUMBERLAND SETTLEMENT,
1779–1780   221

CHAPTER VIII

THE CUMBERLAND SETTLEMENTS TO THE CLOSE OF THE
REVOLUTION, 1781–1783   255

iv Contents

CHAPTER IX

PAGE

WHAT THE WESTERNERS HAD DONE DURING THE REVO-
LUTION, 1783 274

APPENDICES:

APPENDIX A—TO CHAPTER III. 299
APPENDIX B—TO CHAPTER III. 304
APPENDIX C—TO CHAPTER VI. 306
APPENDIX D—TO CHAPTER VIII. 310
APPENDIX E—TO CHAPTER IX. 313
APPENDIX F—TO CHAPTER IX. 316

THE WINNING OF
THE WEST

CHAPTER I

THE MORAVIAN MASSACRE, 1779–1782

AFTER the Moravian Indians were led by
their missionary pastors to the banks of
the Muskingum they dwelt peacefully
and unharmed for several years. In Lord Dunmore's war special care was taken by the white
leaders that these Quaker Indians should not be
harmed; and their villages of Salem, Gnadenhutten, and Schönbrunn received no damage
whatever. During the early years of the Revolutionary struggle they were not molested, but
dwelt in peace and comfort in their roomy cabins
of squared timbers, cleanly and quiet, indus-
triously tilling the soil, abstaining from all strong
drink, schooling their children, and keeping the
Seventh Day as a day of rest. They sought to
observe strict neutrality, harming neither the
Americans nor the Indians, nor yet the allies of

the latter, the British and French at Detroit. They hoped thereby to offend neither side, and to escape unhurt themselves.

But this was wholly impossible. They occupied an utterly untenable position. Their villages lay midway between the white settlements southeast of the Ohio and the towns of the Indians round Sandusky, the bitterest foes of the Americans and those most completely under British influence. They were on the trail that the war-parties followed, whether they struck at Kentucky or at the valleys of the Alleghany and Monongahela. Consequently, the Sandusky Indians used the Moravian villages as half-way houses, at which to halt and refresh themselves whether starting on a foray or returning with scalps and plunder.

By the time the war had lasted four or five years both the wild or heathen Indians and the backwoodsmen had become fearfully exasperated with the unlucky Moravians. The Sandusky Indians were largely Wyandots, Shawnees, and Delawares, the latter being fellow-tribesmen of the Christian Indians; and so they regarded the Moravians as traitors to the cause of their kinsfolk, because they would not take up the hatchet against the whites. As they could not goad them into declaring war, they took malicious pleasure in trying to embroil them against their will, and on returning from raids against the settlements often passed through their towns solely to cast suspicion on them and to draw down the wrath of the backwoodsmen on their heads. The British at Detroit feared lest the Americans might use the Moravian villages as a basis from which to attack the lake posts; they also coveted their men as allies; and so the baser among their officers urged the Sandusky tribes to break up the villages and drive off the missionaries. The other Indian tribes likewise regarded them with angry contempt and hostility; the Iroquois once sent word to the Chippewas and Ottawas that they gave them the Christian Indians "to make broth of."

The Americans became even more exasperated. The war-parties that plundered and destroyed their homes, killing their wives, children, and friends with torments too appalling to mention, got shelter and refreshment from the Moravians,[1] —who, indeed, dared not refuse it. The backwoodsmen, roused to a mad frenzy of rage by the awful nature of their wrongs, saw that the Moravians rendered valuable help to their cruel and inveterate foes, and refused to see that the help was given with the utmost reluctance. Moreover, some of the young Christian Indians backslid and joined their savage brethren, accompanying them

[1] Heckewelder's *Narrative of the Mission of the United Brethren*, Philadelphia, 1820, p. 166.

on their war-parties and ravaging with as much
cruelty as any of their number.[1] Soon the frontiersmen began to clamor for the destruction of
the Moravian towns; yet for a little while they
were restrained by the Continental officers of the
few border forts, who always treated these harmless Indians with the utmost kindness.

On either side were foes, who grew less govern-
able day by day, and the fate of the hapless and
peaceful Moravians, if they continued to dwell on
the Muskingum, was absolutely inevitable. With
blind fatuity their leaders, the missionaries, refused to see the impending doom; and the poor,
simple Indians clung to their homes till destroyed.
The American commander at Pittsburg, Colonel
Gibson, endeavored to get them to come into the
American lines, where he would have the power,
as he already had the wish, to protect them;
he pointed out that where they were they served
in some sort as a shield to the wild Indians,
whom he had to spare so as not to harm the Moravians.[2] The Half King of the Wyandots, from
the other side, likewise tried to persuade them to
abandon their dangerous position, and to come
well within the Indian and British lines, saying:
"Two mighty and angry gods stand opposite to

---

[1] *Pennsylvania Packet* (Philadelphia, April 16, 1782);
Heckewelder, 180; Loskiel's *History of the Mission of the
United Brethren* (London, 1794), p. 172.   [2] Loskiel, p. 137.

each other with their mouths wide open, and you are between them, and are in danger of being crushed by one or the other, or by both." [1] But in spite of these warnings, and heedless of the safety that would have followed the adoption of either course, the Moravians followed the advice of their missionaries and continued where they were. They suffered greatly from the wanton cruelty of their red brethren; and their fate remains a monument to the cold-blooded and cowardly brutality of the borderers, a stain on frontier character that the lapse of time cannot wash away; but it is singular that historians have not yet pointed out the obvious truth, that no small share of the blame for their sad end should be put to the credit of the blind folly of their missionary leaders. Their only hope in such a conflict as was then raging was to be removed from their fatally dangerous position; and this the missionaries would not see. As long as they stayed where they were, it was a mere question of chance and time whether they would be destroyed by the Indians or the whites; for their destruction at the hands of either one party or the other was inevitable.

Their fate was not due to the fact that they were Indians; it resulted from their occupying an absolutely false position. This is clearly shown

[1] State Department MSS., No. 41, vol. iii., pp. 78, 79; extract from diary of Rev. David Zeisburger.

by what happened twenty years previously to a small community of non-resistant Christian whites. They were Dunkards—Quaker-like Germans—who had built a settlement on the Monongahela. As they helped neither side, both distrusted and hated them. The whites harassed them in every way, and the Indians finally fell upon and massacred them.[1] The fates of these two communities, of white Dunkards and red Moravians, were exactly parallel. Each became hateful to both sets of combatants, was persecuted by both, and finally fell a victim to the ferocity of the race to which it did not belong.

The conduct of the backwoodsmen towards these peaceful and harmless Christian Indians was utterly abhorrent, and will ever be a subject of just reproach and condemnation; and at first sight it seems incredible that the perpetrators of so vile a deed should have gone unpunished and almost unblamed. It is a dark blot on the character of a people that otherwise had many fine and manly qualities to its credit. But the extraordinary conditions of life on the frontier must be kept in mind before passing too severe a judgment. In the turmoil of the harassing and long-continued Indian war, and the consequent loosening of social bonds, it was inevitable that, as regards outside matters, each man should do what

[1] Withers, 59.

seemed right in his own eyes. The bad and the good alike were left free and untrammelled to follow the bent of their desires. The people had all they could do to beat off their savage enemies, and to keep order among themselves. They were able to impose but slight checks on ruffianism that was aimed at outsiders. There were plenty of good and upright men who would not harm any Indians wrongfully, and who treated kindly those who were peaceable. On the other hand, there were many of violent and murderous temper. These knew that their neighbors would actively resent any wrong done to themselves, but knew, also, that, under the existing conditions, they would at the worst do nothing more than openly disapprove of an outrage perpetrated on Indians.

The violence of the bad is easily understood. The indifference displayed towards their actions by the better men of the community, who were certainly greatly in the majority, is harder to explain. It rose from varying causes. In the first place, the long continuance of Indian warfare, and the unspeakable horrors that were its invariable accompaniments, had gradually wrought up many even of the best of the backwoodsmen to the point where they barely considered an Indian as a human being. The warrior was not to them a creature of romance. They knew him for what he was—filthy, cruel, lecherous, and faithless. He

sometimes had excellent qualities, but these they
seldom had a chance to see. They always met
him at his worst. To them he was in peace a
lazy, dirty, drunken beggar, whom they despised,
and yet whom they feared; for the squalid, con-
temptible creature might at any moment be
transformed into a foe whose like there was not to
be found in all the wide world for ferocity, cun-
ning, and blood-thirsty cruelty. The greatest Indians, chiefs like Logan and Cornstalk, who were
capable of deeds of the loftiest and most sublime
heroism, were also at times cruel monsters or
drunken good-for-nothings. Their meaner followers had only such virtues as belong to the human wolf—stealth, craft, tireless endurance, and
the courage that prefers to prey on the helpless,
but will fight to the death without flinching if
cornered.

Moreover, the backwoodsmen were a hard people—a people who still lived in an iron age. They
did not spare themselves, nor those who were dear
to them; far less would they spare their real or
possible foes. Their lives were often stern and
grim; they were wonted to hardship and suffering. In the histories or traditions of the different
families there are recorded many tales of how
they sacrificed themselves, and, in time of need,
sacrificed others. The mother who was a captive
among the Indians might lay down her life for her

child; but if she could not save it, and to stay with it forbade her own escape, it was possible that she would kiss it good-by and leave it to its certain fate, while she herself, facing death at every step, fled homewards through hundreds of miles of wilderness.[1] The man who daily imperilled his own life, would, if water was needed in the fort, send his wife and daughter to draw it from the spring round which he knew Indians lurked, trusting that the appearance of the women would make the savages think themselves undiscovered, and that they would therefore defer their attack.[2] Such people were not likely to spare their red-skinned foes. Many of their friends, who had

[1] See Hale's *Trans-Alleghany Pioneers*, the adventures of Mrs. Inglis. She was captured on the head-waters of the Kanawha, at the time of Braddock's defeat. The other inhabitants of the settlement were also taken prisoners or massacred by the savages, whom they had never wronged in any way. She was taken to the Big Bone Lick in Kentucky. On the way her baby was born, but she was not allowed to halt a day on account of this incident. She left it in the Indian camp, and made her escape in company with "an old Dutch woman." They lived on berries and nuts for forty days, while they made their way homewards. Both got in safely, though they separated after the old Dutch woman, in the extremity of hunger, had tried to kill her companion that she might eat her. When Cornstalk's party perpetrated the massacre of the Clendennins during Pontiac's war (see Stewart's "Narrative"), Mrs. Clendennin likewise left her baby to its death, and made her escape; her husband had previously been killed and his bloody scalp tied across her jaws as a gag.

[2] As at the siege of Bryan's Station.

never hurt the savages in any way, had perished, the victims of wanton aggression. They themselves had seen innumerable instances of Indian treachery. They had often known the chiefs of a tribe to profess warm friendship at the very moment that their young men were stealing and murdering. They grew to think of even the most peaceful Indians as merely sleeping wild beasts, and while their own wrongs were ever vividly before them, they rarely heard of or heeded those done to their foes. In a community where every strong, courageous man was a bulwark to the rest, he was sure to be censured lightly for merely killing a member of a loathed and hated race.

Many of the best of the backwoodsmen were Bible-readers, but they were brought up in a creed that made much of the Old Testament, and laid slight stress on pity, truth, or mercy. They looked at their foes as the Hebrew prophets looked at the enemies of Israel. What were the abominations because of which the Canaanites were destroyed before Joshua, when compared with the abominations of the red savages whose lands they, another chosen people, should in their turn inherit? They believed that the Lord was king for ever and ever, and they believed no less that they were but obeying His commandment as they strove mightily to bring about the day when the heathen should have perished out of the land;

for they had read in The Book that he was accursed who did the work of the Lord deceitfully, or kept his sword back from blood. There was many a stern frontier zealot who deemed all the red men, good and bad, corn ripe for the reaping. Such a one rejoiced to see his followers do to the harmless Moravians as the Danites once did to the people of Laish, who lived quiet and secure, after the manner of the Sidonians, and had no business with any man, and who yet were smitten with the edge of the sword, and their city burnt with fire.

Finally, it must not be forgotten that there were men on the frontier who did do their best to save the peaceful Indians, and that there were also many circumstances connected with the latter that justly laid them open to suspicion. When young backsliding Moravians appeared in the war-parties, as cruel and murderous as their associates, the whites were warranted in feeling doubtful as to whether their example might not infect the remainder of their people. War-parties, whose members in dreadful derision left women and children impaled by their trail to greet the sight of the pursuing husbands and fathers, found food and lodging at the Moravian towns. No matter how reluctant the aid thus given, the pursuers were right in feeling enraged, and in demanding that the towns should be removed to where they could no longer give comfort to the enemy. When the missionaries refused to consent to this removal, they thereby became helpers of the hostile Indians; they wronged the frontiersmen, and they still more grievously wronged their own flocks.

They certainly had ample warning of the temper of the whites.   Colonel Brodhead was in command at Fort Pitt until the end of 1781.   At the time that General Sullivan ravaged the country of the Six Nations, he had led a force up the Alleghany and created a diversion by burning one or two Iroquois towns.   In 1781, he led a successful expedition against a town of hostile Delawares on the Muskingum, taking it by surprise and surrounding it so completely that all within were captured.   Sixteen noted warriors and marauders were singled out and put to death.   The remainder fared but little better, for, while marching back to Fort Pitt, the militia fell on them and murdered all the men, leaving only the women and children.   The militia also started to attack the Moravians, and were only prevented by the strenuous exertions of Brodhead.   Even this proof of the brutality of their neighbors was wasted on the missionaries.

The first blow the Moravians received was from the wild Indians.   In the fall of this same year (1781) their towns were suddenly visited by a horde of armed warriors, horsemen and footmen,

from Sandusky and Detroit. Conspicuous among
them were the Wyandots under the Half King;
the Delawares, also led by a famous chief, Captain
Pipe; and a body of white rangers from Detroit,
including British, French, and tories, commanded
by the British Captain Elliott, and flying the British flag.[1] With them came also Shawnees, Chippewas, and Ottawas. All were acting in pursuance
of the express orders of the commandant at Detroit.[2] These warriors insisted on the Christian
Indians abandoning their villages and accompanying them back to Sandusky and Detroit; and they
destroyed many of the houses, and much of the
food for the men and the fodder for the horses and
cattle. The Moravians begged humbly to be left
where they were, but without avail. They were
forced away to Lake Erie, the missionaries being
taken to Detroit, while the Indians were left on
the plains of Sandusky. The wild Indians were
very savage against them, but the British commandant would not let them be seriously maltreated,[3] though they were kept in great want and
almost starved.

A few Moravians escaped, and remained in their
villages; but these, three or four weeks later, were

[1] State Department MSS., No. 41, vol. iii., p. 77.
[2] Haldimand MSS.   De Peyster to Haldimand, October 5th
and 21st, 1781; McKee to De Peyster, October 18th.
[3] *Ibid.*   December 11, 1781.

captured by a small detachment of American militia, under Colonel David Williamson, who had gone out to make the Moravians either move farther off or else come in under the protection of Fort Pitt.   Williamson accordingly took the Indians to the fort, where the Continental commander, Colonel John Gibson, at once released them, and sent them back to the villages unharmed.[1]   Gibson had all along been a firm friend of the Moravians.   He had protected them against the violence of the borderers, and had written repeated and urgent letters to Congress and to his superior officers, asking that some steps might be taken to protect the friendly Christian Indians.[2] In the general weakness and exhaustion, however, nothing was done; and, as neither the State nor Federal government took any steps to protect them, and as their missionaries refused to learn wisdom, it was evident that the days of the Moravians were numbered.   The failure of the government to protect them was perhaps inevitable, but was certainly discreditable.

The very day after Gibson sent the Christian Indians back to their homes, several murders were committed near Pittsburg, and many of the fron-

[1] Gibson was the old friend of the chief Logan.   It is only just to remember that the Continental officers at Fort Pitt treated the Moravians even better than did the British officers at Detroit.

[2] Haldimand MSS. Jan. 22, 1780 (*Intercepted letters*).

tiersmen insisted that they were done with the good will or connivance of the Moravians. The settlements had suffered greatly all summer long, and the people clamored savagely against all the Indians, blaming both Gibson and Williamson for not having killed or kept captive their prisoners. The ruffianly and vicious, of course, clamored louder than any; the mass of people who are always led by others chimed in, in a somewhat lower key; and many good men were silent for the reasons given already. In a frontier democracy, military and civil officers are directly dependent upon popular approval, not only for their offices, but for what they are able to accomplish while filling them. They are therefore generally extremely sensitive to either praise or blame. Ambitious men flatter and bow to popular prejudice or opinion, and only those of genuine power and self-reliance dare to withstand it. Williamson was physically a fairly brave officer and not naturally cruel; but he was weak and ambitious, ready to yield to any popular demand, and, if it would advance his own interests, to connive at any act of barbarity.[1] Gibson, however, who was a very different man, paid no heed to the cry raised against him.

---

[1] This is the most favorable estimate of his character, based on what Doddridge says (p. 260). He was a very despicable person, but not the natural brute the missionaries painted him.

With incredible folly, the Moravians refused to heed even such rough warnings as they had received. During the long winter they suffered greatly from cold and hunger; at Sandusky, and before the spring of 1782 opened, a hundred and fifty of them returned to their deserted villages.

That year the Indian outrages on the frontiers began very early. In February, there was some fine weather; and while it lasted, several families of settlers were butchered, some under circumstances of peculiar atrocity. In particular, four Sandusky Indians having taken some prisoners, impaled two of them, a woman and a child, while on their way to the Moravian towns, where they rested and ate, prior to continuing their journey with their remaining captives. When they left they warned the Moravians that white men were on their trail.[1] A white man who had just escaped this same impaling party also warned the Moravians that the exasperated borderers were preparing a party to kill them; and Gibson, from Fort Pitt, sent a messenger to them, who, however, arrived too late. But the poor Christian Indians, usually very timid, now, in the presence of a real danger, showed a curious apathy; their senses were numbed and dulled by their misfortunes, and they quietly awaited their doom.[2]

It was not long deferred. Eighty or ninety

[1] Heckewelder, 311.   [2] Loskiel, 176.

frontiersmen, under Williamson, hastily gathered together to destroy the Moravian towns. It was, of course, just such an expedition as most attracted the brutal, the vicious, and the ruffianly; but a few decent men, to their shame, went along. They started in March, and on the third day reached the fated villages. That no circumstance might be wanting to fill the measure of their infamy, they spoke the Indians fair, assuring them that they meant well, and spent an hour or two in gathering together those who were in Salem and Gnadenhutten, putting them all in two houses at the latter place. Those at the third town of Schönbrunn got warning and made their escape.

As soon as the unsuspecting Indians were gathered in the two houses, the men in one, the women and children in the other, the whites held a council as to what should be done with them. The great majority were for putting them instantly to death. Eighteen men protested, and asked that the lives of the poor creatures should be spared; and then withdrew, calling God to witness that they were innocent of the crime about to be committed. By rights they should have protected the victims at any hazard. One of them took off with him a small Indian boy, whose life was thus spared. With this exception, only two lads escaped.

When the murderers told the doomed Moravians their fate, they merely requested a short delay in which to prepare themselves for death. They asked one another's pardon for whatever wrongs they might have done, knelt down and prayed, kissed one another farewell, "and began to sing hymns of hope and of praise to the Most High." Then the white butchers entered the houses and put to death the ninety-six men, women, and children that were within their walls. More than a hundred years have passed since this deed of revolting brutality; but even now a just man's blood boils in his veins at the remembrance. It is impossible not to regret that fate failed to send some strong war-party of savages across the path of these inhuman cowards, to inflict on them the punishment they so richly deserved. We know that a few of them were afterwards killed by the Indians; it is a matter of keen regret that any escaped.

When the full particulars of the affair were known all the best leaders of the border, almost all the most famous Indian fighters, joined in denouncing it.[1] Nor is it right that the whole of the frontier folk should bear the blame for the deed.

---

[1] Colonel James Smith, then of Kentucky, in 1799 calls it "an act of barbarity equal to any thing I ever knew to be committed by the savages themselves, except the burning of prisoners."

It is a fact, honorable and worthy of mention, that the Kentuckians were never implicated in this or any similar massacre.[1]

But at the time, and in their own neighborhood —the corner of the Upper Ohio valley where Pennsylvania and Virginia touch—the conduct of the murderers of the Moravians roused no condemnation. The borderers at first felt about it as the English whigs originally felt about the massacre of Glencoe. For some time the true circumstances of the affair were not widely known among them. They were hot with wrath against all the red-skinned race; and they rejoiced to hear of the death of a number of treacherous Indians who pretended to be peaceful, while harboring and giving aid and comfort to, and occasionally letting

[1] The Germans of up-country North Carolina were guilty of as brutal massacres as the Scotch-Irish backwoodsmen of Pennsylvania. See Adair, 245. There are two or three individual instances of the barbarity of Kentuckians—one being to the credit of McGarry,—but they are singularly few when the length and the dreadful nature of their Indian wars are taken into account. Throughout their history the Kentucky pioneers had the right on their side in their dealings with the Indians. They were not wanton aggressors; they entered upon vacant hunting-grounds, to which no tribe had a clear title, and to which most even of the doubtful titles had been fairly extinguished. They fought their foes fiercely, with varying fortune, and eventually wrested the land from them; but they very rarely wronged them; and for the numerous deeds of fearful cruelty that were done on Kentucky soil, the Indians were in almost every case to blame.

their own young men join, bands of avowed murderers. Of course, the large wicked and disorderly element was loud in praise of the deed. The
decent people, by their silence, acquiesced.

A terrible day of reckoning was at hand; the
retribution fell on but part of the real criminals,
and bore most heavily on those who were innocent of any actual complicity in the deed of evil.
Nevertheless, it is impossible to grieve overmuch
for the misfortune that befell men who freely for-
gave and condoned such treacherous barbarity.

In May, a body of four hundred and eighty Pennsylvania and Virginia militia gathered at Mingo
Bottom, on the Ohio, with the purpose of marching against and destroying the towns of the hostile
Wyandots and Delawares in the neighborhood of
the Sandusky River. The Sandusky Indians were
those whose attacks were most severely felt by
that portion of the frontier; and for their repeated and merciless ravages they deserved the
severest chastisement. The expedition against
them was from every point of view just; and it
was undertaken to punish them, and without any
definite idea of attacking the remnant of the Moravians who were settled among them. On the
other hand, the militia included in their ranks
most of those who had taken part in the murderous expedition of two months before; this fact,
and their general character, made it certain that

the peaceable and inoffensive Indians would, if encountered, be slaughtered as pitilessly as their hostile brethren.

How little the militia volunteers disapproved of the Moravian massacre was shown when, as was the custom, they met to choose a leader. There were two competitors for the place, Williamson, who commanded at the massacre, being one, and he was beaten by only five votes. His successful opponent, Colonel William Crawford, was a fairly good officer, a just and upright man, but with no special fitness for such a task as that he had undertaken. Nor were the troops he led of very good stuff [1]; though they included a few veteran Indian fighters.

[1] A minute and exhaustive account of Crawford's campaign is given by Mr. C. W. Butterfield in his *Expedition against Sandusky* (Cincinnati: Robert Clarke & Co., 1873). Mr. Butterfield shows conclusively that the accepted accounts are wholly inaccurate, being derived from the reports of the Moravian missionaries, whose untruthfulness (especially Heckewelder's) is clearly demonstrated. He shows the apocryphal nature of some of the pretended narratives of the expedition, such as two in *The American Pioneer*, etc. He also shows how inaccurate McClung's "sketches" are—for McClung was like a host of other early western annalists, preserving some valuable facts in a good deal of rubbish, and having very little appreciation indeed of the necessity of so much as approximate accuracy. Only a few of these early western historians had the least conception of the value of evidence or of the necessity of sifting it, or of weighing testimony.

On the other hand, Mr. Butterfield is drawn into grave errors, by his excessive partisanship of the borderers. He passes

The party left Mingo Bottom on the 25th of May. After nine days' steady marching through the unbroken forests they came out on the Sandusky plains; billowy stretches of prairie, covered with high coarse grass and dotted with islands of timber. As the men marched across them they roused quantities of prairie fowl, and saw many geese and sand-hill cranes, which circled about in the air, making a strange clamor.

Crawford hoped to surprise the Indian towns; but his progress was slow, and the militia every now and then fired off their guns. The spies of the savages dogged his march and knew all his movements[1]; and runners were sent to Detroit asking help. This the British commandant at once granted. He sent to the assistance of the threatened tribes a number of lake Indians and a body of rangers and Canadian volunteers, under Captain Caldwell.[2]

lightly over their atrocious outrages, colors favorably many of their acts, and praises the generalship of Crawford and the soldiership of his men; when in reality the campaign was badly conducted from beginning to end, and reflected discredit on most who took part in it; Crawford did poorly, and the bulk of his men acted like unruly cowards.

[1] Heckewelder, 336. Butterfield shows conclusively that there is not the slightest ground to accept Heckewelder's assertion that Crawford's people openly declared that "no Indian was to be spared, friend or foe."

[2] Haldimand MSS. De Peyster to Haldimand, May 14, 1782.

On the fourth of June Crawford's troops reached one of the Wyandot towns. It was found to be deserted; and the army marched on to try and find the others. Late in the afternoon, in the midst of the plains, near a cranberry marsh, they encountered Caldwell and his Detroit rangers, together with about two hundred Delawares, Wyandots, and lake Indians.[1] The British and Indians united certainly did not much exceed three hundred men; but they were hourly expecting reinforcements, and decided to give battle. They were posted in a grove of trees, from which they were driven by the first charge of the Americans. A hot skirmish ensued, in which, in spite of Crawford's superiority in force, and of the exceptionally favorable nature of the country, he failed to gain any marked advantage. His troops, containing so large a leaven of the murderers of the Moravians, certainly showed small fighting capacity when matched against armed men who could defend themselves. After the first few minutes neither side gained nor lost ground.

Of the Americans five were killed and nineteen wounded—in all twenty-four. Of their opponents the rangers lost two men killed and three wounded, Caldwell being one of the latter; and

[1] *Ibid.* Official report of Lieutenant John Turney, of the rangers, June 7, 1782.

the Indians four killed and eight wounded—in all seventeen.[1]

That night Crawford's men slept by their watch-fires in the grove, their foes camping round about in the open prairie. Next morning the British and Indians were not inclined to renew the attack; they wished to wait until their numbers were increased. The only chance of the American militia was to crush their enemies before reinforcements arrived, yet they lay supine and idle all day long, save for an occasional harmless skirmish. Crawford's generalship was as poor as the soldiership of his men.

In the afternoon the Indians were joined by one hundred and forty Shawnees. At sight of this accession of strength the disspirited militia gave up all thought of anything but flight, though they were still equal in numbers to their foes. That night they began a hurried and disorderly retreat. The Shawnees and Delawares attacked them in the darkness, causing some loss and great confusion, and a few of the troops got into the marsh. Many thus became scattered, and next morning there were only about three hundred

[1] *Ibid.* Probably some of this loss occurred on the following day. I rely on Butterfield for the American loss, as he quotes Irvine's official report, etc. He of course wrote without knowledge of the British reports; and his account of the Indian losses and numbers is all wrong. He fails signally in his effort to prove that the Americans behaved bravely.

men left together in a body. Crawford himself was among the missing, so Williamson took command, and hastily continued the retreat. The savages did not make a very hot pursuit; nevertheless, in the afternoon of that day a small number of Indians and Detroit rangers overtook the Americans. They were all mounted. A slight skirmish followed, and the Americans lost eleven men, but repulsed their pursuers.[1] After this they suffered little molestation, and reached Mingo Bottom on the thirteenth of the month.[2]

Many of the stragglers came in afterwards. In all about seventy either died of their wounds, were killed outright, or were captured. Of the latter, those who were made prisoners by the Wyandots were tomahawked and their heads stuck on poles; but if they fell into the hands of the Shawnees or Delawares they were tortured to death with fiendish cruelty. Among them was Crawford himself, who had become separated from the main body when it began its disorderly night retreat. After abandoning his jaded horse he started homewards on foot, but fell into the hands of a small party of Delawares, together with a companion named Knight.

[1] Who were probably at this point much fewer in number than the Americans; Butterfield says the reverse, but his account is untrustworthy on these matters.

[2] As Butterfield shows, Heckewelder's account of Crawford's whole expedition is a piece of sheer romancing.

These two prisoners were taken to one of the Delaware villages. The Indians were fearfully exasperated by the Moravian massacre[1]; and some of the former Moravians, who had rejoined their wild tribesmen, told the prisoners that from that time on not a single captive should escape torture. Nevertheless, it is likely that Crawford would have been burned in any event, and that most of the prisoners would have been tortured to death even had the Moravians never been harmed; for such had always been the custom of the Delawares.

The British, who had cared for the remnants of the Moravians, now did their best to stop the cruelties of the Indians,[2] but could accomplish little or nothing. Even the Mingos and Hurons told them that though they would not torture any Americans, they intended thenceforth to put all their prisoners to death.[3]

Crawford was tied to the stake in the presence of a hundred Indians. Among them were Simon Girty, the white renegade, and a few Wyandots. Knight, Crawford's fellow-captive, was a horrified spectator of the awful sufferings which he knew he was destined by his captors ultimately to share. Crawford, stripped naked, and with his hands

[1] Haldimand MSS. De Peyster to Haldimand, June 23, 1782.
[2] *Ibid.* August 18, 1782.   [3] *Ibid.* December 1, 1782.

bound behind him, was fastened to a high stake
by a strong rope; the rope was long enough for
him to walk once or twice round the stake.   The
fire, of small hickory poles, was several yards
from the post, so as only to roast and scorch him.
Powder was shot into his body, and burning
fagots shoved against him, while red embers were
strewn beneath his feet.   For two hours he bore
his torments with manly fortitude, speaking low,
and beseeching the Almighty to have mercy on
his soul.   Then he fell down, and his torturers
scalped him and threw burning coals on his bare
skull.   Rising, he walked about the post once or
twice again, and then died.   Girty and the Wyandots looked on, laughing at his agony, but
taking no part in the torture.   When the news of
his dreadful fate was brought to the settlements,
it excited the greatest horror, not only along the
whole frontier, but elsewhere in the country; for
he was widely known, was a valued friend of Washington, and was everywhere beloved and respected.

Knight, a small and weak-looking man, was
sent to be burned at the Shawnee towns, under the
care of a burly savage.   Making friends with the
latter, he lulled his suspicions, the more easily because the Indian evidently regarded so small a
man with contempt; and then, watching his opportunity, he knocked his guard down and ran off

into the woods, eventually making his way to the settlements.

Another of the captives, Slover by name, made a more remarkable escape. Slover's life history had been curious. When a boy eight years old, living near the springs of the Kanawha, his family was captured by Indians, his brother alone escaping. His father was killed, and his two little sisters died of fatigue on the road to the Indian villages; his mother was afterwards ransomed. He lived twelve years with the savages, at first in the Miami towns, and then with the Shawnees. When twenty years old he went to Fort Pitt, where, by accident, he was made known to some of his relations. They pressed him to rejoin his people, but he had become so wedded to savage life that he at first refused. At last he yielded, however, took up his abode with the men of his own color, and became a good citizen and a worthy member of the Presbyterian Church. At the outbreak of the Revolution he served fifteen months as a Continental soldier, and when Crawford started against the Sandusky Indians, he went along as a scout.

Slover, when captured, was taken round to various Indian towns, and saw a number of his companions, as well as other white prisoners, tomahawked or tortured to death. He was examined publicly about many matters at several Great Councils—for he spoke two or three different

Indian languages fluently. At one of the councils he heard the Indians solemnly resolve to take no more prisoners thereafter, but to kill all Americans, of whatever sex and age, some of the British agents from Detroit signifying their approval of the resolution.[1]

At last he was condemned to be burned, and was actually tied to the stake. But a heavy shower came on, so wetting the wood that it was determined to reprieve him till the morrow. That night he was bound and put in a wigwam under the care of three warriors. They laughed and chatted with the prisoner, mocking him, and describing to him with relish all the torments that he was to suffer. At last they fell asleep, and, just before daybreak, he managed to slip out of his rope and escape, entirely naked.

[1] Slover asserts that it was taken in consequence of a message sent advising it by the commandant at Detroit. This is doubtless untrue; the commandant at Detroit did what he could to stop such outrages, although many of his more reckless and uncontrollable subordinates very probably pursued an opposite course. The ignorant and violently prejudiced backwoodsmen naturally believed all manner of evil of their British foes; but it is singular that writers who ought to be well informed should even now continue to accept all their wild assertions as unquestioned facts. The conduct of the British was very bad; but it is silly to describe it in the terms often used. The year after their escape Slover dictated, and Knight wrote, narratives of their adventures, which were together published in book form at Philadelphia in 1783. They are very interesting.

Catching a horse he galloped away sitting on a piece of old rug, and guiding the animal with the halter. He rode steadily and at speed for seventy miles, until his horse dropped dead under him late in the afternoon. Springing off, he continued the race on foot. At last he halted, sick and weary; but, when he had rested an hour or two, he heard afar off the halloo of his pursuers. Struggling to his feet he continued his flight, and ran until after dark. He then threw himself down and snatched a few hours' restless sleep, but, as soon as the moon rose, he renewed his run for life, carefully covering his trail whenever possible. At last he distanced his enemies. For five days he went straight through the woods, naked, bruised, and torn, living on a few berries and a couple of small crawfish he caught in a stream. He could not sleep nor sometimes even lie down at night because of the mosquitoes. On the morning of the sixth day he reached Wheeling, after experiencing such hardship and suffering as none but an iron will and frame could have withstood.

Until near the close of the year 1782 the frontiers suffered heavily. A terrible and deserved retribution fell on the borderers for their crime in failing to punish the dastardly deed of Williamson and his associates. The Indians were roused to savage anger by the murder of the Moravians, and were greatly encouraged by their easy defeat of

Crawford's troops. They harassed the settlements all along the Upper Ohio, the Alleghany,
and the Monongahela, and far into the interior,[1]
burning, ravaging, and murdering, and bringing
dire dismay to every lonely clearing and every
palisaded hamlet of rough log cabins.

[1] *Virginia State Papers*, iii., 235.

CHAPTER II

THE ADMINISTRATION OF THE CONQUERED FRENCH
SETTLEMENTS, 1779–1783

T HE Virginian Government took immediate
steps to provide for the civil administra-
tion of the country Clark had conquered.
In the fall of 1778 the entire region northwest of the
Ohio was constituted the county of Illinois, with
John Todd as county lieutenant or commandant.

Todd was a firm friend and follower of Clark's
and had gone with him on his campaign against
Vincennes. It therefore happened that he received his commission while at the latter town,
early in the spring of '79. In May, he went to
Kaskaskia, to organize the county; and Clark,
who remained military commandant of the Virginia State troops that were quartered in the district, was glad to turn over the civil government
to the charge of his old friend.

Together with his commission, Todd received a
long and excellent letter of instructions from Governor Patrick Henry. He was empowered to
choose a deputy-commandant and officers for the
militia; but the judges and officers of the court

were to be elected by the people themselves. He
was given large discretionary power, Henry im-
pressing upon him with especial earnestness the
necessity to "cultivate and conciliate the French
and Indians."[1] With this end in view, he was
bidden to pay special heed to the customs of the
creoles, to avoid shocking their prejudices, and to
continually consult with their most intelligent and
upright men. He was to co-operate in every way
with Clark and his troops, while at the same time
the militia were to be exclusively under his own
control. The inhabitants were to have strict
justice done them if wronged by the troops; and
Clark was to put down rigorously any licentious-
ness on the part of the soldiers. The wife and
children of the former British commandant—the
creole Rocheblave—were to be treated with particular respect, and not suffered to want for anything. He was exhorted to use all his diligence
and ability to accomplish the difficult task set
him. Finally, Henry advised him to lose no opportunity of inculcating in the minds of the
French the value of the liberty the Americans

[1] See Colonel John Todd's "Record Book," while County
Lieutenant of Illinois. There is an MS. copy in Colonel
Durrett's library at Louisville. It is our best authority for
these years in Illinois. The substance of it is given on pp.
49–68 of Mr. Edward G. Mason's interesting and valuable
pamphlet on *Illinois in the 18th Century* (Chicago, Fergus
Printing Co., 1881).

brought them, as contrasted with "the slavery to which the Illinois was destined" by the British.

This last sentence was proved by subsequent events to be a touch of wholly unconscious but very grim humor. The French were utterly unsuited for liberty, as the Americans understood the term, and to most of them the destruction of British rule was a misfortune. The bold, self-reliant, and energetic spirits among them, who were able to become Americanized, and to adapt themselves to the new conditions, undoubtedly profited immensely by the change. As soon as they adopted American ways, they were received by Americans on terms of perfect and cordial equality, and they enjoyed a far higher kind of life than could possibly have been theirs formerly, and achieved a much greater measure of success. But most of the creoles were helplessly unable to grapple with the new life. They had been accustomed to the paternal rule of priest and military commandant, and they were quite unable to govern themselves, or to hold their own with the pushing, eager, and often unscrupulous newcomers. So little able were they to understand precisely what the new form of government was, that when they went down to receive Todd as commandant, it is said that some of them, joining in the cheering, from force of habit cried: "*Vive le roi.*"

For the first year of Todd's administration, while Clark still remained in the county as commandant of the State troops, matters went fairly well. Clark kept the Indians completely in check, and when some of them finally broke out, and started on a marauding expedition against Cahokia, he promptly repulsed them, and by a quick march burned their towns on Rock River, and forced them to sue for peace.[1]

Todd appointed a Virginian, Richard Winston, as commandant at Kaskaskia; all his other appointees were Frenchmen. An election was forthwith held for justices—to the no small astonishment of the creoles, unaccustomed as they were to American methods of self-government. Among those whom they elected as judges and court-officers were some of the previously appointed militia captains and lieutenants, who thus held two positions. The judges governed their decisions solely by the old French laws and customs.[2] Todd at once made the court proceed to business. On its recommendation, he granted licenses to trade to men of assured loyalty. He also issued a proclamation in reference to new settlers taking up lands. Being a shrewd man, he clearly foresaw the ruin that was sure to arise from the new Virginia land laws as applied to Kentucky, and he

[1] In the beginning of 1780. Bradford MS.
[2] State Department MSS., No. 48, p. 51.

feared the inrush of a horde of speculators, who would buy land with no immediate intention of settling thereon. Besides, the land was so fertile in the river bottoms that he deemed the amount Virginia allotted to each person excessive. So he decreed that each settler should take up his land in the shape of one of the long narrow French farms that stretched back from the water front, and that no claim should contain a greater number of acres than did one of these same farms. This proclamation undoubtedly had a very good effect.

He next wrestled steadily, but much less successfully, with the financial question. He attempted to establish a land bank, as it were, setting aside a great tract of land to secure certain issues of Continental money. The scheme failed, and in spite of his public assurance that the Continental currency would shortly be equal in value to gold and silver, it swiftly sank until it was not worth two cents on the dollar.

This wretched and worthless paper-money which the Americans brought with them was a perfect curse to the country. Its rapid depreciation made it almost impossible to pay the troops, or to secure them supplies, and as a consequence they became disorderly and mutinous. Two or three prominent creoles, who were devoted adherents to the American cause, made loans of silver to the Virginian Government, as represented by Clark, thereby helping him materially in the prosecution of his campaign. Chief among these public-spirited patriots were Francis Vigo and the priest Gibault, both of them already honorably mentioned. Vigo advanced nearly nine thousand dollars in specie,—piastres or Spanish milled dollars,—receiving in return bills on the "Agent of Virginia," which came back protested for want of funds; and neither he nor his heirs ever got a dollar of what was due them. He did even more. The creoles at first refused to receive anything but peltries or silver for their goods; they would have nothing to do with the paper, and to all explanations as to its uses, simply answered "that their commandants never made money." [1] Finally, they were persuaded to take it on Vigo's personal guaranty, and his receiving it in his store. Even he, however, could not buoy it up long.

Gibault likewise [2] advanced a large sum of money, parted with his titles and beasts, so as to set a good example to his parishioners, and, with the same purpose, furnished goods to the troops at ordinary prices, taking the paper in exchange as if it had been silver. In consequence, he lost

[1] Law's *Vincennes*, pp. 49, 126. For some inscrutable reason, by the way, the Americans for a long time persisted in speaking of the place as *St.* Vincennes.

[2] See his letter to Governor St. Clair, May 1, 1790.

over fifteen hundred dollars, was forced to sell his
only two slaves, and became almost destitute;
though in the end he received from the government a tract of land which partially reimbursed
him.   Being driven to desperate straits, the priest
tried a rather doubtful shift.   He sold, or pretended to sell, a great natural meadow, known as
la prairie du pont, which the people of Cahokia
claimed as a common pasture for their cattle.   His
conduct drew forth a sharp remonstrance from
the Cahokians, in the course of which they frankly
announced that they believed the priest should
confine himself to ecclesiastical matters, and
should not meddle with land grants, especially
when the land he granted did not belong to him.[1]

It grew steadily more difficult to get the creoles
to furnish supplies; Todd had to forbid the ex-
portation of any provisions whatever, and, finally,
the soldiers were compelled to levy on all that they
needed.   Todd paid for these impressed goods, as
well as for what the contractors furnished, at the
regulation prices—one third in paper money and
two thirds in peltries; and thus the garrisons at
Kaskaskia, Cahokia, and Vincennes were supplied
with powder, lead, sugar, flour, and, above all,
hogsheads of taffia, of which they drank an inordi-
nate quantity.

[1] State Department MSS., No. 48, p. 41.   Petition of J. B.
La Croix and A. Girardin.

The justices did not have very much work; in most of the cases that came before them the plaintiff and defendant were both of the same race. One piece of recorded testimony is rather amusing, being to the effect that "Monsieur Smith est un grand vilain coquin."[1]

Yet there are two entries in the proceedings of the creole courts for the summer of 1779, as preserved in Todd's "Record Book," which are of startling significance. To understand them it must be remembered that the creoles were very ignorant and superstitious, and that they one and all, including, apparently, even their priests, firmly believed in witchcraft and sorcery. Some of their negro slaves had been born in Africa, the others had come from the Lower Mississippi or the West Indies; they practised the strange rites of voudooism, and a few were adepts in the art of poisoning. Accordingly, the French were always on the look-out lest their slaves should, by spell or poison, take their lives. It must also be kept in mind that the pardoning power of the commandant did not extend to cases of treason or murder,— a witchcraft trial being generally one for murder, —and that he was expressly forbidden to interfere with the customs and laws, or go counter to the prejudices of the inhabitants.

---

[1] This and most of the other statements for which no authority is quoted are based on Todd's MS. "Record Book."

At this time the creoles were smitten by a sudden epidemic of fear that their negro slaves were trying to bewitch and poison them. Several of the negroes were seized and tried, and in June two were condemned to death. One, named Moreau, was sentenced to be hung outside Cahokia. The other, a Kaskaskian slave named Manuel, suffered a worse fate. He was sentenced "to be chained to a post at the water-side, and there to be burnt alive and his ashes scattered." [1]   These two sentences, and the directions for their immediate execution, reveal a dark chapter in the early history of Illinois. It seems a strange thing that, in the United States, three years after the Declaration of Independence, men should have been burnt and hung for witchcraft, in accordance with the laws and with the decision of the proper court. The fact that the victim, before being burned, was forced to make "honorable fine" at the door of the Catholic church shows that the priest at least acquiesced in the decision. The blame justly resting on the Puritans of seventeenth-century New England must likewise fall on the Catholic French of eighteenth-century Illinois.

Early in the spring of 1780 Clark left the country;

[1] The entries merely record the sentences, with directions that they be immediately executed. But there seems very little doubt that they were for witchcraft, or voudooism, probably with poisoning at the bottom—and that they were actually carried out. See Mason's pamphlet, p. 59.

he did not again return to take command, for after
visiting the fort on the Mississippi, and spending
the summer in the defence of Kentucky, he went
to Virginia to try to arrange for an expedition
against Detroit. Todd also left about the same
time, having been elected a Kentucky delegate
to the Virginia Legislature. He afterwards made
one or two flying visits to Illinois, but exerted
little influence over her destiny, leaving the man-
agement of affairs entirely in the hands of his
deputy, or lieutenant-commandant for the time
being. He usually chose for this position either
Richard Winston, the Virginian, or else a creole
named Thimothé Demunbrunt.

Todd's departure was a blow to the country;
but Clark's was a far more serious calamity. By
his personal influence he had kept the Indians in
check, the creoles contented, and the troops well
fed and fairly disciplined. As soon as he went,
trouble broke out. The officers did not know how
to support their authority; they were very im-
provident, and one or two became implicated in
serious scandals. The soldiers soon grew turbulent, and there was constant clashing between
the civil and military rulers. Gradually the mass
of the creoles became so angered with the Americans that they wished to lay their grievances before the French Minister at Philadelphia; and
many of them crossed the Mississippi and settled

under the Spanish flag. The courts rapidly lost
their power, and the worst people, both Americans
and creoles, practised every kind of rascality with
impunity. All decent men joined in clamoring
for Clark's return; but it was impossible for him
to come back. The freshets and the maladminis-
tration combined to produce a dearth, almost a
famine, in the land. The evils were felt most
severely in Vincennes, where Helm, the captain of
the post, though a brave and capable man, was
utterly unable to procure supplies of any kind.
He did not hear of Clark's success against Piqua
and Chillicothe until October. Then he wrote to
one of the officers at the Falls, saying that he was
"sitting by the fire with a piece of lightwood and
two ribs of an old buflloe, which is all the meat we
have seen this many days. I congratulate your
success against the Shawanohs, but there's never
doubts where that brave Col. Clark commands;
we well know the loss of him in Illinois. . . . Excuse Haste as the Lightwood's Just out and mouth
watering for part of the two ribs." [1]

In the fall of 1780 a Frenchman, named la
Balme, led an expedition composed purely of
creoles against Detroit. He believed that he
could win over the French at that place to his
side, and thus capture the fort as Clark had cap-

[1] Calendar of *Virginia State Papers*, vol. i., pp. 380, 382,
383, October 24–29, 1780.

tured Vincennes. He raised some fifty volunteers round Cahokia and Kaskaskia, perhaps as many more on the Wabash, and marched to the Maumee River. Here he stopped to plunder some British traders; and in November the neighboring Indians fell on his camp, killed him and thirty or forty of his men, and scattered the rest.[1] His march had been so quick and unexpected that it rendered the British very uneasy, and they were much rejoiced at his discomfiture and death.

The following year a new element of confusion was added. In 1779, Spain declared war on Great Britain. The Spanish commandant at New Orleans was Don Bernard de Galvez, one of the very few strikingly able men Spain has sent to the western hemisphere during the past two centuries. He was bold, resolute, and ambitious; there is reason to believe that at one time he meditated a separation from Spain, the establishment of a Spanish-American empire, and the founding of a new imperial house. However this may be, he threw himself heart and soul into the war against Britain; and attacked British West Florida with a fiery energy worthy of Wolfe or Montcalm. He favored the Americans; but it was patent to all that he favored them only the better to harass the British.[2]

Besides the creoles and the British garrisons,

[1] Haldimand MSS. De Peyster to Haldimand, November 16, 1780.   [2] State Department MSS., No. 50, p. 109.

there were quite a number of American settlers in West Florida. In the immediate presence of Spanish and Indian foes, these, for the most part, remained royalists. In 1778, a party of armed Americans, coming down the Ohio and Mississippi, tried to persuade them to turn whig, but, becoming embroiled with them, the militant missionaries were scattered and driven off. Afterwards the royalists fought among themselves; but this was a mere faction quarrel, and was soon healed. Towards the end of 1779, Galvez, with an army of Spanish and French creole troops, attacked the forts along the Mississippi—Manchac, Baton Rouge, Natchez, and one or two smaller places,—speedily carrying them and capturing their garrisons of British regulars and royalist militia. During the next eighteen months he laid siege to and took Mobile and Pensacola. While he was away on his expedition against the latter place, the royalist Americans around Natchez rose and retook the fort from the Spaniards; but at the approach of Galvez they fled in terror, marching overland towards Georgia, then in the hands of the tories. On the way they suffered great loss and damage from the Creeks and Choctaws.

The Spanish commander at St. Louis was inspired by the news of these brilliant victories to try if he, too, could not gain a small wreath at the expense of Spain's enemies. Clark had already become thoroughly convinced of the duplicity of the Spaniards on the upper Mississippi; he believed that they were anxious to have the British retake Illinois, so that they, in their turn, might conquer and keep it.[1]   They never had the chance to execute this plan; but, on January 2, 1781, a Spanish captain, Don Eugénio Pierro, led a hundred and twenty men, chiefly Indians and creoles, against the little French village, or fur post, of St. Joseph, where they burned the houses of one or two British traders, claimed the country round the Illinois River as conquered for the Spanish king, and forthwith returned to St. Louis, not daring to leave a garrison of any sort behind them, and being harassed on their retreat by the Indians. On the strength of this exploit Spain afterwards claimed a large stretch of country to the east of the Mississippi.   In reality it was a mere plundering foray.   The British at once retook possession of the place, and, indeed, were for some time ignorant whether the raiders had been Americans or Spaniards.[2]   Soon after the recapture, the Detroit authorities[3] sent a scouting party to dislodge

[1] Clark to Todd, March, 1780. *Virginia State Papers*, vol. i., p. 338.

[2] Haldimand MSS.   Haldimand to De Peyster, April 10, 1781.   Report of Council at St. Joseph, March 11, 1781.

[3] *Ibid*.   Haldimand to De Peyster, May 19, 1782.   This is the first record of an effort to make a permanent settlement at Chicago.

some Illinois people who had attempted to make a settlement at Chicago.

At the end of the year 1781 the unpaid troops in Vincennes were on the verge of mutiny, and it was impossible longer even to feed them, for the inhabitants themselves were almost starving. The garrison was therefore withdrawn; and immediately the Wabash Indians joined those of the Miami, the Sandusky, and the Lakes in their raids on the settlements.[1] By this time, however, Cornwallis had surrendered at Yorktown, and the British were even more exhausted than the Americans. Some of the French partisans of the British at Detroit, such as Rocheblave and Lamothe, who had been captured by Clark, were eager for revenge, and desired to be allowed to try and retake Vincennes and the Illinois; they saw that the Americans must either be exterminated or else the land abandoned to them.[2] But the British commandant was in no condition to comply with their request, or to begin offensive operations. Clark had not only conquered the land, but he had held it firmly while he dwelt therein; and even when his hand was no longer felt, the order he had established took some little time before crumbling. Meanwhile, his presence at the Falls, his raids into

[1] *Virginia State Papers*, vol. iii., p. 502.

[2] Haldimand MSS. Letter of Rocheblave, October 7, 1781; of Lamothe, April 24, 1782.

the Indian country, and his preparations for an onslaught on Detroit kept the British authorities at the latter place fully occupied, and prevented their making any attempt to recover what they had lost. By the beginning of 1782, the active operations of the Revolutionary War were at an end, and the worn-out British had abandoned all thought of taking the offensive anywhere, though the Indian hostilities continued with unabated vigor. Thus the grasp with which the Americans held the conquered country was not relaxed until all danger that it would be taken from them had ceased.

In 1782, the whole Illinois region lapsed into anarchy and confusion. It was, perhaps, worst at Vincennes, where the departure of the troops had left the French free to do as they wished. Accustomed for generations to a master, they could do nothing with their new-found liberty beyond making it a curse to themselves and their neighbors. They had been provided with their own civil government in the shape of their elective court, but the judges had literally no idea of their proper functions as a governing body to administer justice. At first they did nothing whatever beyond meet and adjourn. Finally, it occurred to them that perhaps their official position could be turned to their own advantage. Their townsmen were much too poor to be plundered;

but there were vast tracts of fertile wild land on every side, to which, as far as they knew, there was no title, and which speculators assured them would ultimately be of great value.   Vaguely remembering Todd's opinion, that he had power to interfere under certain conditions with the settlement of the lands, and concluding that he had delegated this power, as well as others, to themselves, the justices of the court proceeded to make immense grants of territory, reciting that they did so under "*les pouvoirs donnés a Mons'rs Les Magistrats de la cour de Vincennes par le Snr. Jean Todd, colonel et Grand Judge civil pour les États Unis*"; Todd's title having suffered a change and exaltation in their memories.   They granted one another about fifteen thousand square miles of land round the Wabash; each member of the court in turn absenting himself for the day on which his associates granted him his share.

This vast mass of virgin soil they sold to speculators at nominal prices, sometimes receiving a horse or a gun for a thousand acres.   The speculators, of course, knew that their titles were worthless, and made haste to dispose of different lots at very low prices to intending settlers.   These small buyers were those who ultimately suffered by the transaction, as they found they had paid for worthless claims.   The speculators reaped the richest harvest; and it is hard to decide whether to be amused or annoyed at the childish and transparent rascality of the French creoles.[1]

In the Illinois country proper the troops, the American settlers, speculators, and civil officials, and the creole inhabitants all quarrelled together indiscriminately. The more lawless newcomers stole horses from the quieter creoles; the worst among the French, the idle *coureurs de bois*, *voyageurs*, and trappers plundered and sometimes killed the peaceable citizens of either nationality. The soldiers became little better than an unruly mob; some deserted, or else, in company with other ruffians, both French and American, indulged in furious and sometimes murderous orgies, to the terror of the creoles who had property. The civil authorities, growing day by day weaker, were finally shorn of all power by the military. This, however, was in nowise a quarrel between the French and the Americans. As already explained, in Todd's absence the position of deputy was sometimes filled by a creole and sometimes by an American. He had been particular to caution them in writing to keep up a good understanding with the officers and troops, adding, as a final warning: "If this is not the case you will be unhappy." Unfortunately for one of the deputies, Richard Winston, he failed to keep up the

[1] State Department MSS., Nos. 30 and 48. Law's *Vincennes.*

good understanding, and, as Todd had laconically
foretold, he in consequence speedily became very
"unhappy." We have only his own account of
the matter. According to this, in April, 1782, he
was taken out of his house "in despite of the civil
authority, disregarding the laws and on the mali-
tious alugation of Jno. Williams and Michel Pe-
vante." Thus a Frenchman and an American
joined in the accusation, for some of the French
supported the civil, others the military, authorities. The soldiers had the upper hand, however,
and Winston records that he was forthwith "confined by tyrannick military force." From that
time the authority of the laws was at an end, and
as the officers of the troops had but little control,
every man did what pleased him best.

In January, 1781, the Virginia Legislature
passed an act ceding to Congress, for the benefit
of the United States, all of Virginia's claim to the
territory northwest of the Ohio; but the cession
was not consummated until after the close of the
war with Great Britain, and the only immediate
effect of the act was to still further derange affairs
in Illinois. The whole subject of the land ces-
sions of the various States, by which the northwest territory became federal property, and the
heart of the Union, can best be considered in treating of post-Revolutionary times.

The French creoles had been plunged in chaos.

In their deep distress they sent to the powers that the chances of war had set above them petition after petition, reciting their wrongs and praying that they might be righted. There is one striking difference between these petitions and the similar requests and complaints made from time to time by the different groups of American settlers west of the Alleghanies. Both alike set forth the evils from which the petitioners suffered, and the necessity of governmental remedy. But whereas the Americans invariably asked that they be allowed to govern themselves, being delighted to undertake the betterment of their condition on their own account, the French, on the contrary, habituated through generations to paternal rule, were more inclined to request that somebody fitted for the task should be sent to govern them. They humbly asked Congress either to "immediately establish some form of government among them, and appoint officers to execute the same," or else "to nominate commissioners to repair to the Illinois and inquire into the situation." [1]

One of the petitions is pathetic in its showing of the bewilderment into which the poor creoles were thrown as to who their governors really were. It requests "their Sovereign Lords," [2] whether of

[1] State Department MSS., No. 30, p. 453. Memorial of François Carbonneaux, agent for the inhabitants of Illinois.
[2] "*Nos Souverains Seigneurs.*" The letter is ill written

the Congress of the United States or of the Province of Virginia, whichever might be the owner of the country, to nominate "a lieutenant or a governor, whomever it may please our Lords to send us." [1]   The letter goes on to ask that this governor may speak French, so that he may preside over the court; and it earnestly beseeches that the laws may be enforced and crime and wrong-doing put down with a strong hand.

The conquest of the Illinois territory was fraught with the deepest and most far-reaching benefits to all the American people; it likewise benefited, in at least an equal degree, the boldest and most energetic among the French inhabitants, those who could hold their own among freemen, who could swim in troubled waters; but it may well be doubted whether to the mass of the ignorant and simple creoles it was not a curse rather than a blessing.

and worse spelt, in an extraordinary French patois.   State Department MSS., No. 30, page 459.   It is dated December 3, 1782.   Many of the surnames attached are marked with a cross ; others are signed.   Two are given respectively as "*Bienvenus fils*" and "*Blouin fils*."

[1] *Ibid.*,"*de nomer un lieutenant ou un gouverneur tel qu'il plaira a nos Seigneurs de nous l'envoyer.*"

CHAPTER III

SEVENTEEN hundred and eighty-two proved to be Kentucky's year of blood. The British at Detroit had strained every nerve to drag into the war the entire Indian population of the Northwest. They had finally succeeded in arousing even the most distant tribes—not to speak of the twelve thousand savages immediately tributary to Detroit.[1] So lavish had been the expenditure of money and presents to secure the good will of the savages and enlist their active services against the Americans, that it had caused serious complaint at headquarters.[2]

Early in the spring the Indians renewed their forays; horses were stolen, cabins burned, and women and children carried off captive. The people were confined closely to their stockaded forts, from which small bands of riflemen sallied to patrol the country. From time to time these encountered marauding parties, and in the fights

[1] Haldimand MSS. Census for 1782, 11,402.

[2] *Ibid.* Haldimand to De Peyster, April 10, October 6, 1781.

that followed sometimes the whites, sometimes the reds, were victorious.

One of these conflicts attracted wide attention on the border because of the obstinacy with which it was waged and the bloodshed that accompanied it. In March a party of twenty-five Wyandots came into the settlements, passed Boonsborough, and killed and scalped a girl within sight of Estill's Station. The men from the latter, also to the number of twenty-five, hastily gathered under Captain Estill, and after two days' hot pursuit overtook the Wyandots. A fair stand-up fight followed, the better marksmanship of the whites being offset, as so often before, by the superiority their foes showed in sheltering themselves. At last victory declared for the Indians. Estill had despatched a lieutenant and seven men to get round the Wyandots and assail them in the rear; but either the lieutenant's heart or his judgment failed him; he took too long, and meanwhile the Wyandots closed in on the others, killing nine, including Estill, and wounding four, who, with their unhurt comrades, escaped. It is said that the Wyandots themselves suffered heavily.[1]

[1] Of course not as much as their foes. The backwoodsmen (like the regular officers of both the British and American armies in similar cases, as at Grant's and St. Clair's defeats) were fond of consoling themselves for their defeats by snatching at any wild tale of the losses of the victors. In

These various ravages and skirmishes were but the prelude to a far more serious attack. In July, the British captains Caldwell and McKee came down from Detroit with a party of rangers, and gathered together a great army of over a thousand Indians [1]—the largest body of either red men or white that was ever mustered west of the Alleghanies during the Revolution. They meant to strike at Wheeling; but while on their march thither were suddenly alarmed by the rumor that Clark intended to attack the Shawnee towns.[2] They at once countermarched, but on reaching the threatened towns found that the alarm had been groundless. Most of the savages, with characteristic fickleness of temper, then declined to go farther; but a body of somewhat over three hundred Hurons and Lake Indians remained. With these and their Detroit rangers, Caldwell and McKee crossed the Ohio and marched into Kentucky, to attack the small forts of Fayette County.

the present instance, it is even possible that the loss of the Wyandots was very light instead of very heavy.

[1] Haldimand MSS. Letter from Captain Caldwell, August 26, 1782; and letter of Captain McKee, August 28, 1782. These two letters are very important as they give for the first time the British and Indian accounts of the battle of the Blue Licks; I print them as Appendices A and B.

[2] This rumor was caused by Clark's gunboat, which, as will be hereafter mentioned, had been sent up to the mouth of the Licking; some Shawnees saw it, and thought Clark was preparing for an inroad.

Fayette lay between the Kentucky and the Ohio
rivers, and was then the least populous and most
exposed of the three counties into which the growing young commonwealth was divided.   In 1782
it contained but five of the small stockaded towns
in which all the early settlers were obliged to
gather.   The best defended and most central was
Lexington, round which were grouped the other
four—Bryan's (which was the largest), McGee's,
McConnell's, and Boon's.   Boon's Station, sometimes called Boon's new station, where the tranquil, resolute old pioneer at that time dwelt, must
not be confounded with his former fort of Boonsborough, from which it was several miles distant,
north of the Kentucky.   Since the destruction of
Martin's and Ruddle's stations on the Licking,
Bryan's on the south bank of the Elkhorn was left
as the northernmost outpost of the settlers.   Its
stout, loopholed palisades enclosed some forty
cabins, there were strong blockhouses at the corners, and it was garrisoned by fifty good riflemen.

These five stations were held by backwoodsmen
of the usual Kentucky stamp, from the up-
country of Pennsylvania, Virginia, and North
Carolina.   Generations of frontier life had made
them with their fellows the most distinctive and
typical Americans on the continent, utterly different from their old-world kinsfolk.   Yet they still
showed strong traces of the covenanting spirit,

which they drew from the Irish-Presbyterian, the master strain in their mixed blood. For years they had not seen the inside of a church; nevertheless, mingled with men who were loose of tongue and life, there still remained many Sabbath-keepers and Bible-readers, who studied their catechisms on Sundays, and disliked almost equally profane language and debauchery.[1]

An incident that occurred at this time illustrates well their feelings. In June, a fourth of the active militia of the county was ordered on duty, to scout and patrol the country. Accordingly, forty men turned out under Captain Robert Patterson. They were given ammunition, as well as two pack-horses, by the Commissary Department. Every man was entitled to pay for the time he was out. Whether he would ever get it was problematical; at the best it was certain to be given him in worthless paper-money. Their hunters kept them supplied with game, and each man carried a small quantity of parched corn.

The company was ordered to the mouth of the Kentucky to meet the armed row-boat sent by Clark from the Falls. On the way Patterson was much annoyed by a "very profane, swearing man" from Bryan's Station, named Aaron Reynolds. Reynolds was a good-hearted, active young fellow, with a biting tongue, not only given to many

[1] McAfee MSS.

oaths, but likewise skilled in the rough, coarse banter so popular with the backwoodsmen. After having borne with him four days Patterson made up his mind that he would have to reprove him, and, if no amendment took place, send him home. He waited until, at a halt, Reynolds got a crowd round him, and began to entertain them "with oaths and wicked expressions," whereupon he promptly stepped in "and observed to him that he was a very wicked and profane man," and that both the company as well as he, the Captain, would thank him to desist. On the next day, however, Reynolds began to swear again; this time Patterson not only reproved him severely, but also tried the effect of judicious gentleness, promising to give him a quart of spirits on reaching the boat if he immediately "quit his profanity and swearing." Four days afterwards they reached the boat, and Aaron Reynolds demanded the quart of spirits. Patterson suggested a doubt as to whether he had kept his promise, whereupon Reynolds appealed to the company, then on parade, and they pronounced in his favor, saying that they had not heard him swear since he was reproved. Patterson, who himself records the incident, concludes with the remark:[1] "The spirits

[1] Patterson's paper, given by Colonel John Mason Brown, in his excellent pamphlet on the *Battle of the Blue Licks* (Franklin, Ky., 1882). I cannot forbear again commenting

were drank." Evidently the company, who had so
impartially acted as judges between their fellow-
soldier and their superior officer, viewed with the
same equanimity the zeal of the latter and the
mixed system of command, entreaty, and reward by
which he carried his point. As will be seen, the event
had a striking sequel at the battle of the Blue Licks.

Throughout June and July the gunboat patrolled the Ohio, going up to the Licking. Parties
of backwoods riflemen, embodied as militia, likewise patrolled the woods, always keeping their
scouts and spies well spread out, and exercising
the greatest care to avoid being surprised. They
greatly hampered the Indian war bands, but now
and then the latter slipped by and fell on the people
they protected. Early in August such a band
committed some ravages south of the Kentucky,
beating back with loss a few militia who followed
it. Some of the Fayette men were about setting
forth to try and cut off its retreat, when the sudden and unlooked-for approach of Caldwell and
McKee's great war-party obliged them to bend all
their energies to their own defence.

The blow fell on Bryan's Station. The rangers
and warriors moved down through the forest with
the utmost speed and stealth, hoping to take this,

on the really admirable historic work now being done by
Messrs. Brown, Durrett, Speed, and the other members of
the Louisville "Filson Club."

the northernmost of the stockades, by surprise. If they had succeeded, Lexington and the three smaller stations north of the Kentucky would probably likewise have fallen.

The attack was made early on the morning of the 16th of August. Some of the settlers were in the corn-fields, and the rest inside the palisade of standing logs; they were preparing to follow the band of marauders who had gone south of the Kentucky. A few outlying Indian spies were discovered, owing to their eagerness; and the whites being put on their guard, the attempt to carry the fort by the first rush was, of course, foiled. Like so many other stations—but unlike Lexington—Bryan's had no spring within its walls; and as soon as there was reason to dread an attack, it became a matter of vital importance to lay in a supply of water. It was feared that to send the men to the spring would arouse suspicion in the minds of the hiding savages; and, accordingly, the women went down with their pails and buckets, as usual. The younger girls showed some nervousness, but the old housewives marshalled them as coolly as possible, talking and laughing together, and by their unconcern completely deceived the few Indians who were lurking nearby [1]—

[1] Caldwell's letter says that a small party of Indians was sent ahead first; the watering incident apparently took place immediately on this small party being discovered.

for the main body had not yet come up.   This advance guard of the savages feared that, if they attacked the women, all chance of surprising the fort would be lost; and so the water-carriers were suffered to go back unharmed.[1]   Hardly were they within the fort, however, when some of the Indians found that they had been discovered, and the attack began so quickly that one or two of the men who had lingered in the corn-fields were killed, or else were cut off and fled to Lexington; while, at the same time, swift-footed runners were sent

[1] This account rests on tradition; it is recorded by McClung, a most untrustworthy writer; his account of the battle of the Blue Licks is wrong from beginning to end. But a number of gentlemen in Kentucky have informed me that old pioneers whom they knew in their youth had told them that they had themselves seen the incident, and that, as written down, it was substantially true. So with Reynolds's speech to Girty. Of course, his exact words, as given by McClung, are incorrect; but Mr. L. C. Draper informs me that, in his youth, he knew several old men who had been in Bryan's Station and had themselves heard the speech. If it were not for this I should reject it, for the British accounts do not even mention that Girty was along, and do not hint at the incident. It was probably an unauthorized ruse of Girty's. The account of the decoy party of Indians is partially confirmed by the British letters. Both Marshall and McClung get this siege and battle very much twisted in their narratives; they make so many mistakes that it is difficult to know what portion of their accounts to accept. Nevertheless, it would be a great mistake to neglect all, even of McClung's statements. Thus Boon and Levi Todd in their reports make no mention of McGarry's conduct; and it might be supposed to be a traditional myth, but McClung's

out to carry the alarm to the different stockades and summon their riflemen to the rescue.

At first but a few Indians appeared, on the side of the Lexington road; they whooped and danced defiance to the fort, evidently inviting an attack. Their purpose was to lure the defenders into sallying out after them, when their main body was to rush at the stockade from the other side. But they did not succeed in deceiving the veteran Indian fighters who manned the heavy gates of the fort, stood behind the loopholed walls, or scanned the country round about from the high blockhouses at the corners. A dozen active young men were sent out on the Lexington road to carry on a mock skirmish with the decoy party, while the rest of the defenders gathered behind the wall on the opposite side. As soon as a noisy but harmless skirmish had been begun by the sallying party, the main body of warriors burst out of the woods and rushed towards the western gate. A single volley from the loopholes drove them back, while the sallying party returned at a run and entered

account is unexpectedly corroborated by Arthur Campbell's letter, hereafter to be quoted, which was written at the time.

Marshall is the authority for Netherland's feat at the ford. Boon's description in the Filson " Narrative" differs on several points from his earlier official letter, one or two grave errors being made; it is one of the incidents which shows how cautiously the Filson sketch must be used, though it is usually accepted as unquestionable authority.

the Lexington gate unharmed, laughing at the success of their counter stratagem.

The Indians surrounded the fort, each crawling up as close as he could find shelter behind some stump, tree, or fence. An irregular fire began, the whites, who were better covered, having slightly the advantage, but neither side suffering much. This lasted for several hours, until early in the afternoon a party from Lexington suddenly appeared and tried to force its way into the fort.

The runners who slipped out of the fort at the first alarm went straight to Lexington. There they found that the men had just started out to cut off the retreat of the marauding savages who were ravaging south of the Kentucky. Following their trail they speedily overtook the troops, and told of the attack on Bryan's. Instantly forty men under Major Levi Todd countermarched to the rescue. Being ignorant of the strength of the Indians they did not wait for the others, but pushed boldly forward, seventeen being mounted and the others on foot.[1]

The road from Lexington to Bryan's for the last few hundred yards led beside a field of growing corn, taller than a man. Some of the Indians were lying in this field when they were surprised by the sudden appearance of the rescuers, and promptly

[1] *Virginia State Papers*, vol. iii., p. 300. McClung's and Collins's accounts of this incident are pure romance.

fired on them.　Levi Todd and the horsemen, who were marching in advance, struck spurs into their steeds, and, galloping hard through the dust and smoke, reached the fort in safety.　The footmen were quickly forced to retreat towards Lexington; but the Indians were too surprised by the unlooked-for approach to follow, and they escaped with the loss of one man killed and three wounded.[1]

That night the Indians tried to burn the fort, shooting flaming arrows onto the roofs of the cabins and rushing up to the wooden wall with lighted torches.　But they were beaten off at each attempt.　When day broke they realized that it was hopeless to make any further effort, though they still kept up a desultory fire on the fort's defenders; they had killed most of the cattle and pigs and some of the horses, and had driven away the rest.

Girty, who was among the assailants, as a last shift, tried to get the garrison to surrender, assuring them that the Indians were hourly expecting reinforcements, including the artillery brought against Ruddle's and Martin's stations two years previously; and that if forced to batter down the walls no quarter would be given to any one. Among the fort's defenders was young Aaron Reynolds, the man whose profanity had formerly roused Captain Patterson's ire; and he now under-

[1] *Ibid.*

took to be spokesman for the rest. Springing up
into sight, he answered Girty in the tone of rough
banter so dear to the backwoodsmen, telling the
renegade that he knew him well, and despised him,
that the men in the fort feared neither cannon nor
reinforcements, and, if need be, could drive Girty's
tawny followers back from the walls with switches;
and he ended by assuring him that the whites, too,
were expecting help, for the country was roused,
and if the renegade and his followers dared to
linger where they were for another twenty-four
hours, their scalps would surely be sun-dried on
the roofs of the cabins.

The Indians knew well that the riflemen were
mustering at all the neighboring forts; and, as
soon as their effort to treat failed, they withdrew
during the forenoon of the 17th.[1] They were

[1] There are four contemporary official reports of this battle:
two American, those of Boon and Levi Todd; and two British,
those of McKee and Caldwell. All four agree that the fort
was attacked on one day, the siege abandoned on the next,
pursuit made on the third, and the battle fought on the
fourth. Boon and Todd make the siege begin on August 16th
and the battle take place on the 19th; Caldwell makes the
dates the 15th and 18th; McKee makes them the 18th and
21st. I therefore take Boon's and Todd's dates.

McClung and Marshall make the siege last three or four
days instead of less than two.

All the accounts of the battle of the Blue Licks, so far, have
been very inaccurate, because the British reports have never
been even known to exist, and the reports of the American
commanders, printed in the *Virginia State Papers*, have but

angry and sullen at their discomfiture.   Five of
their number had been killed and several wounded.
Of the fort's defenders four had been killed and
three wounded.   Among the children within its
walls during the siege there was one, the youngest,
a Kentucky-born baby, named Richard Johnson;
over thirty years later he led the Kentucky
mounted riflemen at the victory of the Thames,
when they killed not only the great Indian chief
Tecumseh, but also, it is said, the implacable renegade Simon Girty himself, then in extreme old age.

All this time the runners sent out from Bryan's
had been speeding through the woods, summoning help from each of the little walled towns.   The
Fayette troops quickly gathered.   As soon as
Boon heard the news he marched at the head of
the men of his station, among them his youngest
son Israel, destined shortly to be slain before his
eyes.   The men from Lexington, McConnell's, and
McGee's, rallied under John Todd, who was
County Lieutenant, and, by virtue of his commission in the Virginia line, the ranking officer of Kentucky, second only to Clark.   Troops also came
from south of the Kentucky River; Lieutenant-
Colonel Trigg and Majors McGarry and Harlan

recently seen the light.   Mr. Whitsitt, in his recent excellent
Life of Judge Wallace, uses the latter, but makes the great
mistake of incorporating into his narrative some of the most
glaring errors of McClung and Marshall.

led the men from Harrodsburg, who were soonest ready to march, and likewise brought the news that Logan, their County Lieutenant, was raising the whole force of Lincoln in hot haste, and would follow in a couple of days.

These bands of rescuers reached Bryan's Station on the afternoon of the day the Indians had left. The men thus gathered were the very pick of the Kentucky pioneers; sinewy veterans of border strife, skilled hunters and woodsmen, long wonted to every kind of hardship and danger. They were men of the most dauntless courage, but unruly and impatient of all control. Only a few of the cooler heads were willing to look before they leaped; and even their chosen and trusted leaders were forced to advise and exhort rather than to command them. All were eager for battle and vengeance, and were excited and elated by the repulse that had just been inflicted on the savages; and they feared to wait for Logan lest the foe should escape. Next morning they rode out in pursuit, one hundred and eighty-two strong, all on horseback, and all carrying long rifles. There was but one sword among them, which Todd had borrowed from Boon—a rough weapon, with short steel blade and buckhorn hilt. As with most frontier levies, the officers were in large proportion; for, owing to the system of armed settlement and half-military organization, each wooden

fort, each little group of hunters or hard-fighting
backwoods farmers, was forced to have its own
captain, lieutenant, ensign, and sergeant.[1]

The Indians, in their unhurried retreat, followed the great buffalo trace that led to the Blue

[1] For the American side of the battle of Blue Licks, I take
the contemporary reports of Boon, Levi Todd, and Logan,
Virginia State Papers, vol. iii., pp. 276, 280, 300, 333.   Boon
and Todd both are explicit that there were one hundred and
eighty-two riflemen, all on horseback, and substantially agree
as to the loss of the frontiersmen.   Later reports underesti-
mate both the numbers and loss of the whites.   Boon's
"Narrative," written two years after the event, from memory,
conflicts in one or two particulars with his earlier report.
Patterson, writing long afterwards, and from memory, falls
into gross errors, both as to the number of troops and as to
some of them being on foot; his account must be relied on
chiefly for his own adventures.   Most of the historians of Kentucky give the affair very incorrectly.   Butler follows Marshall;
but from the Clark papers he got the right number of men
engaged.   Marshall gives a few valuable facts; but he is all
wrong on certain important points.   For instance, he says
Todd hurried into action for fear Logan would supersede him
in the command; but in reality Todd ranked Logan.   Mc-
Clung's ornate narrative, that usually followed, hangs on the
very slenderest thread of truth; it is mainly sheer fiction.
Prolix, tedious Collins follows the plan he usually does when
his rancorous prejudices do not influence him, and presents
half a dozen utterly inconsistent accounts, with no effort
whatever to reconcile them.   He was an industrious collector
of information, and gathered an enormous quantity, some of
it very useful; he recorded with the like complacency authentic incidents of the highest importance and palpable
fabrications or irrelevant trivialities; and it never entered
his head to sift evidence or to exercise a little critical power
and judgment.

Licks, a broad road, beaten out through the forest by the passing and repassing of the mighty herds through countless generations. They camped on the farther side of the river; some of the savages had left, but there were still nearly three hundred men in all—Hurons and Lake Indians, with the small party of rangers.[1]

The backwoods horsemen rode swiftly on the trail of their foes, and before evening came to where they had camped the night before. A careful examination of the camp-fires convinced the leaders that they were heavily outnumbered; nevertheless they continued the pursuit, and overtook the savages early the following morning, the 19th of August.

As they reached the Blue Licks, they saw a few Indians retreating up a rocky ridge that led from the north bank of the river. The backwoodsmen halted on the south bank, and a short council was held. All turned naturally to Boon, the most

[1] Caldwell says that he had at first "three hundred Indians and Rangers," but that before the battle "nigh 100 Indians left." McKee says that there were at first "upwards of three hundred Hurons and Lake Indians," besides the rangers and a very few Mingos, Delawares, and Shawnees. Later, he says of the battle: "We were not much superior to them in numbers, they being about two hundred."

Levi Todd put the number of the Indians at three hundred, which was pretty near the truth; Boon thought it four hundred; later writers exaggerate wildly, putting it even at one thousand.

experienced Indian fighter present, in whose cool
courage and tranquil self-possession all confided.
The wary old pioneer strongly urged that no attack be made at the moment, but that they
should await the troops coming up under Logan.
The Indians were certainly much superior in
numbers to the whites; they were aware that
they were being followed by a small force, and
from the confident, leisurely way in which they
had managed their retreat, were undoubtedly
anxious to be overtaken and attacked. The hurried pursuit had been quite proper in the first
place, for if the Indians had fled rapidly they
would surely have broken up into different bands,
which could have been attacked on even terms,
while delay would have permitted them to go off
unscathed. But, as it was, the attack would be
very dangerous; while the delay of waiting for
Logan would be a small matter, for the Indians
could still be overtaken after he had arrived.

Well would it have been for the frontiersmen
had they followed Boon's advice.[1]   Todd and

[1] *Virginia State Papers*, iii., 337.   Colonel Campbell's letter
of October 3, 1782.   The letter is interesting as showing by
contemporary authority that Boon's advice and McGarry's
misbehavior are not mere matters of tradition.   It is possible
that there was some jealousy between the troops from Lincoln
and those from Fayette; the latter had suffered much from
the Indians, and were less rash in consequence; while many
of the Lincoln men were hot for instant battle.

Trigg both agreed with him, and so did many of the cooler riflemen—among others a man named Netherland, whose caution caused the young hotheads to jeer at him as a coward. But the decision was not suffered to rest with the three colonels who nominally commanded. Doubtless the council was hasty and tumultuous, being held by the officers in the open, closely pressed upon and surrounded by a throng of eager, unruly soldiers, who did not hesitate to offer advice or express dissatisfaction. Many of the more headlong and impatient among the bold spirits looking on desired instant action; and these found a sudden leader in Major Hugh McGarry. He was a man utterly unsuited to command of any kind; and his retention in office after repeated acts of violence and insubordination shows the inherent weakness of the frontier militia system. He not only chafed at control, but he absolutely refused to submit to it; and his courage was of a kind better fitted to lead him into a fight than to make him bear himself well after it was begun. He wished no delay, and was greatly angered at the decision of the council; nor did he hesitate to at once appeal therefrom. Turning to the crowd of backwoodsmen he suddenly raised the thrilling war-cry, and spurred his horse into the stream, waving his hat over his head and calling on all who were not cowards to follow him. The effect was electrical. In an instant all the hunter-soldiers plunged in after him with a shout, and splashed across the ford of the shallow river in huddled confusion.

Boon and Todd had nothing to do but follow. On the other side they got the men into order, and led them on, the only thing that was possible under the circumstances. These two leaders acted excellently throughout; and they now did their best to bring the men with honor through the disaster into which they had been plunged by their own headstrong folly.

As the Indians were immediately ahead, the array of battle was at once formed. The troops spread out into a single line. The right was led by Trigg, the centre by Colonel-Commandant Todd in person, with McGarry under him, and an advance guard of twenty-five men under Harlan in front; while the left was under Boon. The ground was equally favorable to both parties, the timber being open and good. But the Indians had the advantage in numbers, and were able to outflank the whites.

In a minute the spies brought word that the enemy were close in front.[2] The Kentuckians

[1] Levi Todd's letter, August 26, 1782.

[2] It is absolutely erroneous to paint the battle as in any way a surprise. Boon says: "We discovered the enemy lying in wait for us; on this discovery we formed our columns into a single line, and marched up in their front." There

galloped up at speed to within sixty yards of their
foes, leaped from their horses, and instantly gave
and received a heavy fire.[1] Boon was the first to
open the combat; and under his command the
left wing pushed the Indians opposite them back
for a hundred yards. The old hunter, of course,
led in person; his men stoutly backed him up,
and their resolute bearing and skilful marksmanship gave to the whites in this part of the line
a momentary victory. But on the right of the
Kentucky advance affairs went badly from the
start. The Indians were thrown out so as to completely surround Trigg's wing. Almost as soon
as the firing became heavy in front, crowds of
painted warriors rose from some hollows of long
grass that lay on Trigg's right and poured in a
close and deadly volley. Rushing forward, they
took his men in rear and flank, and rolled them
up on the centre, killing Trigg himself. Harlan's
advance guard was cut down almost to a man,
their commander being among the slain. The
centre was then assailed from both sides by over-
whelming numbers. Todd did all he could by
voice and example to keep his men firm and cover

was no ambush, except that of course the Indians, as usual,
sheltered themselves behind trees or in the long grass. From
what Boon and Levi Todd say, it is evident that the firing began on both sides at the same time. Caldwell says the Indians fired one gun, whereupon the Kentuckians fired a volley.

[1] Levi Todd's letter.

Boon's successful advance, but in vain.   Riding
to and fro on his white horse he was shot through
the body, and mortally wounded.   He leaped on
his horse again, but his strength failed him; the
blood gushed from his mouth; he leaned forward,
and fell heavily from the saddle.   Some say that
his horse carried him to the river, and that he fell
into its current.   With his death the centre gave
way; and of course Boon and the men of the left
wing, thrust in advance, were surrounded on
three sides.   A wild rout followed, every one pushing in headlong haste for the ford.   "He that
could remount a horse was well off; he that could
not, had no time for delay," wrote Levi Todd.
The actual fighting had only occupied five minutes.[1]

In a mad and panic race the Kentuckians
reached the ford, which was fortunately but a
few hundred yards from the battle-field, the Indians being mixed in with them.   Among the first
to cross was Netherland, whose cautious advice
had been laughed at before the battle.   No sooner
had he reached the south bank, than he reined up
his horse and leaped off, calling on his comrades
to stop and cover the flight of the others; and
most of them obeyed him.   The ford was choked
with a struggling mass of horsemen and footmen,
fleeing whites and following Indians.   Nether-

[1] *Ibid.*

land and his companions opened a brisk fire upon
the latter, forcing them to withdraw for a moment
and let the remainder of the fugitives cross in
safety. Then the flight began again. The check
that had been given the Indians allowed the
whites time to recover heart and breath. Retreating in groups or singly through the forest,
with their weapons reloaded, their speed of foot
and woodcraft enabled such as had crossed the
river to escape without further serious loss.

Boon was among the last to leave the field. His
son Israel was slain, and he himself was cut off
from the river; but, turning abruptly to one side,
he broke through the ranks of the pursuers, out-
ran them, swam the river, and returned unharmed
to Bryan's Station.

Among the men in the battle were Captain
Robert Patterson and young Aaron Reynolds.
When the retreat began Patterson could not get
a horse. He was suffering from some old and un-
healed wounds received in a former Indian fight,
and he speedily became exhausted. As he was on
the point of sinking, Reynolds suddenly rode up
beside him, jumped off his horse, and, without
asking Patterson whether he would accept, bade
him mount the horse and flee. Patterson did so,
and was the last man over the ford. He escaped
unhurt, though the Indians were running alongside and firing at him. Meanwhile Reynolds, who

possessed extraordinary activity, reached the river in safety and swam across. He then sat down to take off his buckskin trousers, which, being soaked through, hampered him much, and two Indians suddenly pounced on and captured him. He was disarmed and left in charge of one. Watching his chance, he knocked the savage down, and running off into the woods escaped with safety. When Patterson thanked him for saving his life, and asked him why he had done it, he answered, that ever since Patterson had reproved him for swearing, he had felt a strong and continued attachment for him. The effect of the reproof, combined with his narrow escape, changed him completely, and he became a devout member of the Baptist Church. Patterson, to show the gratitude he felt, gave him a horse and saddle and a hundred acres of prime land, the first he had ever owned.

The loss of the defeated Kentuckians had been very great. Seventy were killed outright, including Colonel Todd and Lieutenant-Colonel Trigg, the first and third in command. Seven were captured, and twelve of those who escaped were badly wounded.[1] The victors lost one of the Detroit Rangers (a Frenchman), and six Indians

[1] Those are the figures of Boon's official report, and must be nearly accurate. The later accounts give all sorts of numbers.

killed and ten Indians wounded.[1]   Almost their whole loss was caused by the successful advance of Boon's troops, save what was due to Netherland when he rallied the flying backwoodsmen at the ford.

Of the seven white captives four were put to death with torture, three eventually rejoining their people.   One of them owed his being spared to a singular and amusing feat of strength and daring.   When forced to run the gauntlet he, by his activity, actually succeeded in reaching the council-house unharmed; when almost to it, he turned, seized a powerful Indian and hurled him violently to the ground, and then, thrusting his head between the legs of another pursuer, he tossed him clean over his back, after which he sprang on a log, leaped up and knocked his heels together, crowed in the fashion of backwoods victors, and rallied the Indians as a pack of cowards.   One of the old chiefs immediately adopted him into the tribe as his son.

All the little forted villages north of the Kentucky, and those lying near its southern bank,

[1] Caldwell's letter.   But there are some slight discrepancies between the letters of McKee and Caldwell.   Caldwell makes the loss at Bryan's Station and the Blue Licks together twelve killed and twelve wounded; McKee says eleven killed and fourteen wounded.   Both exaggerate the American loss, but not as much as the Americans exaggerated that of the Indians, Boon in his "Narrative" giving the wildest of all the estimates.

were plunged into woe and mourning by the defeat.[1] In every stockade, in almost every cabin, there was weeping for husband or father, son, brother, or lover, The best and bravest blood in the land had been shed like water. There was no one who had not lost some close and dear friend, and the heads of all the people were bowed and their hearts sore stricken.

The bodies of the dead lay where they had fallen, on the hill-slope, and in the shallow river, torn by wolf, vulture, and raven, or eaten by fishes. In a day or two Logan came up with four hundred men from south of the Kentucky, tall Simon Kenton marching at the head of the troops, as captain of a company.[2] They buried the bodies of the slain on the battle-field, in long trenches, and heaped over them stones and logs. Meanwhile, the victorious Indians, glutted with vengeance, recrossed the Ohio and vanished into the northern forests.

[1] Arthur Campbell, in the letter already quoted, comments with intense bitterness on the defeat, which, he says, was due largely to McGarry's "vain and seditious expressions." He adds that Todd and Trigg had capacity but no experience, and Boon experience but no capacity, while Logan was "a dull and narrow body," and Clark "a sot, if nothing worse." Campbell was a Holston Virginian, an able but very jealous man, who disliked the Kentucky leaders and indeed had no love for Kentucky itself; he had strenuously opposed its first erection as a separate county.

[2] McBride's *Pioneer Biography*, i., 210.

The Indian ravages continued throughout the early fall months; all the outlying cabins were destroyed, the settlers were harried from the clearings, and a station on Salt River was taken by surprise, thirty-seven people being captured. Stunned by the crushing disaster at the Blue Licks, and utterly disheartened and cast down by the continued ravages, many of the settlers threatened to leave the country. The county officers sent long petitions to the Virginia Legislature, complaining that the troops posted at the Falls were of no assistance in checking the raids of the Indians, and asserting that the operations carried on by order of the Executive for the past eighteen months had been a detriment rather than a help. The utmost confusion and discouragement prevailed everywhere.[1]

At last the news of repeated disaster roused

[1] *Virginia State Papers*, iii., pp. 301, 331. Letter of William Christian, September 28th. Petition of Boon, Todd, Netherland, etc., September 11th. In Morehead's Address is a letter from Nathaniel Hart. He was himself, as a boy, witness of what he describes. His father, who had been Henderson's partner and bore the same name as himself, was from North Carolina. He founded in Kentucky a station known as White Oak Springs, and was slain by the savages during this year. The letter runs: "It is impossible at this day to make a just impression of the sufferings of the pioneers about the period spoken of. The White Oak Springs fort in 1782, with perhaps one hundred souls in it, was reduced in August to three fighting white men—and I can say with truth that for two or three weeks my mother's family never

Clark into his old-time energy.   He sent outrun-
ners through the settlements, summoning all the
able-bodied men to make ready for a blow at
the Indians.   The pioneers turned with eager relief towards the man who had so often led them to

unclothed themselves to sleep, nor were all of them within
that time at their meals together, nor was any household
business attempted.   Food was prepared and placed where
those who chose could eat.   It was the period when Bryant's
station was besieged, and for many days before and after that
gloomy event we were in constant expectation of being made
prisoners.   We made application to Col. Logan for a
guard and obtained one, but not until the danger was
measurably over.   It then consisted of two men only.
Col. Logan did everything in his power, as County Lieutenant, to sustain the different forts—but it was not a very
easy matter to order a married man from a fort where his
family was to defend some other when his own was in imminent danger.

"I went with my mother in January, 1783, to Logan's
station to prove my father's will.   He had fallen in the preceding July.   Twenty armed men were of the party.   Twenty-
three widows were in attendance upon the court to obtain
letters of administration on the estates of their husbands
who had been killed during the past year."

The letter also mentions that most of the original settlers
of the fort were from Pennsylvania, "orderly respectable
people and the men good soldiers.   But they were unaccustomed to Indian warfare, and the consequence was that
of some ten or twelve men all were killed but two or three."
This incident illustrates the folly of the hope, at one time
entertained, that the Continental troops, by settling in the
West on lands granted them, would prove a good barrier
against the Indians; the best Continentals in Washington's
army would have been almost as helpless as British grenadiers
in the woods.

success. They answered his call with quick enthusiasm; beeves, pack-horses, and supplies were offered in abundance, and every man who could shoot and ride marched to the appointed meeting-places. The men from the eastern stations gathered at Bryan's, under Logan; those from the western, at the Falls, under Floyd. The two divisions met at the mouth of the Licking, where Clark took supreme command. On the 4th of November, he left the banks of the Ohio, and struck off northward through the forest, at the head of one thousand and fifty mounted riflemen. On the tenth he attacked the Miami towns. His approach was discovered just in time to prevent a surprise. The Indians hurriedly fled to the woods, those first discovered raising the alarm-cry, which could be heard an incredible distance, and thus warning their fellows. In consequence, no fight followed, though there was sharp skirmishing between the advance guard and the hindermost Indians. Ten scalps were taken and seven prisoners, besides two whites being recaptured. Of Clark's men, one was killed and one wounded. The flight of the Indians was too hasty to permit them to save any of their belongings. All the cabins were burned, together with an immense quantity of corn and provisions—a severe loss at the opening of winter. McKee, the Detroit partisan, attempted to come to the rescue with what

Indians he could gather, but was met and his force promptly scattered.[1]   Logan led a detachment to the head of the Miami, and burned the stores of the British traders.   The loss to the savages at the beginning of cold weather was very great; they were utterly cast down and panic-stricken at such a proof of the power of the whites, coming as it did so soon after the battle of the Blue Licks. The expedition returned in triumph, and the Kentuckians completely regained their self-confidence; and though for ten years longer Kentucky suffered from the inroads of small parties of savages, it was never again threatened by a serious invasion.[2]

At the beginning of 1783, when the news of peace was spread abroad, immigration began to flow to Kentucky down the Ohio, and over the Wilderness Road, in a flood of which the volume dwarfed all former streams into rivulets.   Indian hostilities continued at intervals throughout this year,[3] but they were not of a serious nature. Most of the tribes concluded at least a nominal

[1] Haldimand MSS.   Letter of Alex. McKee, November 15, 1782.   He makes no attempt to hide the severity of the blow; his letter shows a curious contrast in tone to the one he wrote after the Blue Licks.   He states that the victory has opened the road to Detroit to the Americans.

[2] *Virginia State Papers*, p. 381.   Clark's letter of November 27, 1782.

[3] *Ibid.*, p. 522.   Letter of Benjamin Logan, August 11, 1783.

peace, and liberated over two hundred white prisoners, though they retained nearly as many more.[1] Nevertheless in the spring one man of note fell victim to the savages, for John Floyd was waylaid and slain as he was riding out with his brother. Thus, within the space of eight months, two of the three county lieutenants had been killed, in battle or ambush.

The inrush of new settlers was enormous,[2] and Kentucky fairly entered on its second stage of growth. The days of the first game-hunters and Indian fighters were over. By this year the herds of the buffalo, of which the flesh and hides had been so important to the early pioneers, were nearly exterminated; though bands still lingered in the remote recesses of the mountains, and they were plentiful in Illinois. The land claims began to clash, and interminable litigation followed. This rendered very important the improvement in the judiciary system which was begun in March by the erection of the three counties into the "District of Kentucky," with a court of common law and chancery jurisdiction co-extensive with its limits. The name of Kentucky, which had been dropped when the original county was divided into three, was thus permanently revived. The first court sat at Harrodsburg, but as there was

[1] *Pennsylvania Packet*, No. 1079, August 12, 1783.
[2] McAfee MSS.

no building where it could properly be held, it adjourned to the Dutch Reformed Meeting-house six miles off. The first grand jury empanelled presented nine persons for selling liquor without license, eight for adultery and fornication, and the clerk of Lincoln County for not keeping a table of fees; besides several for smaller offences.[1] A log court-house and a log jail were immediately built.

Manufactories of salt were started at the Licks, where it was sold at from three to five silver dollars a bushel.[2] This was not only used by the settlers for themselves, but for their stock, which ranged freely in the woods; to provide for the latter a tree was chopped down and the salt placed in notches or small troughs cut in the trunk, making it what was called a lick-log. Large grist-mills were erected at some of the stations; wheat crops were raised; and small distilleries were built. The gigantic system of river commerce of the Mississippi had been begun the preceding year by one Jacob Yoder, who loaded a flat-boat at the old Redstone fort, on the Monongahela, and drifted down to New Orleans, where he sold his goods and returned to the Falls of the Ohio by a roundabout course, leading through Havana, Philadelphia, and Pittsburg.   Several regular schools were started.   There were already

[1] Marshall, i., 159.   [2] McAfee MSS.

meeting-houses of the Baptist and Dutch Reformed congregations, the preachers spending the
week-days in clearing and tilling the fields, splitting rails, and raising hogs; in 1783 a permanent
Presbyterian minister arrived, and a log church
was speedily built for him. The sport-loving Kentuckians this year laid out a race-track at Shallow-
ford Station. It was a straight quarter-of-a-mile
course, within two hundred yards of the stockade;
at its farther end was a canebrake, wherein an
Indian once lay hid and shot a rider, who was
pulling up his horse at the close of a race. There
was still but one ferry, that over the Kentucky
River at Boonsborough; the price of ferriage was
three shillings for either man or horse. The surveying was still chiefly done by hunters, and much
of it was in consequence very loose indeed.[1]

The first retail store Kentucky had seen since
Henderson's, at Boonsborough, was closed in
1775, was established this year at the Falls; the
goods were brought in wagons from Philadelphia
to Pittsburg, and thence down the Ohio in flat-
boats. The game had been all killed off in the
immediate neighborhood of the town at the Falls,
and Clark undertook to supply the inhabitants
with meat, as a commercial speculation. Accordingly he made a contract with John Saunders,
the hunter who had guided him on his march to

[1] McAfee MSS. Marshall, Collins, Brown's pamphlets.

the Illinois towns; the latter had presumably forgiven his chief for having threatened him with death when he lost the way.   Clark was to furnish Saunders with three men, a pack-horse, salt, and ammunition; while Saunders agreed to do his best and be "assiduously industrious" in hunting. Buffalo beef, bear's meat, deer hams, and bear oil were the commodities most sought after.   The meat was to be properly cured and salted in camp, and sent from time to time to the Falls, where Clark was to dispose of it in market, a third of the price going to Saunders.   The hunting season was to last from November 1st to January 15th.[1]

Thus the settlers could no longer always kill their own game; and there were churches, schools, mills, stores, race-tracks, and markets in Kentucky.

[1] Original agreement in Durrett MSS.; bound volume of "Papers Relating to G. R. Clark." This particular agreement is for 1784; but apparently he entered into several such in different years.

CHAPTER IV

THE HOLSTON SETTLEMENTS, 1777–1779

THE history of Kentucky and the Northwest
has now been traced from the date of the
Cherokee war to the close of the Revolution. Those portions of the southwestern lands
that were afterwards made into the State of Tennessee had meanwhile developed with almost
equal rapidity. Both Kentucky and Tennessee
grew into existence and power at the same time,
and were originally settled and built up by precisely the same class of American backwoodsmen.
But there were one or two points of difference in
their methods of growth. Kentucky sprang up
afar off in the wilderness, and as a separate entity
from the beginning. The present State has
grown steadily from a single centre, which was
the part first settled; and the popular name of
the commonwealth has always been Kentucky.
Tennessee, on the other hand, did not assume her
present name until a quarter of a century after
the first exploration and settlement had begun;
and the State grew from two entirely distinct
centres. The first settlements, known as the

Watauga, or afterwards more generally as the
Holston, settlements, grew up while keeping close
touch with the Virginians, who lived around the
Tennessee headwaters, and also in direct communication with North Carolina, to which State
they belonged.   It was not until 1779 that a portion of these Holston people moved to the bend of
the Cumberland River and started a new community, exactly as Kentucky had been started
before.   At first this new community, known as
the Cumberland settlement, was connected by
only the loosest tie with the Holston settlements.
The people of the two places were not grouped together; they did not even have a common name.
The three clusters of Holston, Cumberland, and
Kentucky settlements developed independently of
one another, and though their founders were in
each case of the same kind, they were at first only
knit one to another by a lax bond of comradeship.

In 1776, the Watauga pioneers probably numbered some six hundred souls in all.   Having at
last found out the State in which they lived, they
petitioned North Carolina to be annexed thereto
as a district or county.   The older settlements
had evidently been jealous of them, for they
found it necessary to deny that they were, as had
been asserted, "a lawless mob"; it may be remarked that the Transylvanian colonists had been
obliged to come out with a similar statement.   In

their petition they christened their country "Washington District," in honor of the great chief whose name already stood first in the hearts of all Americans. The document was written by Sevier. It set forth the history of the settlers, their land purchases from the Indians, their successful effort at self-government, their military organization, with Robertson as captain, and finally their devotion to the Revolutionary cause; and recited their lack of proper authority to deal promptly with felons, murderers, and the like, who came in from the neighboring States, as the reason why they wished to become a self-governing portion of North Carolina.[1] The legislature of the State granted the prayer of the petitioners, Washington District was annexed, and four representatives therefrom, one of them Sevier, took their seats that fall in the Provincial Congress at Halifax. But no change whatever was made in the government of the Watauga people until 1777. In the spring of that year laws were passed providing for the establishment of courts of pleas and quarter sessions in the district, as well as for the appointment of justices of the peace, sheriffs, and militia officers; and in the fall the district was made a county, under the same name. The

[1] The petition, drawn up in the summer of '76, was signed by 112 men. It is given in full by Ramsey, p. 138. See also Phelan, p. 40.

boundaries of Washington County were the same
as those of the present State of Tennessee, and
seem to have been outlined by Sevier, the only
man who at that time had a clear idea as to what
should be the logical and definite limits of the
future State.

The nominal change of government worked
little real alteration in the way the Holston people
managed their affairs. The members of the old
committee became the justices of the new court,
and, with a slight difference in forms, proceeded
against all offenders with their former vigor.
Being eminently practical men, and not learned in
legal technicalities, their decisions seem to have
been governed mainly by their own ideas of justice, which, though genuine, were rough. As the
war progressed and the Southern States fell into
the hands of the British, the disorderly men who
had streamed across the mountains became
openly defiant towards the law. The tories gathered in bands, and every man who was impatient
of legal restraint, every murderer, horse-thief,
and highway robber in the community flocked to
join them. The militia who hunted them down
soon ceased to discriminate between tories and
other criminals, and the courts rendered decisions to the same effect. The caption of one in-
dictment that has been preserved reads against
the defendant "in toryism." He was condemned

to imprisonment during the war, half his goods was confiscated to the use of the State, and the other half was turned over for the support of his family. In another case the court granted a still more remarkable order, upon the motion of the State attorney, which set forth that fifteen hundred pounds, due to a certain H., should be retained in the hands of the debtor, because "there is sufficient reason to believe that the said H's estate will be confiscated to the use of the State for his misdemeanours."

There is something refreshing in the solemnity with which these decisions are recorded, and the evident lack of perception on the part of the judges that their records would, to their grandchildren, have a distinctly humorous side. To tories and evil-doers generally, the humor was doubtless very grim; but, as a matter of fact, the decisions, though certainly of unusual character, were needful and just. The friends of order had to do their work with rough weapons, and they used them most efficiently. Under the stress of so dire an emergency as that they confronted they were quite right in attending only to the spirit of law and justice, and refusing to be hampered by the letter. They would have discredited their own energy and hard common sense had they acted otherwise, and, moreover, would have inevitably failed to accomplish their purpose.

In the summer of '78, when Indian hostilities
almost entirely ceased, most of the militia were
disbanded, and, in consequence, the parties of
tories and horse-thieves sprang into renewed
strength, and threatened to overawe the courts
and government officers. Immediately the leaders
among the whigs, the friends of order and liberty,
gathered together and organized a vigilance committee. The committee raised two companies of
mounted riflemen, who were to patrol the country
and put to death all suspicious characters who re-
sisted them or who refused to give security to
appear before the committee in December. The
proceedings of the committee were thus perfectly
open; the members had no idea of acting secretly
or against order. It was merely that in a time of
general confusion they consolidated themselves
into a body which was a most effective, though
irregular, supporter of the cause of law. The
mounted riflemen scoured the country and broke
up the gangs of evil-doers, hanging six or seven of
the leaders, while a number of the less prominent
were brought before the committee, who fined
some and condemned others to be whipped or
branded. All of doubtful loyalty were compelled
to take the test oath.[1]

[1] Haywood, p. 58. As Haywood's narrative is based
largely on what the pioneers in their old age told him, his
dates, and especially his accounts of the numbers and losses

Such drastic measures soon brought about peace; but it was broken again and again by similar risings and disturbances. By degrees, most of the worst characters fled to the Cherokees or joined the British as their forces approached the up country. Until the battle of King's Mountain, the pioneers had to watch the tories as closely as they did the Indians; there was a constant succession of murders, thefts, and savage retaliations. Once a number of tories attempted to surprise and murder Sevier in his own house; but the plot was revealed by the wife of the leader, to whom Sevier's wife had shown great kindness in her time of trouble. In consequence, the tories were themselves surprised and their ringleaders slain. Every man in the country was obliged to bear arms the whole time, not only because of the Indian warfare, but also on account of the inveterate hatred and constant collisions between the whigs and the loyalists. Many dark deeds were done, and though the tories, with whom the criminal classes were in close alliance, were generally the first and chief offenders, yet the patriots cannot be held guiltless of murderous and ferocious

of the Indians in their battles, are often very inaccurate. In this very chapter he gives, with gross inaccuracy of detail, an account of one of Sevier's campaigns as taking place in 1779, whereas it really occurred after his return from King's Mountain. There is, therefore, need to be cautious in using him.

reprisals. They often completely failed to distinguish between the offenders against civil order and those whose only crime was an honest, if mistaken, devotion to the cause of the king.

Early in '78 a land office was opened in the Holston settlements, and the settlers were required to make entries according to the North Carolina land laws. Hitherto they had lived on their clearings undisturbed, resting their title upon purchase from the Indians and upon their own mutual agreements. The old settlers were given the prior right to the locations, and until the beginning of '79 in which to pay for them. Each head of a family was allowed to take up six hundred and forty acres for himself, one hundred for his wife, and one hundred for each of his children, at the price of forty shillings per hundred acres, while any additional amount cost at the rate of one hundred shillings, instead of forty. All of the men of the Holston settlements were at the time in the service of the State as militia, in the campaign against the Indians; and when the land office was opened, the money that was due them sufficed to pay for their claims. They thus had no difficulty in keeping possession of their lands, much to the disappointment of the land speculators, many of whom had come out at the opening of the office. Afterwards, large tracts were given as bounty, or in lieu of pay, to the Revolutionary soldiers. All the struggling colonies used their wild land as a sort of military chest; it was often the only security of value in their possession.

The same year that the land office was opened, it was enacted that the bridle-path across the mountains should be chopped out and made into a rough wagon-road.[1] The following spring the successful expedition against the Chicka-maugas temporarily put a stop to Indian troubles. The growing security, the opening of the land office, and the increase of knowledge concerning the country, produced a great inflow of settlers in 1779, and from that time onward the volume of immigration steadily increased.

Many of these new-comers were "poor whites," or crackers; lank, sallow, ragged creatures, living in poverty, ignorance, and dirt, who regarded all strangers with suspicion as "outlandish folks."[2] With every chance to rise, these people remained mere squalid cumberers of the earth's surface, a rank, up-country growth, containing within itself the seeds of vicious, idle pauperism and semi-criminality. They clustered in little groups, scattered throughout the backwoods settlements, in strong contrast to the vigorous and manly people around them.

[1] However this was not actually done until some years later.

[2] Smyth's *Tour*, i., 103, describes the up-country crackers of North Carolina and Virginia.

By far the largest number of the new-comers were of the true hardy backwoods stock, fitted to grapple with the wilderness and to hew out of it a prosperous commonwealth. The leading settlers began, by thrift and industry, to acquire what in the backwoods passed for wealth. Their horses, cattle, and hogs throve and multiplied. The stumps were grubbed out of the clearings, and different kinds of grains and roots were planted. Wings were added to the houses, and sometimes they were roofed with shingles. The little town of Jonesboro, the first that was not a mere stockaded fort, was laid off midway between the Watauga and the Nolichucky.

As soon as the region grew at all well settled, clergymen began to come in. Here, as elsewhere, most of the frontiersmen who had any religion at all professed the faith of the Scotch-Irish; and the first regular church in this cradle-spot of Tennessee was a Presbyterian log meeting-house built near Jonesboro in 1777, and christened Salem Church. Its pastor was a pioneer preacher, who worked with fiery and successful energy to spread learning and religion among the early settlers of the Southwest. His name was Samuel Doak. He came from New Jersey, and had been educated in Princeton. Possessed of the vigorous energy that marks the true pioneer spirit, he determined to cast in his lot with the frontier folk. He walked

through Maryland and Virginia, driving before
him an old "flea-bitten grey" horse, loaded with
a sackful of books; crossed the Alleghanies, and
came down along blazed trails to the Holston
settlements. The hardy people among whom he
took up his abode were able to appreciate his
learning and religion as much as they admired his
adventurous and indomitable temper; and the
stern, hard, God-fearing man became a most
powerful influence for good throughout the whole
formative period of the Southwest.[1]

Not only did he found a church, but near it he
built a log high school, which soon became Washington College, the first institution of the kind
west of the Alleghanies. Other churches, and
many other schools, were soon built. Any young
man or woman who could read, write, and cipher
felt competent to teach an ordinary school; higher
education, as elsewhere at this time in the West,
was in the hands of the clergy.

As elsewhere, the settlers were predominantly
of Calvinistic stock; for of all the then prominent
faiths Calvinism was nearest to their feelings and
ways of thought. Of the great recognized creeds
it was the most republican in its tendencies, and
so the best suited to the backwoodsmen. They
disliked Anglicanism as much as they abhorred

---

[1] See *East Tennessee a Hundred Years ago*, by the Honorable
John Allison, Nashville, 1887, p. 8.

and despised Romanism—theoretically at least, for practically then, as now, frontiersmen were liberal to one another's religious opinions, and the staunch friend and good hunter might follow whatever creed he wished, provided he did not intrude it on others. But backwoods Calvinism differed widely from the creed as first taught. It was professed by thorough-going Americans, essentially free and liberty-loving, who would not for a moment have tolerated a theocracy in their midst. Their social, religious, and political systems were such as naturally flourished in a country remarkable for its temper of rough and self-asserting equality. Nevertheless, the old Calvinistic spirit left a peculiar stamp on this wild border democracy. More than anything else, it gave the backwoodsmen their code of right and wrong. Though they were a hard, narrow, dogged people, yet they intensely believed in their own standards and ideals. Often warped and twisted, mentally and morally, by the strain of their existence, they at least always retained the fundamental virtues of hardihood and manliness.

Presbyterianism was not, however, destined even here to remain the leading frontier creed. Other sects still more democratic, still more in keeping with backwoods life and thought, largely supplanted it. Methodism did not become a power until after the close of the Revolution; but

the Baptists followed close on the heels of the
Presbyterians.   They, too, soon built log meeting-
houses here and there, while their preachers
cleared the forest and hunted elk and buffalo like
the other pioneer settlers.[1]

To all the churches the preacher and congregation alike went armed, the latter leaning their
rifles in their pews or near their seats, while the
pastor let his stand beside the pulpit.   On week-
days the clergymen usually worked in the fields
in company with the rest of the settlers; all with
their rifles close at hand and a guard stationed.
In more than one instance when such a party was
attacked by Indians the servant of the Lord
showed himself as skilled in the use of carnal
weapons as were any of his warlike parishioners.

The leaders of the frontiersmen were drawn
from among several families, which, having taken
firm root, were growing into the position of backwoods gentry.   Of course, the use of this term
does not imply any sharp social distinctions in
backwoods life, for there were none such.   The
poorest and richest met on terms of perfect equality, slept in one another's houses and dined at one
another's tables.   But certain families, by dint
of their thrift, the ability they showed in civil
affairs, or the prowess of some of their members in
time of war, had risen to acknowledged headship.

[1] Ramsey, 144.

The part of Washington County northwest of the Holston was cut off and made into the county of Sullivan by the North Carolina Legislature in 1779. In this part the Shelbys were the leading family; and Isaac Shelby was made County Lieutenant. It had been the debatable ground between Virginia and North Carolina, the inhabitants not knowing to which province they belonged, and sometimes serving the two governments alternately. When the line was finally drawn, old Evan Shelby's estate was found to lie on both sides of it; and as he derived his title from Virginia, he continued to consider himself a Virginian, and held office as such.[1]

In Washington County Sevier was treated as practically commander of the militia some time before he received his commission as County Lieutenant. He was rapidly becoming the leader of the whole district. He lived in a great, rambling one-story log-house on the Nolichucky, a rude, irregular building with broad verandas and great stone fireplaces. The rooms were in two groups, which were connected by a covered porch—a "dog alley," as old settlers still call it, because the dogs are apt to sleep there at night. Here he kept open house to all comers, for he was lavishly hospitable, and every one was welcome to bed and board, to apple-jack and cider, hominy and

[1] Campbell MSS. "Notes," by Governor David Campbell.

corn-bread, beef, venison, bear meat, and wild fowl. When there was a wedding or a merry-making of any kind he feasted the neighborhood, barbecuing oxen—that is, roasting them whole on great spits—and spreading board tables out under the trees. He was ever on the alert to lead his mounted riflemen against the small parties of marauding Indians that came into the country. He soon became the best commander against Indians that there was on this part of the border, moving with a rapidity that enabled him again and again to overtake and scatter their roving parties, recovering the plunder and captives, and now and then taking a scalp or two himself. His skill and daring, together with his unfailing courtesy, ready tact, and hospitality, gained him unbounded influence with the frontiersmen, among whom he was universally known as "Nolichucky Jack." [1]

The Virginian settlements on the Holston, adjoining those of North Carolina, were in 1777 likewise made into a county of Washington. The people were exactly the same in character as those across the line; and for some years the fates of all these districts were bound up together. Their inhabitants were still of the usual backwoods type, living by tilling their clearings and hunting; the

[1] MSS. "Notes of Conversations with Old Pioneers," by Ramsey, in Tennessee Historical Society. Campbell MSS.

elk and buffalo had become very scarce, but there were plenty of deer and bear, and in winter countless wild swans settled down on the small lakes and ponds. The boys followed these eagerly; one of them, when an old man, used to relate how his mother gave him a pint of cream for every swan he shot, with the result that he got the pint almost every day.[1]

The leading family among these Holston Virginians was that of the Campbells, who lived near Abingdon. They were frontier farmers, who chopped down the forest and tilled the soil with their own hands. They used the axe and guided the plough as skilfully as they handled their rifles; they were also mighty hunters, and accustomed from boyhood to Indian warfare. The children received the best schooling the back country could afford, for they were a book-loving race, fond of reading and study as well as of outdoor sports. The two chief members were cousins, Arthur and William. Arthur was captured by the northern Indians when sixteen, and was kept a prisoner among them several years; when Lord Dunmore's war broke out he made his escape, and acted as scout to the Earl's army. He served as militia colonel in different Indian campaigns, and

[1] *Sketch of Mrs. Elizabeth Russell*, by her grandson, Thomas L. Preston, Nashville, 1888, p. 29. An interesting pamphlet.

was for thirty years a magistrate of the county; he was a man of fine presence, but of jealous, ambitious, overbearing temper. He combined with his fondness for Indian and hunter life a strong taste for books, and gradually collected a large library. So keen were the jealousies, bred of ambition, between himself and his cousin William Campbell, they being the two ranking officers of the local forces, that they finally agreed to go alternately on the different military expeditions; and thus it happened that Arthur missed the battle of King's Mountain, though he was at the time County Lieutenant.

William Campbell stood next in rank. He was a man of giant strength, standing six feet two inches in height, and straight as a spear-shaft, with fair complexion, red hair, and piercing, light blue eyes. A firm friend and staunch patriot, a tender and loving husband and father, gentle and courteous in ordinary intercourse with his fellows, he was, nevertheless, if angered, subject to fits of raging wrath that impelled him to any deed of violence.[1] He was a true type of the Roundheads of the frontier, the earnest, eager men who pushed the border ever farther westward across the continent. He followed Indians and tories with relentless and undying hatred; for the long list of backwoods virtues did not include pity for either

[1] Campbell MSS. "Notes," by Governor David Campbell.

public or private foes. The tories threatened his life and the lives of his friends and families; they were hand in glove with the outlaws who infested the borders, the murderers, horse-thieves, and passers of counterfeit money. He hunted them down with a furious zest, and did his work with merciless thoroughness, firm in the belief that he thus best served the Lord and the nation. One or two of his deeds illustrate admirably the grimness of the times, and the harsh contrast between the kindly relations of the border folks with their friends and their ferocity towards their foes. They show how the better backwoodsmen,—the upright, churchgoing men, who loved their families, did justice to their neighbors, and sincerely tried to serve God—not only waged an unceasing war on the red and white foes of the State and of order, but carried it on with a certain ruthlessness that indicated less a disbelief in, than an utter lack of knowledge of, such a virtue as leniency to enemies.

One Sunday, Campbell was returning from church with his wife and some friends, carrying his baby on a pillow in front of his saddle, for they were all mounted. Suddenly a horseman crossed the road close in front of them, and was recognized by one of the party as a noted tory. Upon being challenged, he rode off at full speed. Instantly Campbell handed the baby to a negro slave, struck spur into his horse, and galloping after the fugitive, overtook and captured him. The other men of the party came up a minute later. Several recognized the prisoner as a well-known tory; he was riding a stolen horse; he had on him letters to the British agents among the Cherokees, arranging for an Indian rising. The party of returning churchgoers were accustomed to the quick and summary justice of lynch law. With stern gravity they organized themselves into a court. The prisoner was adjudged guilty, and was given but a short shrift; for the horsemen hung him to a sycamore-tree before they returned to the road where they had left their families.

On another occasion, while Campbell was in command of a camp of militia, at the time of a Cherokee outbreak, he wrote a letter to his wife, a sister of Patrick Henry, that gives us a glimpse of the way in which he looked at Indians. His letter began, "My dearest Betsy"; in it he spoke of his joy at receiving her "sweet and affectionate letter"; he told how he had finally got the needles and pins she wished, and how pleased a friend had been with the apples she had sent him. He urged her to buy a saddle-horse, of which she had spoken, but to be careful that it did not start nor stumble, which were bad faults, "especially in a woman's hackney." In terms of endearment that showed he had not sunk the lover in the husband, he spoke of his delight at being again in the house where he had for the first time seen her loved face, "from which happy moment he dated the hour of all his bliss," and besought her not to trouble herself too much about him, quoting to her Solomon's account of a good wife, as reminding him always of her; and he ended by commending her to the peculiar care of Heaven. It was a letter that it was an honor to a true man to have written; such a letter as the best of women and wives might be proud to have received. Yet in the middle of it he promised to bring a strange trophy to show his tender and God-fearing spouse. He was speaking of the Indians; how they had murdered men, women, and children nearby, and how they had been beaten back; and he added: "I have now the scalp of one who was killed eight or nine miles from my house about three weeks ago. The first time I go up I shall take it along to let you see it." Evidently, it was as natural for him to bring home to his wife and children the scalp of a slain Indian as the skin of a slain deer.[1]

The times were hard, and they called for men of flinty fibre. Those of softer, gentler mould would have failed in the midst of such surroundings. The iron men of the border had a harsh and terrible task allotted them; and though they did it roughly, they did it thoroughly and on the whole well. They may have failed to learn that it is

[1] See Preston's pamphlet on Mrs. Russell, pp. 11-18.

good to be merciful, but at least they knew that it is still better to be just and strong and brave; to see clearly one's rights, and to guard them with a ready hand.

These frontier leaders were generally very jealous of one another. The ordinary backwoodsmen vied together as hunters, axemen, or wrestlers; as they rose to leadership their rivalries grew likewise, and the more ambitious, who desired to become the civil and military chiefs of the community, were sure to find their interests clash. Thus old Evan Shelby distrusted Sevier; Arthur Campbell was jealous of both Sevier and Isaac Shelby; and the two latter bore similar feelings to William Campbell. When a great crisis occurred all these petty envies were sunk; the nobler natures of the men came uppermost; and they joined with unselfish courage, heart and hand, to defend their country in the hour of her extreme need. But when the danger was over the old jealousies cropped out again.

Some one or other of the leaders was almost always employed against the Indians. The Cherokees and Creeks were never absolutely quiet and at peace. After the chastisement inflicted upon the former by the united forces of all the southern backwoodsmen, treaties were held with them,[1] in the spring and summer of 1777. The

[1] See *ante*, Vol. II., Chap. III.

negotiations consumed much time, the delegates form both sides meeting again and again to complete the preliminaries. The credit of the State being low, Isaac Shelby furnished on his own responsibility the goods and provisions needed by the Virginians and Holston people in coming to an agreement with the Otari, or Upper Cherokees [1]; and some land was formally ceded to the whites.

But the chief Dragging Canoe would not make peace. Gathering the boldest and most turbulent of the young braves about him, he withdrew to the great whirl in the Tennessee,[2] at the crossing-place of the Creek war-parties, when they followed the trail that led to the bend of the Cumberland River. Here he was joined by many Creeks, and also by adventurous and unruly members from almost all the western tribes [3]—Chickasaws, Choctaws, and Indians from the Ohio. He soon had a great band of red outlaws round him. These freebooters were generally known as the Chickamaugas, and they were the most dangerous and least controllable of all the foes who menaced the western settlements. Many tories and white refugees from border justice joined them, and shared in their misdeeds. Their shifting villages

[1] Shelby's MS. Autobiography, copy in Col. Durrett's library.

[2] *Virginia State Papers*, iii., 271; the settlers always spoke of it as the "suck" or "whirl."

[3] Shelby MSS.

stretched from Chickamauga Creek to Running Water. Between these places the Tennessee twists down through the sombre gorges by which the chains of the Cumberland ranges are riven in sunder. Some miles below Chickamauga Creek, near Chattanooga, Lookout Mountain towers aloft into the clouds; at its base the river bends round Moccasin Point, and then rushes through a gap between Walden's Ridge and the Raccoon Hills. Then for several miles it foams through the winding Narrows between jutting cliffs and sheer rock walls, while in its boulder-strewn bed the swift torrent is churned into whirlpools, cataracts, and rapids. Near the Great Crossing, where the war-parties and hunting-parties were ferried over the river, lies Nick-a-jack Cave, a vast cavern in the mountain-side. Out of it flows a stream, up which a canoe can be paddled two or three miles into the heart of the mountain. In these high fast-nesses, inaccessible ravines, and gloomy caverns the Chickamaugas built their towns, and to them they retired with their prisoners and booty after every raid on the settlements.

No sooner had the preliminary treaty been agreed to in the spring of '77 than the Indians again began their ravages. In fact, there never was any real peace. After each treaty the settlers would usually press forward into the Indian lands, and if they failed to do this the young braves were

sure themselves to give offence by making forays
against the whites.   On this occasion the first
truce or treaty was promptly broken by the red
men.   The young warriors refused to be bound by
the promises of the chiefs and headmen, and they
continued their raids for scalps, horses, and plunder.   Within a week of the departure of the Indian
delegates from the treaty ground in April, twelve
whites were murdered and many horses stolen.
Robertson, with nine men, followed one of these
marauding parties, killed one Indian, and retook
ten horses; on his return he was attacked by a
large band of Creeks and Cherokees, and two of
his men were wounded; but he kept hold of the
recaptured horses and brought them safely in.[1]
On the other hand, a white scoundrel killed an
Indian on the treaty ground in July, the month
in which the treaties were finally completed in
due form.   By act of the Legislature, the Holston
militia were kept under arms throughout most of
the year, companies of rangers, under Sevier's
command, scouring the woods and canebrakes,
and causing such loss to the small Indian war-
parties that they finally almost ceased their forays.
Bands of these Holston rangers likewise crossed
the mountains by Boon's trail, and went to the
relief of Boonsborough and St. Asaphs, in Ken-

[1] Charles Robertson to Captain-General of North Carolina,
April 27, 1777.

tucky, then much harassed by the northwestern warriors.[1] Though they did little or no fighting, and stayed but a few days, they yet by their presence brought welcome relief to the hard-pressed Kentuckians.[2]   Kentucky, during her earliest and most trying years, received compara-tively little help from sorely beset Virginia; but the backwoodsmen of the upper Tennessee valley —on both sides of the boundary—did her real and lasting service.

In 1778, the militia were disbanded, as the set-tlements were very little harried; but as soon as the vigilance of the whites was relaxed the depre-dations and massacres began again, and soon be-came worse than ever.   Robertson had been made superintendent of Indian affairs for North Carolina; and he had taken up his abode among the Cherokees at the town of Chota in the latter half of the year 1777.   He succeeded in keeping them comparatively quiet and peaceable during 1778 and until his departure, which took place the following year, when he went to found the settle-ments on the Cumberland River.

But the Chickamaugas refused to make peace, and in their frequent and harassing forays they

[1] See *ante*, Vol. II., Chap. v.

[2] Monette (followed by Ramsey and others) hopelessly con-fuses these small relief expeditions; he portrays Logan as a messenger from Boon's Station, is in error as to the siege of the latter, etc.

were from time to time joined by parties of young
braves from all the Cherokee towns that were beyond the reach of Robertson's influence—that is,
by all save those in the neighborhood of Chota.
The Chickasaws and Choctaws likewise gave active support to the king's cause; the former
scouted along the Ohio, the latter sent bands of
young warriors to aid the Creeks and Cherokees
in their raids against the settlements.[1]

The British agents among the southern Indians
had received the letters Hamilton sent them after
he took Vincennes; in these they were urged at
once to send out parties against the frontier, and
to make ready for a grand stroke in the spring. In
response, the chief agent, who was the Scotch captain Cameron, a noted royalist leader, wrote to
his official superior that the instant he heard of
any movement of the northwestern Indians he
would see that it was backed up, for the Creeks
were eager for war, and the Cherokees likewise
were ardently attached to the British cause; as a
proof of the devotion of the latter, he added[2]:
"They keep continually killing and scalping in
Virginia, North Carolina, and the frontier of
Georgia, although the rebels are daily threatening

[1] Haldimand MSS.   Letter of Rainsford and Tait to Hamilton, April 9, 1779.

[2] *Ibid.*, Series B, vol. cxvii., p. 131.   Letter of Alexander
Cameron, July 15, 1779.

to send in armies from all quarters and extirpate
the whole tribe." It would certainly be impossible to desire better proof than that thus furnished by this royal officer, both of the ferocity of
the British policy towards the frontiersmen, and
of the treachery of the Indians, who so richly deserved the fate that afterwards befell them.

While waiting for the signal from Hamilton,
Cameron organized two Indian expeditions against
the frontier, to aid the movements of the British
army that had already conquered Georgia. A
great body of Creeks, accompanied by the British
commissaries and most of the white traders (who
were, of course, tories), set out in March to join
the king's forces at Savannah; but when they
reached the frontier they scattered out to plunder
and ravage. A body of Americans fell on one of
their parties and crushed it; whereupon the rest
returned home in a fright, save about seventy,
who went on and joined the British. At the
same time three hundred Chickamaugas, likewise
led by the resident British commissaries, started
out against the Carolina frontier. But Robertson, at Chota, received news of the march, and
promptly sent warning to the Holston settlements [1]; and the Holston men, both of Virginia

---

[1] *Ibid.* "A rebel commissioner in Chote being informed of
their movements here sent express into Holston river." This
"rebel commissioner" was in all probability Robertson.

and North Carolina, decided immediately to send an expedition against the homes of the war-party. This would not only at once recall them from the frontier, but would give them a salutary lesson.

Accordingly, the backwoods levies gathered on Clinch River, at the mouth of Big Creek, April 10th, and embarked in pirogues and canoes to descend the Tennessee. There were several hundred of them [1] under the command of Evan Shelby; Isaac Shelby having collected the supplies for the expedition by his individual activity and on his personal credit. The backwoodsmen went down the river so swiftly that they took the Chickamaugas completely by surprise, and the few warriors who were left in the villages fled to the wooded mountains without offering any resistance. Several Indians were killed [2] and a

[1] State Department MSS. No. 51, vol. ii., p. 17, a letter from the British agents among the Creeks to Lord George Germain, of July 12, 1779. It says "near 300 rebels"; Haywood, whose accounts are derived from oral tradition, says one thousand. Cameron's letter of July 15th in the Haldimand MSS. says seven hundred. Some of them were Virginians who had been designed for Clark's assistance in his Illinois campaign, but who were not sent him. Shelby made a very clever stroke, but it had no permanent effect, and it is nonsense to couple it, as has been recently done, with Clark's campaigns.

[2] Cameron in his letter says four, which is probably near the truth. Haywood says forty, which merely represents the backwoods tradition on the subject, and is doubtless a great exaggeration.

number of their towns were burnt, together with a great deal of corn; many horses and cattle were recaptured, and among the spoils were large piles of deer-hides, owned by a tory trader. The troops then destroyed their canoes and returned home on foot, killing game for their food; and they spread among the settlements many stories of the beauty of the lands through which they had passed, so that the pioneers became eager to possess them. The Chickamaugas were alarmed and confounded by this sudden stroke; their great war band returned at once to the burned towns, on being informed by swift runners of the destruction that had befallen them. All thoughts of an immediate expedition against the frontier were given up; peace-talks were sent to Evan Shelby [1]; and throughout the summer the settlements were but little molested.

Yet all the while they were planning further attacks; at the same time that they sent peace-talks to Shelby they sent war-talks to the northwestern Indians, inviting them to join in a great combined movement against the Americans. [2] When the

[1] State Department MSS. No. 71, vol. i., p. 255, letter of Evan Shelby, June 4, 1779.

[2] Haldimand MSS., Series B, vol. cxvii., p. 157. A talk from the Cherokees to the envoy from the Wabash and other Indians, July 12, 1779. One paragraph is interesting: "We cannot forget the talk you brought us some years ago into this Nation, which was to take up the hatchet against the

news of Hamilton's capture was brought it
wrought a momentary discouragement; but the
efforts of the British agents were unceasing, and
by the end of the year most of the southwestern
Indians were again ready to take up the hatchet.
The rapid successes of the royal armies in the
Southern States had turned the Creeks into open
antagonists of the Americans, and their war-parties were sent out in quick succession, the British
agents keeping alive the alliance by a continued
series of gifts—for the Creeks were a venal, fickle
race whose friendship could not otherwise be permanently kept.[1]

Virginians. We heard and listened to it with great attention
and before the time that was appointed to lift it we took it
up and struck the Virginians. Our Nation was alone and
surrounded by them. They were numerous and their hatchets
were sharp; and after we had lost some of our best warriors,
we were forced to leave our towns and corn to be burnt by
them, and now we live in the grass as you see us. But we
are not yet conquered, and to convince you that we have
not thrown away your talk here are 4 strands of whampums
we received from you when you came before as a messenger
to our Nation."

[1] State Department MSS. Papers Continental Congress.
Intercepted Letters, No. 51, vol. ii. Letter of British agents
Messrs. Rainsford, Mitchell, and McCullough, of July 12, 1779.
"The present unanimity of the Creek Nation is no doubt
greatly owing to the rapid successes of His Majesty's forces
in the Southern provinces, as they have now no cause to apprehend the least danger from the Rebels . . . We have
found by experience that without presents the Indians are
not to be depended on."

As for the Cherokees, they had not confined themselves to sending the war-belt to the northwestern tribes, while professing friendship for the Americans; they had continued in close communication with the British Indian agents, assuring them that their peace negotiations were only shams, intended to blind the settlers, and that they would be soon ready to take up the hatchet.[1] This time Cameron himself marched into the Cherokee country with his company of fifty tories, brutal outlaws, accustomed to savage warfare, and ready to take part in the worst Indian outrages.[2] The ensuing Cherokee war was due not to the misdeeds of the settlers—though doubtless a few lawless whites occasionally did wrong to their red neighbors—but to the shortsighted treachery and ferocity of the savages themselves, and especially to the machinations of the tories and British agents. The latter unceasingly incited the Indians to ravage the

[1] *Ibid.*, No. 71, vol. ii., p. 189. Letter of David Tait to Oconostota. "I believe what you say about telling lies to the Virginians to be very right."

[2] *Ibid.*, No. 51, vol. ii. Letter of the three agents. "The Cherokees are now exceedingly well disposed. Mr. Cameron is now among them. . . . Captain Cameron has his company of Loyal Refugees with him, who are well qualified for the service they are engaged in. . . . He carried up with him a considerable quantity of presents and ammunition which are absolutely necessary to engage the Indians to go upon service."

frontier with torch and scalping-knife. They deliberately made the deeds of the torturers and woman-killers their own, and this they did with the approbation of the British Government, and to its merited and lasting shame.

Yet by the end of 1779 the inrush of settlers to the Holston regions had been so great that, as with Kentucky, there was never any real danger after this year that the whites would be driven from the land by the red tribes whose hunting-ground it once had been.

CHAPTER V

D URING the Revolutionary War the men of the West for the most part took no share in the actual campaigning against the British and Hessians. Their duty was to conquer and hold the wooded wilderness that stretched westward to the Mississippi; and to lay therein the foundations of many future commonwealths. Yet at a crisis in the great struggle for liberty, at one of the darkest hours for the patriot cause, it was given to a band of western men to come to the relief of their brethren of the seaboard and to strike a telling and decisive blow for all America. When the three southern provinces lay crushed and helpless at the feet of Cornwallis, the Holston backwoodsmen suddenly gathered to assail the triumphant conqueror. Crossing the mountains that divided them from the beaten and despairing people of the tidewater region, they killed the ablest lieutenant of the British commander, and at a single stroke undid all that he had done.

By the end of 1779 the British had reconquered Georgia. In May, 1780, they captured Charleston, speedily reduced all South Carolina to submission, and then marched into the old North State. Cornwallis, much the ablest of the British generals, was in command over a mixed force of British, Hessian, and loyal American regulars, aided by Irish volunteers and bodies of refugees from Florida. In addition, the friends to the king's cause, who were very numerous in the southernmost States, rose at once on the news of the British successes, and thronged to the royal standards; so that a number of regiments of tory militia were soon embodied. McGillivray, the Creek chief, sent bands of his warriors to assist the British and tories on the frontier, and the Cherokees likewise came to their help. The patriots for the moment abandoned hope, and bowed before their victorious foes.

Cornwallis himself led the main army northward against the American forces. Meanwhile, he entrusted to two of his most redoubtable officers the task of scouring the country, raising the loyalists, scattering the patriot troops that were still embodied, and finally crushing out all remaining opposition. These two men were Tarleton, the dashing cavalryman, and Ferguson the rifleman, the skilled partisan leader.

Patrick Ferguson, the son of Lord Pitfour, was a Scotch soldier, at this time about thirty-six years old, who had been twenty years in the British

army. He had served with distinction against
the French in Germany, had quelled a Carib uprising in the West Indies, and in 1777 was given
the command of a company of riflemen in the
army opposed to Washington.[1] He played a
good part at Brandywine and Monmouth. At the
former battle he was wounded by an American
sharpshooter, and had an opportunity, of which
he forbore taking advantage, to himself shoot an
American officer of high rank, who unsuspectingly
approached the place where he lay hid; he always
insisted that the man he thus spared was no less a
person than Washington. While suffering from
his wound, Sir William Howe disbanded his rifle
corps, distributing it among the light companies
of the different regiments; and its commander in
consequence became an unattached volunteer in
the army. But he was too able to be allowed
to remain long unemployed. When the British
moved to New York he was given the command
of several small independent expeditions, and was
successful in each case; once, in particular, he
surprised and routed Pulaski's legion, committing
great havoc with the bayonet, which was always
with him a favorite weapon. His energy and

---

[1] *Biographical Sketch or Memoir of Lieutenant-Colonel
Patrick Ferguson*, by Adam Ferguson, LL.D., Edinburgh,
1817, p. 11. The copy was kindly lent me by Mr. George
H. Moore of the Lenox Library.

valor attracted much attention; and when a
British army was sent against Charleston and
the South he went along as a lieutenant-colonel
of a recently raised regular regiment, known as
the American Volunteers.[1]

Cornwallis speedily found him to be peculiarly
fitted for just such service as was needed; for he
possessed rare personal qualities.   He was of middle height and slender build, with a quiet serious
face and a singularly winning manner; and withal,
he was of literally dauntless courage, of hopeful,
eager temper, and remarkably fertile in shifts and
expedients.   He was particularly fond of night attacks, surprises, and swift, sudden movements
generally, and was unwearied in drilling and dis-
ciplining his men.   Not only was he an able leader,
but he was also a finished horseman, and the best
marksman with both pistol and rifle in the British
army.   Being of quick, inventive mind, he con-
structed a breech-loading rifle, which he used in
battle with deadly effect.   This invention had
been one of the chief causes of his being brought
into prominence in the war against America, for
the British officers especially dreaded the American

[1] Though called volunteers, they were simply a regular
regiment raised in America instead of England; Ferguson's
Memoir, p. 30, etc., always speaks of them as regulars.
The British gave an absurd number of titles to their various
officers; thus Ferguson was a brigadier-general of militia,
lieutenant-colonel of volunteers, a major in the army, etc.

sharpshooters.[1]   It would be difficult to imagine
a better partisan leader, or one more fitted by his
feats of prowess and individual skill to impress
the minds of his followers.   Moreover, his courtesy
stood him in good stead with the people of the
country; he was always kind and civil, and would
spend hours in talking affairs over with them and
pointing out the mischief of rebelling against their
lawful sovereign.   He soon became a potent force
in winning the doubtful to the British side, and
exerted a great influence over the tories; they
gathered eagerly to his standard, and he drilled
them with patient perseverance.

After the taking of Charleston Ferguson's volunteers and Tarleton's legion, acting separately or
together, speedily destroyed the different bodies
of patriot soldiers.   Their activity and energy
was such that the opposing commanders seemed
for the time being quite unable to cope with them,
and the American detachments were routed and
scattered in quick succession.[2]   On one of these
occasions, the surprise at Monk's Corners, where
the American commander, Huger, was slain, Ferguson's troops again had a chance to show their
skill in the use of the bayonet.

[1] Ferguson's *Memoir*, p. 11.
[2] *History of the Campaigns of 1780 and 1781*, Lieutenant-
Colonel Tarleton, London (1787).   See also the *Strictures*
thereon, by Roderick Mackenzie, London, same date.

Tarleton did his work with brutal ruthlessness; his men plundered and ravaged, maltreated prisoners, outraged women, and hung without mercy all who were suspected of turning from the loyalist to the whig side. His victories were almost always followed by massacres; in particular, when he routed with small loss a certain Captain Buford, his soldiers refused to grant quarter, and mercilessly butchered the beaten Americans.[1]

Ferguson, on the contrary, while quite as valiant and successful a commander, showed a generous heart, and treated the inhabitants of the country fairly well. He was especially incensed at any outrage upon women, punishing the offender with the utmost severity, and as far as possible he spared his conquered foes. Yet even Ferguson's tender mercies must have seemed cruel to the whigs, as may be judged by the following extract from a diary kept by one of his lieutenants[2] : "This day Col. Ferguson got the rear guard in order to do his King and country justice by protecting friends and widows, and destroying rebel property; also to collect live stock for the use of the army. All of which we effect as we go

[1] It is worth while remembering that it was not merely the tories who were guilty of gross crimes; the British regulars, including even some of their officers, often behaved with abhorrent brutality.

[2] Diary of Lieutenant Anthony Allaire, entry for March 24, 1780.

by destroying furniture, breaking windows, etc.,
taking all their horned cattle, horses, mules, sheep,
etc., and their negroes to drive them." When
such were the authorized proceedings of troops
under even the most merciful of the British commanders, it is easy to guess what deeds were done
by uncontrolled bodies of stragglers bent on
plunder.

When Ferguson moved into the back country
of the two Carolinas still worse outrages followed.
In the three southernmost of the thirteen rebel-
lious colonies there was a very large tory party.[1]
In consequence, the struggle in the Carolinas and
Georgia took the form of a ferocious civil war.
Each side in turn followed up its successes by a
series of hangings and confiscations, while the
lawless and violent characters fairly revelled in the
confusion. Neither side can be held guiltless of
many and grave misdeeds; but, for reasons already
given, the bulk—but by no means the whole—of
the criminal and disorderly classes espoused the
king's cause in the regions where the struggle was
fiercest. They murdered, robbed, or drove off
the whigs in their hour of triumph; and in turn

[1] Gates MSS., *passim*, for July–October, 1780. *E. g.*, letter
of Mr. Ramsey, August 9, 1780, describes how "the Scotch
are all lying out," the number of tories in the "Drowning
Creek region," their resistance to the levy of cattle, etc. In
these colonies, as in the middle colonies, the tory party was
very strong.

brought down ferocious reprisals on their own heads and on those of their luckless associates.

Moreover, Cornwallis and his under-officers tried to cow and overawe the inhabitants by executing some of the men whom they deemed the chief and most criminal leaders of the rebellion, especially such as had sworn allegiance and then again taken up arms [1]; of course, retaliation in kind followed. Ferguson himself hung some men; and though he did his best to spare the country people, there was much plundering and murdering by his militia.

In June, he marched to upper South Carolina, moving to and fro, calling out the loyal militia. They responded enthusiastically, and three or four thousand tories were embodied in different bands. Those who came to Ferguson's own standard were divided into companies and regiments, and taught the rudiments of discipline by himself and his subalterns. He soon had a large but fluctuating force under him, in part composed of good men, loyal adherents of the king (these being very frequently recent arrivals from England, or else Scotch highlanders), in part also of cut-throats, horse-thieves, and desperadoes of all kinds who wished for revenge on the whigs and were eager to plunder them. His own regular

[1] Gates MSS. See letter from Sumter, August 12th, and *passim*, for instances of hanging by express command of the British officers.

force was also mainly composed of Americans, although it contained many Englishmen. His chief subordinates were Lieutenant-Colonels De Peyster [1] and Cruger; the former usually serving under him, the latter commanding at Ninety-Six. They were both New York loyalists, members of old Knickerbocker families; for in New York many of the gentry and merchants stood by the king.

Ferguson moved rapidly from place to place, breaking up the bodies of armed whigs; and the latter now and then skirmished fiercely with similar bands of tories, sometimes one side winning, sometimes the other. Having reduced South Carolina to submission, the British commander then threatened North Carolina; and Colonel McDowell, the commander of the whig militia in that district, sent across the mountains to the Holston men, praying that they would come to his help. Though suffering continually from Indian ravages, and momentarily expecting a formidable inroad, they responded nobly to the call. Sevier remained to patrol the border and watch the Cherokees, while Isaac Shelby crossed the mountains with a couple of hundred mounted riflemen early in July. The mountain men were joined by McDowell, with whom they found also a handful of Georgians and some South Carolinians

[1] A relative of the Detroit commander.

who, when their States were subdued, had fled northward, resolute to fight their oppressors to the last.

The arrival of the mountain men put new life into the dispirited whigs. On July 30th, a mixed force, under Shelby and two or three local militia colonels, captured Thickett's fort, with ninety tories, near the Pacolet. They then camped at the Cherokee ford of Broad River, and sent out parties of mounted men to carry on a guerilla or partisan warfare against detachments, not choosing to face Ferguson's main body. After a while they moved south to Cedar Spring. Here, on the 8th of August, they were set upon by Ferguson's advanced guard of dragoons and mounted riflemen. These they repulsed, handling the British rather roughly; but, as Ferguson himself came up, they fled, and though he pursued them vigorously, he could not overtake them.[1]

[1] Shelby's MS. Autobiography, and the various accounts he wrote of these affairs in his old age (which Haywood and most of the other local American historians follow or amplify) certainly greatly exaggerate the British force and loss, as well as the part Shelby himself played, compared to the Georgia and Carolina leaders. The Americans seemed to have outnumbered Ferguson's advance guard, which was less than two hundred strong, about three to one. Shelby's account of the Musgrove affair is especially erroneous. See p. 120 of L. C. Draper's *King's Mountain and Its Heroes* (Cincinnati, 1881). Mr. Draper has with infinite industry and research gathered all the published and unpublished accounts and all

On the 18th of the month, the mountain men, assisted as usual by some parties of local militia, all under their various colonels, performed another feat—one of those swift, sudden strokes so dear to the hearts of these rifle-bearing horsemen. It was of a kind peculiarly suited to their powers; for they were brave and hardy, able to thread their way unerringly through the forests and fond of surprises; and, though they always fought on foot, they moved on horseback, and therefore with great celerity. Their operations should be carefully studied by all who wish to learn the possibilities of mounted riflemen. Yet they were impatient of discipline or of regular service, and they really had no one commander. The different militia officers combined to perform some definite piece of work, but, like their troops, they were incapable of long-continued campaigns; and there

the traditions concerning the battle; his book is a mine of information on the subject. He is generally quite impartial but some of his conclusions are certainly biassed; and the many traditional statements, as well as those made by very old men concerning events that took place fifty or sixty years previously, must be received with extreme caution. A great many of them should never have been put in the book at all. When they take the shape of anecdotes, telling how the British are overawed by the mere appearance of the Americans on some occasion (as pp. 94, 95, etc.), they must be discarded at once as absolutely worthless, as well as ridiculous. The British and tory accounts, being forced to explain ultimate defeat, are, if possible, even more untrustworthy, when taken solely by themselves, than the American.

were frequent and bitter quarrels between the several commanders, as well as between the bodies of men they led.

It seems certain that the mountaineers were, as a rule, more formidable fighters than the lowland militia, beside or against whom they battled; and they formed the main strength of the attacking party that left the camp at the Cherokee ford before sunset on the seventeenth. Ferguson's army was encamped southwest of them, at Fair Forest Shoals; they marched round him, and went straight on, leaving him in their rear. Sometimes they rode through open forest, more often they followed the dim wood roads; their horses pacing or cantering steadily through the night. As the day dawned they reached Musgrove's Ford, on the Enoree, having gone forty miles. Here they hoped to find a detachment of tory militia; but it had been joined by a body of provincial regulars, the united force being probably somewhat more numerous than that of the Americans. The latter were discovered by a patrol, and the British after a short delay marched out to attack them. The Americans in the meantime made good use of their axes, felling trees for a breastwork, and when assailed they beat back and finally completely routed their assailants.[1]

[1] Shelby's account of this action, written in his old age, is completely at fault; he not only exaggerates the British

However, the victory was of little effect, for just
as it was won word was brought to Shelby that the
day before Cornwallis had met Gates at Camden,
and had not only defeated but practically destroyed the American army; and on the very day
of the fight on the Enoree, Tarleton surprised
Sumter, and scattered his forces to the four winds.
The panic among the whigs was tremendous, and
the mountaineers shared it. They knew that
Ferguson, angered at the loss of his detachment,
would soon be in hot pursuit, and there was no
time for delay. The local militia made off in
various directions; while Shelby and his men
pushed straight for the mountains, crossed them,
and returned each man to his own home. Ferguson speedily stamped out the few remaining
sparks of rebellion in South Carolina, and crossing
the boundary into the North State he there repeated the process. On September 12th, he
caught McDowell and the only remaining body of
militia at Cane Creek, of the Catawba, and beat

force and loss, but he likewise greatly overestimates the
number of the Americans—always a favorite trick of his.
Each of the militia colonels, of course, claimed the chief share
of the glory of the day. Haywood, Ramsey, and even Phelan
simply follow Shelby. Draper gives all the different accounts;
it is quite impossible to reconcile them, but all admit that the
British were defeated.

I have used the word "British"; but though there were
some Englishmen and Scotchmen among the tories and pro-
vincials, they were mainly loyalist Americans.

them thoroughly,[1] the survivors, including their commander, fleeing over the mountains to take refuge with the Holston men. Except for an occasional small guerilla party, there was not a single organized body of American troops left south of Gates's broken and dispirited army.

All the southern lands lay at the feet of the conquerors. The British leaders, overbearing and arrogant, held almost unchecked sway throughout the Carolinas and Georgia; and looking northward they made ready for the conquest of Virginia.[2] Their right flank was covered by the waters of the ocean, their left by the high mountain barrier-chains, beyond which stretched the interminable forest; and they had as little thought of danger from one side as from the other.

Suddenly and without warning, the wilderness sent forth a swarm of stalwart and hardy riflemen, of whose very existence the British had hitherto been ignorant.[3] Riders spurring in hot haste

[1] Draper apparently endorses the absurd tradition that makes this a whig victory instead of a defeat. It seems certain (see Draper), contrary to the statements of the Tennessee historians, that Sevier had no part in these preliminary operations.

[2] The northern portion of North Carolina was still in possession of the remainder of Gates's army, but they could have been brushed aside without an effort.

[3] "A numerous army now appeared on the frontier drawn from Nolachucky and other settlements beyond the mountains, whose very names had been unknown to us." Lord

brought word to the king's commanders that the
backwater men had come over the mountains.
The Indian fighters of the frontier, leaving un-
guarded their homes on the western waters, had
crossed by wooded and precipitous defiles, and
were pouring down to the help of their brethren
of the plains.

Ferguson had pushed his victories to the foot of
the Smoky and the Yellow mountains.   Here he
learned, perhaps for the first time, that there were
a few small settlements beyond the high ranges he
saw in his front; and he heard that some of these
backwoods mountaineers had already borne arms
against him, and were now harboring men who
had fled from before his advance.   By a prisoner
whom he had taken he at once sent them warning
to cease their hostilities, and threatened that if
they did not desist he would march across the
mountains, hang their leaders, put their fighting
men to the sword, and waste their settlements
with fire.   He had been joined by refugee tories
from the Watauga, who could have piloted him
thither; and perhaps he intended to make his
threats good.   It seems more likely that he paid
little heed to the mountaineers, scorning their

Rawdon's letter of October 24, 1780.   Clarke of Georgia had
plundered a convoy of presents intended for the Indians, at
Augusta, and the British wrongly supposed this to be likewise the aim of the mountaineers.

power to do him hurt; though he did not regard
them with the haughty and ignorant disdain usually felt for such irregulars by the British army
officers.

When the Holston men learned that Ferguson
had come to the other side of the mountains, and
threatened their chiefs with the halter and their
homes with the torch, a flame of passionate anger
was kindled in all their hearts.   They did not wait
for his attack; they sallied from their strongholds
to meet him.   Their crops were garnered, their
young men were ready for the march; and though
the Otari war bands lowered like thunder-clouds
on their southern border, they determined to leave
only enough men to keep the savages at bay for
the moment, and with the rest to overwhelm Ferguson before he could retreat out of their reach.
Hitherto, the war with the British had been something afar off; now it had come to their thresholds,
and their spirits rose to the danger.

Shelby was the first to hear the news.   He at
once rode down to Sevier's home on the Nolichucky; for they were the two County Lieutenants,[1] who had control of all the militia of the
district.   At Sevier's log-house there was feasting

[1] Shelby was regularly commissioned as County Lieutenant.
Sevier's commission was not sent him until several weeks
later; but he had long acted as such by the agreement of the
settlers, who paid very little heed to the weak and disorganized North Carolina government.

and merrymaking, for he had given a barbecue,
and a great horserace was to be run, while the
backwoods champions tried their skill as marksmen and wrestlers. In the midst of the merry-
making Shelby appeared, hot with hard riding, to
tell of the British advance, and to urge that the
time was ripe for fighting, not feasting. Sevier
at once entered heartily into his friend's plan, and
agreed to raise his rifle-rangers, and to gather the
broken and disorganized refugees who had fled
across the mountains under McDowell. While
this was being done, Shelby returned to his home
to call out his own militia and to summon the
Holston Virginians to his aid. With the latter
purpose he sent one of his brothers to Arthur
Campbell, the County Lieutenant of his neighbors
across the border. Arthur at once proceeded to
urge the adoption of the plan on his cousin, William Campbell, who had just returned from a
short and successful campaign against the tories
round the head of the Kanawha, where he had
speedily quelled an attempted uprising.

Gates had already sent William Campbell an
earnest request to march down with his troops
and join the main army. This he could not do,
as his militia had only been called out to put down
their own internal foes,[1] and their time of service

[1] Gates MSS. Letter of William Campbell, September 6,
1780. He evidently at the time failed to appreciate the

had expired. But the continued advance of the British at last thoroughly alarmed the Virginians of the mountain region. They promptly set about raising a corps of riflemen,[1] and as soon as this course of action was determined on Campbell was foremost in embodying all the Holston men who could be spared, intending to march westward and join any Virginia army that might be raised to oppose Cornwallis. While thus employed he received Shelby's request, and, for answer, at first sent word that he could not change his plans; but on receiving a second and more urgent message he agreed to come as desired.[2]

The appointed meeting-place was at the Syca-

pressing danger; but he ended by saying that "if the Indians were not harassing their frontier," and a corps of riflemen were formed, he would do all in his power to forward them to Gates.

[1] Gates MSS. Letter of William Preston, September 18, 1780. The corps was destined to join Gates, as Preston says; hence Campbell's reluctance to go with Shelby and Sevier. There were to be from five hundred to one thousand men. See letter of William Davidson, September 18, 1780.

[2] Shelby's MS. Autobiography. Campbell MSS., especially MS. letters of Colonel Arthur Campbell of September 3, 1810, October 18, 1810, etc.; MS. notes on Sevier in Tennessee Historical Society. The latter consist of memoranda by his old soldiers, who were with him in the battle; many of their statements are to be received cautiously, but there seems no reason to doubt their account of his receiving the news while giving a great barbecue. Shelby is certainly entitled to the credit of planning and starting the campaign against Ferguson.

more Shoals of the Watauga. There the riflemen
gathered on the 25th of September, Campbell
bringing four hundred men, Sevier and Shelby
two hundred and forty each, while the refugees
under McDowell amounted to about one hundred
and sixty. With Shelby came his two brothers,
one of whom was afterwards slightly wounded at
King's Mountain; while Sevier had in his regiment no less than six relations of his own name,
his two sons being privates, and his two brothers
captains. One of the latter was mortally wounded
in the battle.

To raise money for provisions, Sevier and Shelby
were obliged to take, on their individual guaranties
the funds in the entry-taker's offices that had
been received from the sale of lands. They
amounted in all to nearly thirteen thousand dollars, every dollar of which they afterward re-
funded.

On the twenty-sixth [1] they began the march,
over a thousand strong, most of them mounted
on swift, wiry horses. They were led by leaders
they trusted, they were wonted to Indian warfare,

[1] *State of the Proceedings of the Western Army from Sept.
25, 1780, to the Reduction of Major Ferguson and the Army
under his Command*, signed by Campbell, Shelby, and Cleavland. The official report ; it is in the Gates MSS. in the
New York Historical Society. It was published complete at
the time, except the tabulated statement of loss, which has
never been printed; I give it farther on.

they were skilled as horsemen and marksmen, they knew how to face every kind of danger, hardship, and privation. Their fringed and tasselled hunting-shirts were girded in by bead-worked belts, and the trappings of their horses were stained red and yellow. On their heads they wore caps of coonskin or minkskin, with the tails hanging down, or else felt hats, in each of which was thrust a bucktail or a sprig of evergreen. Every man carried a small-bore rifle, a tomahawk, and a scalping-knife. A very few of the officers had swords. and there was not a bayonet nor a tent in the army.[1] Before leaving their camping-ground at the Sycamore Shoals they gathered in an open grove to hear a stern old Presbyterian preacher[2] invoke on the enterprise the blessing of Jehovah. Leaning on their long rifles, they stood in rings round the black-frocked minister, a grim and wild congregation, who listened in silence to his words of burning zeal as he called on them to stand stoutly in the battle and to smite their foes with the sword of the Lord and of Gideon.

The army marched along Doe River, driving

[1] General William Lenoir's account, prepared for Judge A. D. Murphy's intended history of North Carolina. Lenoir was a private in the battle.

[2] Reverend Samuel Doak. Draper, 176. A tradition, but probably truthful, being based on the statements of Sevier and Shelby's soldiers in their old age. It is the kind of an incident that tradition will often faithfully preserve.

their beef cattle with them, and camped that night at the " Resting-Place," under Shelving Rock, beyond Crab Orchard. Next morning they started late, and went up the pass between Roan and Yellow mountains. The table-land on the top was deep in snow.[1] Here two tories who were in Sevier's band deserted and fled to warn Ferguson; and the troops, on learning of the desertion, abandoned their purpose of following the direct route, and turned to the left, taking a more northerly trail. It was of so difficult a character that Shelby afterwards described it as "the worst route ever followed by an army of horsemen." [2] That afternoon they partly descended the east side of the range, camping in Elk Hollow, near Roaring Run. The following day they went down through the ravines and across the spurs by a stony and precipitous path, in the midst of magnificent scenery, and camped at the mouth of Grassy Creek. On the 29th they crossed the Blue Ridge at Gillespie's Gap, and saw afar off, in the mountain coves and rich valleys of the upper Catawba, the advanced settlements of the Carolina pioneers,—for hitherto they had gone through an uninhabited waste. The mountaineers, fresh from their bleak and rugged hills, gazed with delight on the soft and fertile beauty of the landscape. That night they camped on the North

[1] " Diary " of Ensign Robert Campbell.   [2] Shelby MS.

Fork of the Catawba, and next day they went down the river to Quaker Meadows, McDowell's home.

At this point they were joined by three hundred and fifty North Carolina militia from the counties of Wilkes and Surrey, who were creeping along through the woods, hoping to fall in with some party going to harass the enemy.[1] They were under Colonel Benjamin Cleavland, a mighty hunter and Indian fighter, and an adventurous wanderer in the wilderness. He was an uneducated backwoodsman, famous for his great size and his skill with the rifle, no less than for the curious mixture of courage, rough good-humor, and brutality in his character. He bore a ferocious hatred to the royalists, and in the course of the vindictive civil war carried on between the whigs and tories in North Carolina he suffered much. In return he persecuted his public and private foes with ruthless ferocity, hanging and mutilating any tories against whom the neighboring whigs chose to bear evidence. As the fortunes of the war veered about he himself received

[1] Shelby MS. Autobiography. See also Gates MSS. Letter of William Davidson, September 14, 1780. Davidson had foreseen that there would be a fight between the western militia and Ferguson, and he had sent word to his militia subordinates to join any force—as McDowell's—that might go against the British leader. The alarm caused by the latter had prevented the militia from joining Davidson himself.

many injuries. His goods were destroyed, and his friends and relations were killed or had their ears cropped off. Such deeds often repeated roused to a fury of revenge his fierce and passionate nature, to which every principle of self-control was foreign. He had no hope of redress, save in his own strength and courage, and on every favorable opportunity he hastened to take more than ample vengeance. Admitting all the wrongs he suffered, it still remains true that many of his acts of brutality were past excuse. His wife was a worthy helpmeet. Once, in his absence, a tory horse-thief was brought to their home and, after some discussion, the captors, Cleavland's sons, turned to their mother, who was placidly going on with her ordinary domestic avocations, to know what they should do with the prisoner. Taking from her mouth the corn-cob pipe she had been smoking, she coolly sentenced him to be hung, and hung he was without further delay or scruple.[1] Yet Cleavland was a good friend and neighbor, devoted to his country, and also a staunch Presbyterian.[2]

The tories were already on the alert. Some of them had been harassing Cleavland, and they had ambushed his advance guard, and shot his brother, crippling him for life. But they did not dare try

[1] Draper, 448.
[2] Allaire's "Diary," entry for October 29, 1780.

to arrest the progress of so formidable a body of men as had been gathered together at Quaker Meadows; and contented themselves with sending repeated warnings to Ferguson.

On October 1st the combined forces marched past Pilot Mountain, and camped near the heads of Cane and Silver creeks. Hitherto each colonel had commanded his own men, there being no general head, and every morning and evening the colonels had met in concert to decide the day's movements. The whole expedition was one of volunteers, the agreement between the officers and the obedience rendered them by the soldiers simply depending on their own free-will; there was no legal authority on which to go, for the commanders had called out the militia without any instructions from the executives of their several States.[1] Disorders had naturally broken out. The men of the different companies felt some rivalry towards one another; and those of bad character, sure to be found in any such gathering, could not be properly controlled. Some of Cleavland's and McDowell's people were very unruly; and a few of the Watauga troops also behaved badly, plundering both whigs and tories,[2] and even

[1] Gates MSS. Letter of Campbell, Shelby, Cleavland, etc., October 4, 1780.

[2] Deposition of Colonel Matthew Willoughby (who was in the fight), April 30, 1823, *Richmond Enquirer*, May 9, 1823.

starting to drive the stolen stock back across the mountains.

At so important a crisis the good sense and sincere patriotism of the men in command made them sink all personal and local rivalries. On the 2d of October they all gathered to see what could be done to stop the disorders and give the army a single head; for it was thought that in a day or two they would close in with Ferguson. They were in Colonel Charles McDowell's district, and he was the senior officer; but the others distrusted his activity and judgment, and were not willing that he should command. To solve the difficulty, Shelby proposed that supreme command should be given to Colonel Campbell, who had brought the largest body of men with him, and who was a Virginian, whereas the other four colonels were North Carolinians.[1] Meanwhile, McDowell should go to Gates's army to get a general to command them, leaving his men under the charge of his brother Joseph, who was a major. This proposition was at once agreed to; and its adoption did much to ensure the subsequent success. Shelby not only acted wisely, but magnanimously; for he was himself of superior rank to Campbell, and

[1] Though by birth three were Virginians, and one, Shelby, a Marylander. All were Presbyterians. McDowell, like Campbell, was of Irish descent, Cleavland of English, Shelby of Welsh, and Sevier of French Huguenot. The families of the first two had originally settled in Pennsylvania.

moreover was a proud, ambitious man, desirous of military glory.

The army had been joined by two or three squads of partisans, including some refugee Georgians. They were about to receive a larger reinforcement; for at this time several small guerilla bands of North and South Carolina whigs were encamped at Flint Hill, some distance west of the encampment of the mountain men. These Flint Hill bands numbered about four hundred men, all told, under the leadership of various militia colonels—Hill, Lacey, Williams, Graham, and Hambright.[1] Hill and Lacey were two of Sumter's lieutenants, and had under them some of his men; Williams,[2] who was also a South Carolinian, claimed command of them because he had just been commissioned a brigadier-general of militia. His own force was very small, and he did not wish

[1] Hambright was a Pennsylvania German, the father of eighteen children. Hill, who was suffering from a severe wound, was unfit to take an active part in the King's Mountain fight. His MS. narrative of the campaign is largely quoted by Draper.

[2] Bancroft gives Williams an altogether undeserved prominence. As he had a commission as brigadier-general, some of the British thought he was in supreme command at King's Mountain; in a recent magazine article, General De Peyster again sets forth his claims. In reality he only had a small subordinate or independent command, and had no share whatever in conducting the campaign, and very little in the actual battle, though he behaved with much courage and was killed.

to attack Ferguson, but to march southwards to
Ninety-Six. Sumter's men, who were more numerous, were eager to join the mountaineers, and
entirely refused to submit to Williams. A hot
quarrel, almost resulting in a fight, ensued, Hill
and Lacey accusing Williams of being bent merely
on plundering the wealthy tories and of desiring
to avoid a battle with the British. Their imputa-
tion on his courage was certainly unjust; but they
were probably quite right when they accused him
of a desire to rob and plunder the tories. A succession of such quarrels speedily turned this assem-
blage of militia into an armed and warlike rabble.
Fortunately, Hill and Lacey prevailed, word was
sent to the mountaineers, and the Flint Hill bands
marched in loose order to join them at the Cowpens.[1]

The mountain army had again begun its march
on the afternoon of the third day of the month.
Before starting, the colonels summoned their men,
told them the nature and danger of the service,
and asked such as were unwilling to go farther to
step to the rear; but not a man did so. Then
Shelby made them a short speech, well adapted to
such a levy. He told them when they encountered
the enemy not to wait for the word of command,
but each to "be his own officer," and do all he

[1] Gates MSS. Letter of General William Davidson, October 3, 1780. Also Hill's "Narrative."

could, sheltering himself as far as possible, and not to throw away a chance; if they came on the British in the woods they were "to give them Indian play," and advance from tree to tree, pressing the enemy unceasingly. He ended by promising them that their officers would shrink from no danger, but would lead them everywhere, and, in their turn, they must be on the alert and obey orders.

When they set out their uncertainty as to Ferguson's movements caused them to go slowly, their scouts sometimes skirmishing with lurking tories. They reached the mouth of Cane Creek, near Gilbert Town, on October 4th. With the partisans that had joined them they then numbered fifteen hundred men. McDowell left them at this point to go to Gates with the request for the appointment of a general to command them.[1]

[1] Gates MSS. (in New York Historical Society). It is possible that Campbell was not chosen chief commander until this time; Ensign Robert Campbell's account (MSS. in Tennessee Historical Society) explicitly states this to be the case. The Shelby MS. and the official report make the date the 1st or 2d. One letter in the Gates MSS. has apparently escaped all notice from historians and investigators; it is the document which McDowell bore with him to Gates. It is dated "October 4th, 1780, near Gilbert town," and is signed by Cleavland, Shelby, Sevier, Campbell, Andrew Hampton, and J. Winston. It begins: "We have collected at this place 1500 good men drawn from the counties of Surrey, Wilkes, Burk, Washington, and Sullivan counties [sic] in this State and Washington County in Virginia." It says that they expect to be joined in a few days by Clarke of Georgia and Williams

For some days the men had been living on the ears of green corn which they plucked from the fields, but at this camping-place they slaughtered some beeves and made a feast.

The mountaineers had hoped to catch Ferguson at Gilbert Town, but they found that he had fled towards the northeast, so they followed after him. Many of their horses were crippled and exhausted, and many of the footmen footsore and weary; and the next day they were able to go but a dozen miles to the ford of Green River.

That evening Campbell and his fellow-officers held a council to decide what course was best to

of South Carolina with one thousand men (in reality, Clarke, who had nearly six hundred troops, never met them); asks for a general; says they have great need of ammunition, and remarks on the fact of their "troops being all militia, and but little acquainted with discipline." It was this document that gave the first impression to contemporaries that the battle was fought by 1500 Americans. Thus General Davidson's letter of October 10th to Gates, giving him the news of the victory, has served as a basis for most subsequent writers about the numbers. He got his particulars from one of Sumter's men, who was in the fight; but he evidently mixed them up in his mind, for he speaks of Williams, Lacey, and their companions as joining the others at Gilbert Town, instead of the Cowpens; makes the total number 3000, whereas, by the official report of October 4th, Campbell's party only numbered 1500, and Williams, Lacey, etc., had but 400, or 1900 in all; says that 1600 good horses were chosen out, evidently confusing this with the number at Gilbert Town; credits Ferguson with 1400 men, and puts the American loss at only 20 killed.

follow.   Lacey, riding over from the militia companies who were marching from Flint Hill, had just reached their camp; he told them the direction in which Ferguson had fled, and at the same time appointed the Cowpens as the meeting-place for their respective forces.   Their whole army was so jaded that the leaders knew they could not possibly urge it on fast enough to overtake Ferguson, and the flight of the latter made them feel all the more confident that they could beat him, and extremely reluctant that he should get away. In consequence, they determined to take seven or eight hundred of the least tired, best armed, and best mounted men, and push rapidly after their foe, picking up on the way any militia they met, and leaving the other half of their army to follow as fast as it could.

At daybreak on the morning of the sixth the picked men set out, about seven hundred and fifty in number.[1]   In the afternoon they passed by several large bands of tories, who had assembled to join Ferguson; but the Holston men were reso-

[1] MS. " Narrative " of Ensign Robert Campbell (see also Draper, 221) says seven hundred; and about fifty of the footmen who were in good training followed so quickly after them that they were able to take part in the battle.   Lenoir says the number was only five or six hundred.   The modern accounts generally fail to notice this Green River weeding out of the weak men, or confuse it with what took place at the Cowpens; hence many of them greatly exaggerate the number of Americans who fought in the battle.

lute in their determination to strike at the latter, and would not be diverted from it, nor waste time by following their lesser enemies.

Riding all day they reached the Cowpens when the sun had already set, a few minutes after the arrival of the Flint Hill militia under Lacey, Hill, and Williams. The tired troops were speedily engaged in skinning beeves for their supper, roasting them by the blazing camp-fires; and fifty acres of corn, belonging to the rich tory who owned the Cowpens, materially helped the meal. Meanwhile a council was held, in which all the leading officers, save Williams, took part. Campbell was confirmed as commander-in-chief, and it was decided to once more choose the freshest soldiers, and fall on Ferguson before he could either retreat or be reinforced. The officers went round, picking out the best men, the best rifles, and the best horses. Shortly after nine o'clock the choice had been made, and nine hundred and ten [1] picked riflemen, well mounted, rode out of the circle of

---

[1] The official report says 900; Shelby, in all his earlier narratives, 910; Hill, 933. The last authority is important because he was one of the 400 men who joined the mountaineers at the Cowpens, and his testimony confirms the explicit declaration of the official report that the 900 men who fought in the battle were chosen after the junction with Williams, Lacey, and Hill. A few late narratives, including that of Shelby in his old age, make the choice take place before the junction, and the total number then amount to 1300; evi-

flickering firelight, and began their night journey. A few determined footmen followed, going almost as fast as the horse, and actually reached the battle-field in season to do their share of the fighting.

All this time Ferguson had not been idle.   He first heard of the advance of the backwoodsmen on September 30th from the two tories who deserted Sevier on Yellow Mountain.   He had furloughed many of his loyalists, as all formidable resistance seemed at an end; and he now sent out messengers in every direction to recall them to his standard.   Meanwhile, he fell slowly back from the foothills, so that he might not have to face the mountaineers until he had time to gather his own troops.   He instantly wrote for reinforcements to Cruger, at Ninety-Six.   Cruger had just returned from routing the Georgian Colonel Clarke, who was besieging Augusta.   In the chase a number of Americans were captured, and thirteen were hung. The British and tories interpreted the already sufficiently severe instructions of their commander-in-chief with the utmost liberality, even the officers chronicling the hanging with exultant pleasure,

dently the choice at the Cowpens is by these authors confused with the choice at Green River. Shelby's memory when he was old was certainly very treacherous; in similar fashion he, as has been seen, exaggerated greatly his numbers at the Enoree. On the other hand, Robert Campbell puts the number at only 700, and Lenoir between 600 and 700. Both of these thus err in the opposite direction.

as pointing out the true way by which to end the war.[1]

Cruger, in his answer to Ferguson, explained that he did not have the number of militia regiments with which he was credited; and he did not seem to quite take in the gravity of the situation,[2] expressing his pleasure at hearing how strongly the loyalists of North Carolina had rallied to Ferguson's support, and speaking of the hope he had felt that the North Carolina tories would by themselves have proved "equal to the mountain lads." However, he promptly set about forwarding the reinforcements that were demanded; but before they could reach the scene of action the fate of the campaign had been decided.

Ferguson had not waited for outside help. He threw himself into the work of rallying the people of the plains, who were largely loyalists,[3] against the over-mountain men, appealing not only to their royalist sentiments, but to their strong local prejudices, and to the dread many of them felt for the wild border fighters. On the 1st of October he sent out a proclamation, of which copies were scattered broadcast among the loyalists. It was

[1] Draper, p. 201, quotes a printed letter from a British officer to this effect.

[2] Probably Ferguson himself failed to do so at this time.

[3] Gates MSS. Letter of Davidson, September 14th, speaks of the large number of tories in the counties where Ferguson was operating.

instinct with the fiery energy of the writer, and
well suited to goad into action the rough tories
and the doubtful men to whom it was addressed.
He told them that the backwater men had
crossed the mountains, with chieftains at their
head who would surely grant mercy to none who
had been loyal to the king. He called on them
to grasp their arms on the moment and run to his
standard, if they desired to live and bear the name
of men; to rally without delay, unless they wished
to be eaten up by the incoming horde of cruel barbarians, to be themselves robbed and murdered,
and to see their daughters and wives abused by
the dregs of mankind. In ending, he told them
scornfully that if they chose to be spat [1] upon and
degraded forever by a set of mongrels, to say so at
once, that their women might turn their backs
on them and look out for real men to protect
them.

Hoping to be joined by Cruger's regiments, as
well as by his own furloughed men and the neighboring tories, he gradually drew off from the mountains, doubling and turning, so as to hide his
route and puzzle his pursuers.   Exaggerated
reports of the increase in the number of his foes
were brought to him, and, as he saw how slowly
they marched, he sent repeated messages to
Cornwallis, asking for reinforcements; promising

[1] The word actually used was still stronger.

speedily to "finish the business," if three or four
hundred soldiers, part dragoons, were given him,
for the Americans were certainly making their
"last push in this quarter." [1] He was not willing
to leave the many loyal inhabitants of the district
to the vengeance of the whigs [2]; and his hopes of
reinforcements were well founded. Every day
furloughed men rejoined him, and bands of loyalists came into camp; and he was in momentary
expectation of help from Cornwallis or Cruger. It
will be remembered that the mountaineers on
their last march passed several tory bands. One
of these alone, near the Cowpens, was said to have
contained six hundred men; and in a day or two
they would all have joined Ferguson. If the
whigs had come on in a body, as there was every
reason to expect, Ferguson would have been given
the one thing he needed—time; and he would
certainly have been too strong for his opponents.
His defeat was due to the sudden push of the
mountain chieftains; to their long, swift ride from
the ford of Green River, at the head of their
picked horse-riflemen.

The British were still in the dark as to the exact
neighborhood from which their foes—the "swarm
of backwoodsmen," as Tarleton called them [3]—

---

[1] See letter quoted by Tarleton.

[2] Ferguson's *Memoir*, p. 32.

[3] Tarleton's *Campaigns*, p. 169.

really came.   It was generally supposed that they
were in part from Kentucky, and that Boon himself was among the number.[1]   However, Ferguson probably cared very little who they were;
and keeping, as he supposed, a safe distance away
from them, he halted at King's Mountain in South
Carolina on the evening of October 6th, pitching
his camp on a steep, narrow hill just south of the
North Carolina boundary.   The King's Mountain
range itself is about sixteen miles in length, extend-
ing in a southwesterly course from one State into
the other.   The stony, half-isolated ridge on which
Ferguson camped was some six or seven hundred
yards long and half as broad from base to base, or
two thirds that distance on top.   The steep sides
were clad with a growth of open woods, including
both saplings and big timber.   Ferguson parked
his baggage-wagons along the northeastern part
of the mountain.   The next day he did not move;

[1] British historians to the present day repeat this.   Even
Lecky, in his *History of England*, speaks of the backwoodsmen as in part from Kentucky.   Having pointed out this
trivial fault in Lecky's work, it would be ungracious not to
allude to the general justice and impartiality of its accounts
of these Revolutionary campaigns; they are very much more
trustworthy than Bancroft's, for instance.   Lecky scarcely
gives the right color to the struggle in the South; but when
Bancroft treats of it, it is not too much to say that he puts
the contest between the whigs and the British and tories in
a decidedly false light.   Lecky fails to do justice to Washington's military ability, however; and overrates the French
assistance.

he was as near to the army of Cornwallis at Char-
lotte as to the mountaineers, and he thought it
safe to remain where he was.   He deemed the
position one of great strength,—as indeed it would
have been, if assailed in the ordinary European
fashion,—and he was confident that even if the
rebels attacked him he could readily beat them
back.   But, as General Lee, "Light-Horse Harry,"
afterwards remarked, the hill was much easier
assaulted with the rifle than defended with the
bayonet.

The backwoodsmen, on leaving the camp at
the Cowpens, marched slowly through the night,
which was dark and drizzly; many of the men
got scattered in the woods, but joined their commands in the morning—the morning of October
7th.   The troops bore down to the southward, a
little out of the straight route, to avoid any patrol
parties;   and at sunrise they splashed across
the Cherokee ford.[1]   Throughout the forenoon the
rain continued, but the troops pushed steadily onwards without halting,[2] wrapping their blankets

[1] *American Pioneer*, ii., 67.   An account of one of the soldiers, Benjamin Sharp, written in his old age; full of contra-
dictions of every kind (he, for instance, forgets they joined
Williams at the Cowpens); it cannot be taken as an authority,
but supplies some interesting details.

[2] Late in life Shelby asserted that this steadiness in pushing
on was due to his own influence.   The other accounts do not
bear him out.

and the skirts of their hunting-shirts round their gun-locks, to keep them dry. Some horses gave out, but their riders, like the thirty or forty foot-men who had followed from the Cowpens, struggled onwards and were in time for the battle. When near King's Mountain they captured two tories, and from them learned Ferguson's exact position; that "he was on a ridge between two branches,[1]" where some deer-hunters had camped the previous fall. These deer-hunters were now with the oncoming backwoodsmen, and declared that they knew the ground well. Without halting, Campbell and the other colonels rode forward together, and agreed to surround the hill so that their men might fire upwards without risk of hurting one another. It was a bold plan; for they knew their foes probably outnumbered them; but they were very confident of their own prowess and were anxious to strike a crippling blow. From one or two other captured tories, and from a staunch whig friend, they learned the exact disposition of the British and loyalist force, and were told that their noted leader wore a light parti-colored hunting-shirt; and he was forthwith doomed to be a special target for the backwoods rifles. When within a mile of the hill a halt was called, and after a hasty council of the different colonels—in which Williams did not take part,—

[1] _I. e._, brooks.

the final arrangements were made, and the men, who had been marching in loose order, were formed in line of battle. They then rode forward in absolute silence and, when close to the west slope of the battle-hill, beyond King's Creek, drew rein and dismounted. They tied their horses to trees, and fastened their great coats and blankets to the saddles, for the rain had cleared away. A few of the officers remained mounted. The countersign of the day was "Buford," the name of the colonel whose troops Tarleton had defeated and butchered. The final order was for each man to look carefully at the priming of his rifle, and then to go into battle and fight till he died.

The foes were now face to face. On the one side were the American backwoodsmen, under their own leaders, armed in their own manner, and fighting after their own fashion, for the freedom and the future of America; on the opposite side were other Americans—the loyalists, led by British officers, armed and trained in the British fashion, and fighting on behalf of the empire of Britain and the majesty of the monarchy. The Americans numbered, all told, about nine hundred and fifty men.[1] The British forces were composed,

[1] Nine hundred and ten horsemen (possibly 900, or perhaps 933) started out; and the footmen who kept up were certainly less than 50 in number. There is really no question as to the American numbers; yet a variety of reasons have conspired to cause them to be generally greatly overstated, even by Ameri-

in bulk, of the Carolina loyalists—troops similar
to the Americans who joined the mountaineers at
Quaker Meadows and the Cowpens [1]; the differ-

can historians.   Even Phelan gives them 1500 men, following
the ordinary accounts.   At the time, many outsiders supposed
that all the militia who were at the Cowpens fought in the
battle; but this is not asserted by any one who knew the
facts.   General J. Watts De Peyster, in the *Magazine of
American History* for 1880,—"The Affair at King's Mountain,"
—gives the extreme tory view.   He puts the number of the
Americans at from 1300 to 1900.   His account, however, is
only based on Shelby's later narratives, told thirty years after
the event, and these are all that need be considered.   When
Shelby grew old he greatly exaggerated the numbers on both
sides in all the fights in which he had taken part.   In his
account of King's Mountain, he speaks of Williams and the
400 Flint Hill men joining the attacking body *after*, not *before*,
the 910 picked men started.   But his earlier accounts, including the official report which he signed, explicitly contradict
this.   The question is thus purely as to the time of the junction: as to whether it was after or before this that the body
of 900 actual fighters was picked out.   Shelby's later report
contains the grossest self-contradictions.   Thus it enumerates
the companies which fought the battle in detail, the result
running up several hundred more than the total he gives.   The
early and official accounts are in every way more worthy of
credence; but the point is settled beyond dispute by Hill's
"Narrative."   Hill was one of the 400 men with Williams,
and he expressly states that after the junction at the Cowpens
the force, from both commands, that started out numbered
933.   The question is thus definitely settled.   Most of the
later accounts simply follow the statements Shelby made in
his old age.

[1] There were many instances of brothers and cousins in
the opposing ranks at King's Mountain; a proof of the simi-
larity in the character of the forces.

ence being that besides these lowland militia,
there were arrayed on one side the men from the
Holston, Watauga, and Nolichucky, and on the
other the loyalist regulars. Ferguson had, all told,
between nine hundred and a thousand troops, a
hundred and twenty or thirty of them being the
regulars or "American Volunteers," the remainder
tory militia.[1] The forces were very nearly equal
in number. What difference there was, was probably in favor of the British and tories. There was

---

[1] The American official account says that they captured
the British provision returns, according to which their force
amounted to 1125 men. It further reports, of the regulars,
19 killed, 35 wounded and left on the ground as unable to
march, and 78 captured; of the tories, 206 killed, 128 wounded
and left on the ground, unable to march, and 648 captured.
The number of tories killed must be greatly exaggerated.
Allaire, in his "Diary," says Ferguson had only 800 men, but
almost in the same sentence enumerates 906, giving of the
regulars 19 killed, 33 wounded, and 64 captured (116 in all,
instead of 132, as in the American account), and of the tories
100 killed, 90 wounded, and "about" 600 captured. This
does not take account of those who escaped. From Ramsey
and De Peyster down most writers assert that every single
individual on the defeated side was killed or taken; but in
Colonel Chesney's admirable *Military Biography* there is
given the autobiography or memoir of a South Carolina
loyalist who was in the battle. His account of the battle is
meagre and unimportant, but he expressly states that at the
close he and a number of others escaped through the American
lines by putting sprigs of white paper in their caps, as some
of the whig militia did—for the militia had no uniforms, and
were dressed alike on both sides. A certain number of men
who escaped must thus be added.

not a bayonet in the American army, whereas
Ferguson trusted much to this weapon. All his
volunteers and regulars were expert in its use, and
with his usual ingenuity he had trained several of
his loyalist companies in a similar manner, im-
provising bayonets out of their hunting-knives.
The loyalists whom he had had with him for
some time were well drilled. The North Carolina
regiment was weaker on this point, as it was composed of recruits who had joined him but recently.[1]

[1] There were undoubtedly very many horse-thieves, murderers, and rogues of every kind with Ferguson, but equally
undoubtedly the bulk of his troops were loyalists from principle and men of good standing, especially those from the seaboard. Many of the worst tory bandits did not rally to him,
preferring to plunder on their own account. The American
army itself was by no means free from scoundrels. Most
American writers belittle the character of Ferguson's force
and sneer at the courage of the tories, although entirely unable
to adduce any proof of their statements, the evidence being
the other way. Apparently they are unconscious of the fact
that they thus wofully diminish the credit to be given to the
victors. It may be questioned if there ever was a braver or
finer body of riflemen than the nine hundred who surrounded
and killed or captured a superior body of well-posted, well-
led, and courageous men, in part also well-drilled, on King's
Mountain. The whole world now recognizes how completely
the patriots were in the right; but it is especially incumbent
on American historians to fairly portray the acts and character of the tories, doing justice to them as well as to the whigs,
and condemning them only when they deserve it. In study-
ing the Revolutionary War in the Southern States, I have
been struck by the way in which the American historians
alter the facts by relying purely on partisan accounts, sup-

The Americans were discovered by their foes when only a quarter of a mile away. They had formed their forces as they marched. The right centre was composed of Campbell's troops; the left centre of Shelby's. These two bodies separated slightly so as to come up opposite sides of the narrow southwestern spur of the mountain. The right wing was led by Sevier, with his own and McDowell's troops. On the extreme right Major Winston, splitting off from the main body a few minutes before, had led a portion of Cleavland's men by a roundabout route to take the mountain in the rear, and cut off all retreat. He and his

pressing the innumerable whig excesses and outrages, or else palliating them. They thus really destroy the force of the many grave accusations which may be truthfully brought against the British and tories. I regret to say that Bancroft is among the offenders. Hildreth is an honorable exception. Most of the British historians of the same events are even more rancorous and less trustworthy than the American writers; and while fully admitting the many indefensible outrages committed by the whigs, a long-continued and impartial examination of accessible records has given me the belief that in the districts where the Civil War was most ferocious, much the largest number of the criminal class joined the tories, and the misdeeds of the latter were more numerous than those of the whigs. But the frequency with which both whigs and tories hung men for changing sides, shows that quite a number of the people shifted from one party to the other; and so there must have been many men of exactly the same stamp in both armies. Much of the nominal changing of sides, however, was due to the needless and excessive severity of Cornwallis and his lieutenants.

followers "rode like fox-hunters," as was afterwards reported by one of their number who was accustomed to following the buck and the gray fox with horn and hound. They did not dismount until they reached the foot of the mountain, galloping at full speed through the rock-strewn woods; and they struck exactly the right place, closing up the only gap by which the enemy could have retreated. The left wing was led by Cleavland. It contained not only the bulk of his own Wilkes and Surrey men, but also the North and South Carolinians who had joined the army at the Cowpens under the command of Williams, Lacey, Hambright, Chronicle, and others.[1] The different leaders cheered on their troops by a few last words as they went into the fight; being especially careful to warn them how to deal with the British bayonet charges. Campbell had visited each separate band, again requesting every man who felt like flinching not to go into the battle. He bade them hold on to every inch of ground as long as possible, and when forced back to rally and return at once to the fight. Cleavland gave much the same advice; telling his men that when once engaged they were not to wait for

[1] Draper gives a good plan of the battle. He also gives some pictures of the fighting, in which the backwoodsmen are depicted in full Continental uniform, which probably not a man—certainly very few of them—wore.

the word of command, but to do as he did, for he would show them by his example how to fight, and they must then act as their own officers. The men were to fire quickly, and stand their ground as long as possible, if necessary sheltering themselves behind trees. If they could do no better they were to retreat, but not to run quite off; but to return and renew the struggle, for they might have better luck at the next attempt.[1]

So rapid were the movements of the Americans, and so unexpected the attack, that a loyalist officer, who had been out reconnoitring, had just brought word to the British commander that there was no sign of danger, when the first shots were heard; and by the time the officer had paraded and posted his men, the assault had begun, his horse had been killed, and he himself wounded.[2]

[1] Ramsey (*Revolution in South Carolina*), writing in 1785, gives the speech verbatim, apparently from Cleavland himself. It is very improbable that it is verbally correct, but doubtless it represents the spirit of his remarks.

[2] *Essays in Military Biography*, Colonel Charles Cornwallis Chesney, London, 1874. On p. 323 begins a memoir of "A Carolina Loyalist in the Revolutionary War." It is written by the loyalist himself, who was presumably a relation of Colonel Chesney's. It was evidently written after the event, and there are some lapses. Thus he makes the war with the Cherokees take place in 1777, instead of '76. His explanation of Tarleton's defeat at the Cowpens must be accepted with much reserve. At King's Mountain he says the Americans had fifteen hundred men, instead of twenty-five hundred, of

When Ferguson learned that his foes were on him, he sprang on his horse, his drums beat to arms, and he instantly made ready for the fight. Though surprised by the unexpected approach of the Americans, he exerted himself with such energy that his troops were in battle array when the attack began.   The outcrops of slaty rock on the hillsides made ledges which, together with the boulders strewn on top, served as breastworks for the less disciplined tories; while he in person led his regulars and such of the loyalist companies as were furnished with the hunting-knife bayonets. He hoped to be able to repulse his enemies by himself taking the offensive, with a succession of bayonet charges—a form of attack in which his experience with Pulaski and Huger had given him great confidence.

At three o'clock in the afternoon the firing began, as the Americans drove in the British pickets. The brunt of the battle fell on the American centre, composed of Campbell's and Shelby's men, who sustained the whole fight for nearly ten minutes [1] until the two wings had time to get into place and surround the enemy.   Campbell began the assault, riding on horseback along the line of his

which Allaire speaks.   Allaire probably consciously exaggerated the number.

[1] Campbell MSS.   Letter of Colonel William Campbell, October 10, 1780, says ten minutes: the official report (Gates MSS.) says five minutes.

riflemen. He ordered them to raise the Indian war-whoop, which they did with a will, and made the woods ring.[1] They then rushed upwards and began to fire, each on his own account; while their war-cries echoed along the hillside. Ferguson's men on the summit responded with heavy volley firing, and then charged, cheering lustily. The mountain was covered with smoke and flame, and seemed to thunder.[2] Ferguson's troops advanced steadily, their officers riding at their head, with their swords flashing; and the mountaineers, who had no bayonets, could not withstand the shock. They fled down the hillside and being sinewy, nimble men, swift of foot, they were not overtaken, save a few of sullen temper, who would not retreat and were bayoneted. One of their officers, a tall backwoodsman, six feet in height, was cut down by Lieutenant Allaire, a New York loyalist, as the latter rode at the head of his platoon. No sooner had the British charge spent itself than Campbell, who was riding midway between the

[1] *Richmond Enquirer* (November 12, 1822 and May 9, 1823), certificates of King's Mountain survivors—of James Crow, May 6, 1813; David Beattie, May 4, 1813, etc. All the different commanders in after-life claimed the honor of beginning the battle; the official report decides it in favor of Campbell and Shelby, the former being the first actually engaged, as is acknowledged by Shelby in his letter to Arthur Campbell on October 12, 1780.

[2] Haywood, 71; doubtless he uses the language of one of the actors.

enemy and his own men, called out to the latter in a voice of thunder to rally and return to the fight, and in a minute or two they were all climbing the hill again, going from tree to tree, and shooting at the soldiers on the summit. Campbell's horse, exhausted by the breakneck galloping hither and thither over the slope, gave out; he then led the men on foot, his voice hoarse with shouting, his face blackened with powder; for he was always in the front of the battle and nearest the enemy.

No sooner had Ferguson returned from his charge on Campbell than he found Shelby's men swarming up to the attack on the other side. Shelby himself was at their head. He had refused to let his people return the dropping fire of the tory skirmishers until they were close up. Ferguson promptly charged his new foes and drove them down the hillside; but the instant he stopped, Shelby, who had been in the thick of the fight, closest to the British, brought his marksmen back, and they came up nearer than ever, and with a deadlier fire.[1] While Ferguson's bayonet-men—both regulars and militia—charged to and fro, the rest of the loyalists kept up a heavy fire from behind the rocks on the hill-top. The battle raged in every part, for the Americans had by this time surrounded their foes, and they advanced rapidly under cover of the woods. They

[1] Shelby, MS.

inflicted much more damage than they suffered,
for they were scattered out while the royalist
troops were close together, and, moreover, were
continually taken in flank.   Ferguson, conspicuous from his hunting-shirt,[1] rode hither and
thither with reckless bravery, his sword in his left
hand—for he had never entirely regained the use
of his wounded right—while he made his presence
known by the shrill, ear-piercing notes of a silver
whistle which he always carried.   Whenever the
British and tories charged with the bayonet, under
Ferguson, De Peyster, or some of their lieutenants,
the mountaineers were forced back down the hill;
but the instant the red lines halted and returned
to the summit, the stubborn riflemen followed
close behind, and from every tree and boulder
continued their irregular and destructive fire.
The peculiar feature of the battle was the success
with which, after every retreat, Campbell, Shelby,
Sevier, and Cleavland rallied their followers on
the instant; the great point was to prevent the
men from becoming panic-stricken when forced to
flee.   The pealing volleys of musketry at short
intervals drowned the incessant clatter of the less
noisy but more deadly backwoods rifles.   The
wild whoops of the mountain men, the cheering of

[1] The *South Carolina Loyalist* speaks as if the hunting-shirt
were put on for disguise; it says Ferguson was recognized,
"although wearing a hunting-shirt."

the loyalists, the shouts of the officers, and the
cries of the wounded mingled with the reports of
the firearms, and shrill above the din rose the calling of the silver whistle.   Wherever its notes were
heard the wavering British line came on, and the
Americans were forced back.   Ferguson dashed
from point to point, to repel the attacks of his foes,
which were made with ever-increasing fury.   Two
horses were killed under him [1] ; but he continued
to lead the charging parties, slashing and hewing
with his sword until it was broken off at the hilt.
At last, as he rode full speed against a part of
Sevier's men, who had almost gained the hill crest,
he became a fair mark for the vengeful backwoods
riflemen.   Several of them fired together and he
fell suddenly from his horse, pierced by half a
dozen bullets almost at the same instant.   The
gallant British leader was dead, while his foot yet
hung in the stirrup.[2]

[1] Ferguson's *Memoir*, p. 32.

[2] The *South Carolina Loyalist* says he was killed just as he
had slain Colonel Williams "with his left hand."   Ramsey,
on the other side, represents Colonel Williams as being shot
while dashing forward to kill Ferguson.   Williams certainly
was not killed by Ferguson himself, and in all probability
the latter was slain earlier in the action and in an entirely
different part of the line.   The *Loyalist* is also in error as to
Cleavland's regiment being the first that was charged.   There
is no ground whatever for the statement that Ferguson was
trying to escape when shot; nor was there any attempt at a
charge of horsemen, made in due form.   The battle was

The silver whistle was now silent, but the disheartened loyalists were rallied by De Peyster, who bravely continued the fight.[1] It is said that he himself led one of the charges which were at this time made on Cleavland's line; the "South Fork" men from the Catawba, under Hambright and Chronicle, being forced back, Chronicle being killed and Hambright wounded. When the Americans fled, they were scarcely a gun's length ahead of their foes; and the instant the latter faced about the former were rallied by their officers, and again went up the hill. One of the backwoodsmen was in the act of cocking his rifle when a loyalist, dashing at him with the bayonet, pinned his hand to his thigh; the rifle went off, the ball going through the loyalist's body, and the two men fell together. Hambright, though wounded, was able to sit in the saddle, and continued in the battle. Cleavland had his horse shot under him, and then led his men on foot. As the lines came close together, many of the whigs recognized in the tory ranks their former neighbors, friends, or relatives; and the men taunted and jeered one another with

purely one of footmen and the attempt to show an effort at a cavalry charge at the end is a simple absurdity.

[1] In his *Historical Magazine* article, General Watts De Peyster clears his namesake's reputation from all charge of cowardice; but his account of how De Peyster counselled and planned all sorts of expedients that might have saved the loyalists is decidedly mythical.

bitter hatred. In more than one instance brother was slain by brother or cousin by cousin. The lowland tories felt an especial dread of the mountaineers; looking with awe and hatred on their tall, gaunt, rawboned figures, their long, matted hair and wild faces. One wounded tory, as he lay watching them, noticed their deadly accuracy of aim, and saw also that the loyalists, firing from the summit, continually overshot their foes.

The British regulars had lost half their number; the remainder had been scattered and exhausted in their successive charges. The bayonet companies of the loyalist militia were in the same plight; and the North Carolina tories, the least disciplined, could no longer be held to their work. Sevier's men gained the summit at the same time with Campbell's and part of Shelby's. The three colonels were heading their troops; and as Sevier saw Shelby, he swore, by God, the British had burned off part of his hair; for it was singed on one side of his head.

When the Holston and Watauga men gained the crest the loyalists broke and fled to the east end of the mountain, among the tents and baggage-wagons, where they again formed. But they were huddled together, while their foes surrounded them on every hand. The fighting had lasted an hour; all hope was gone; and De Peyster hoisted a white flag.

In the confusion the firing continued in parts of the lines on both sides. Some of the backwoodsmen did not know what a white flag meant; others disregarded it, savagely calling out, "Give them Buford's play," in allusion to Tarleton's having refused quarter to Buford's troops.[1] Others of the men as they came up began shooting before they learned what had happened; and some tories who had been out foraging returned at this moment, and also opened fire. A number of the loyalists escaped in the turmoil, putting badges in their hats like those worn by certain of the American militia and thus passing in safety through the whig lines.[2] It was at this time, after the white flag had been displayed, that Colonel Williams was shot, as he charged a few of the tories who were still firing. The flag was hoisted again, and white handkerchiefs were also waved from guns and ramrods. Shelby, spurring up to part of their line, ordered the tories to lay down their arms, which they did.[3] Campbell, at the same moment, running among his men with his sword pointed to the ground, called on them for God's sake to cease firing; and turning to the prisoners he bade the officers rank by themselves, and the men to take off their hats and sit down. He then ordered De Peyster to dismount; which the latter did, and handed his sword

---

[1] Deposition of John Long, in *Enquirer*, as quoted.
[2] Chesney, p. 333.   [3] Shelby MS.

to Campbell.[1] The various British officers likewise surrendered their swords to different Americans, many of the militia commanders who had
hitherto only possessed a tomahawk or scalping-
knife thus for the first time getting possession of
one of the coveted weapons.

Almost the entire British and tory force was
killed or captured; the only men who escaped were
the few who got through the American lines by
adopting the whig badges. About three hundred
of the loyalists were killed or disabled; the slightly
wounded do not seem to have been counted.[2] The
colonel-commandant was among the slain; of the
four militia colonels present, two were killed, one
wounded,[3] and the other captured—a sufficient
proof of the obstinacy of the resistance. The
American loss in killed and wounded amounted
to less than half, perhaps only a third, that of

[1] Campbell MSS. Letter of General George Rutledge (who
was in the battle, an eye-witness of what he describes), May
27, 1813. But there is an irreconcilable conflict of testimony
as to whether Campbell or Evan Shelby received De Peyster's
sword.

[2] For the loyalist losses, see *ante*, note discussing their
numbers. The *South Carolina Loyalist* says they lost about
a third of their number. It is worthy of note that the actual
fighting at King's Mountain bore much resemblance to that
at Majuba Hill a century later; a backwoods levy was much
like a Boer commando.

[3] In some accounts, this officer is represented as a major, in
some, as a colonel; at any rate he was in command of a small
regiment, or fragment of a regiment.

their foes.[1] Campbell's command suffered more
than any other, the loss among the officers being
especially great, for it bore the chief part in

[1] The official report as published gave the American loss as
twenty-eight killed and sixty wounded. The original document (in the Gates MSS., New York Historical Society) gives
the loss in tabulated form in an appendix, which has not here-
tofore been published. It is as follows:

RETURN OF KILLED AND WOUNDED.

REGIMENTS.	KILLED.								WOUNDED.								Grand Total.
	Col.	Major.	Capt.	Lieut.	Ensign.	Sergt.	Private.	Total.	Col.	Major.	Capt.	Lieut.	Ensign.	Sergt.	Private.	Total.	
Campbell's			1	2	4		5	12		1	3				17	21	33
McDowell's							4	4							4	4	8
Thomas's															8	8	8
Cleavland's							8	8		1	2				10	13	21
Shelby's																	
Sevier's							2	2							10	10	12
Hayes's		1						1							3	3	4
Brannon's															3	3	3
Col. Williams's	1							1									1
	1	1	1	2	4		19	28		1	3	3			55	62	90

It will be seen that these returns are imperfect. They do
not include Shelby's loss; yet his regiment was alongside of
Campbell's, did its full share of the work, and probably suffered as much as Sevier's, for instance. But it is certain
that in the hurry not all the killed and wounded were enumer-
ated (compare Draper, pp. 302–304). Hayes's, Thomas's, and
"Brannon's" (Brandon's) commands were some of those
joining at the Cowpens. Winston's loss is doubtless included
under Cleavland's. It will be seen that Williams's troops
could have taken very little part in the action.

withstanding the successive bayonet charges of the regulars, and the officers had been forced to expose themselves with the utmost freedom in order to rally their men when beaten back.[1]

The mountain men had done a most notable deed. They had shown in perfection the best qualities of horse-riflemen. Their hardihood and perseverance had enabled them to bear up well under fatigue, exposure, and scanty food. Their long, swift ride, and the suddenness of the attack took their foes completely by surprise. Then leaving their horses, they had shown in the actual battle such courage, marksmanship, and skill in woodland fighting, that they had not only defeated but captured an equal number of well-armed, well-led, resolute men, in a strong position. The victory was of far-reaching importance and ranks among the decisive battles of the Revolution. It was the first great success of the

[1] It would be quite impossible to take notice of the countless wild absurdities of the various writers who have given "histories," so-called, of the battle. One of the most recent of them, Mr. Kirke, having accepted as the number of the British dead two hundred and twenty-five, and the wounded one hundred and eighty-five, says that the disproportion shows "the wonderful accuracy of the backwoods rifle"—the beauty of the argument being that it necessarily implies that the backwoodsmen only fired some 410 shots. Mr. Kirke's account of the battle having been "won" owing to a remarkable ride taken by Sevier to rally the men at the critical moment is, of course, without any historic basis whatever.

Americans in the South, the turning-point in the southern campaign, and it brought cheer to the patriots throughout the Union. The loyalists of the Carolinas were utterly cast down, and never recovered from the blow; and its immediate effect was to cause Cornwallis to retreat from North Carolina, abandoning his first invasion of that State.[1]

The expedition offered a striking example of the individual initiative so characteristic of the back-woodsmen. It was not ordered by any one authority; it was not even sanctioned by the central or State governments. Shelby and Sevier were the two prime movers in getting it up, Campbell exercised the chief command, and the various other leaders, with their men, simply joined the mountaineers, as they happened to hear of them and come across their path. The ties of discipline were of the slightest. The commanders elected their own chief without regard to rank or seniority; in fact the officer [2] who was by rank entitled to the place was hardly given any share in the conduct of the campaign. The authority of the commandant over the other officers, and of the various colonels over their troops, resembled rather the control exercised by Indian chiefs over their warriors than the discipline obtained in the regular army. But the men were splendid individual fighters, who

[1] Tarleton's *Campaigns*, p. 166.   [2] Williams.

liked and trusted their leaders; and the latter were bold, resolute, energetic, and intelligent.

Cornwallis feared that the mountain men would push on and attack his flank; but there was no such danger. By themselves they were as little likely to assail him in force in the open as Andreas Hofer's Tyrolese—with whom they had many points in common—were to threaten Napoleon on the Danubian plains. Had they been Continental troops, the British would have had to deal with a permanent army. But they were only militia [1] after all, however formidable from their patriotic purpose and personal prowess. The backwoods armies were not unlike the armies of the Scotch Highlanders; tumultuous gatherings of hardy and warlike men, greatly to be dreaded under certain

[1] The striking nature of the victory and its important consequences must not blind us to the manifold shortcomings of the Revolutionary militia. The mountaineers did well in spite of being militia; but they would have done far better under another system. The numerous failures of the militia as a whole must be balanced against the few successes of a portion of them. If the States had possessed wisdom enough to back Washington with Continentals, or with volunteers such as those who fought in the Civil War, the Revolutionary contest would have been over in three years. The trust in militia was a perfect curse. Many of the backwoods leaders knew this. The old Indian fighter, Andrew Lewis, about this time wrote to Gates (see Gates MSS., September 30, 1780), speaking of the "dastardly conduct of the militia," calling them "a set of poltroons," and longing for Continentals.

circumstances, but incapable of a long campaign
and almost as much demoralized by a victory as
by a defeat. Individually, or in small groups, they
were perhaps even more formidable than the Highlanders; but in one important respect they were
inferior, for they totally lacked the regimental organization which the clan system gave the Scotch
Celts.

The mountaineers had come out to do a certain
thing—to kill Ferguson and scatter his troops.
They had done it, and now they wished to go
home. The little log-huts in which their families
lived were in daily danger of Indian attack; and it
was absolutely necessary that they should be on
hand to protect them. They were, for the most
part, very poor men, whose sole sources of liveli-
hood were the stock they kept beyond the mountains. They loved their country greatly, and had
shown the sincerity of their patriotism by the
spontaneous way in which they risked their lives
on this expedition. They had no hope of reward;
for they neither expected nor received any pay
except in liquidated certificates, worth two cents
on the dollar. Shelby's share of these, for his
services as colonel throughout '80 and '81, was
sold by him for "six yards of middling broad-
cloth" [1]; so it can be readily imagined how little

---

[1] Shelby's MS. Autobiography.

each private got for the King's Mountain expedition.[1]

The day after the battle the Americans fell back towards the mountains, fearing lest, while cumbered by prisoners and wounded, they should be struck by Tarleton or perhaps Cruger. The prisoners were marched along on foot, each carrying one or two muskets, for twelve hundred stands of arms had been captured. The Americans had little to eat, and were very tired; but the plight of the prisoners was pitiable. Hungry, footsore, and heartbroken, they were hurried along by the fierce and boastful victors, who gloried in the vengeance they had taken, and recked little of such a virtue as magnanimity to the fallen. The only surgeon in either force was Ferguson's. He did what he could for the wounded; but that was little enough, for, of course, there were no medical stores whatever. The Americans buried their dead in graves, and carried their wounded along on horse-litters. The wounded loyalists were left on the field, to be cared for by the neighboring people. The conquerors showed neither respect nor sympathy for the leader who had so gallantly fought them.[2] His body and the bodies of his slain followers were cast

[1] Among these privates was the father of Davy Crockett.

[2] But the accounts of indignity being shown him are not corroborated by Allaire and Ryerson, the two contemporary British authorities, and are probably untrue.

into two shallow trenches, and loosely covered
with stones and earth. The wolves, coming to
the carnage, speedily dug up the carcasses, and
grew so bold from feasting at will on the dead that
they no longer feared the living. For months
afterwards King's Mountain was a favorite resort
for wolf-hunters.

The victory once gained, the bonds of discipline
over the troops were forthwith loosened; they had
been lax at the best, and only the strain of the
imminent battle with the British had kept them
tense for the fortnight the mountaineers had been
away from their homes. All the men of the different commands were bragging as to their respective
merits in the battle, and the feats performed by
the different commanders.[1] The general break-up
of authority, of course, allowed full play to the
vicious and criminal characters. Even before the
mountaineers came down, the unfortunate Carolinas had suffered from the misdeeds of different
bodies of ill-disciplined patriot troops,[2] almost as
much as from the British and tories. The case was
worse now. Many men deserted from the returning army for the especial purpose of plundering
the people of the neighborhood, paying small heed

[1] Certificate of Matthew Willoughby, in *Richmond Enquirer*,
as quoted.

[2] Gates MSS., deposition of John Satty and others, September 7, 1780; of William Hamilton, September 12th, etc.

which cause the victims had espoused; and parties
continually left camp avowedly with this object.
Campbell's control was of the slightest; he was
forced to entreat rather than command the troops,
complaining that they left their friends in "almost
a worse situation than the enemy would have
done," and expressing what was certainly a moderate "wish," that the soldiers would commit no
"unnecessary injury" on the inhabitants of the
country.[1] Naturally, such very mild measures
produced little effect in stopping the plundering.

However, Campbell spoke in stronger terms of
an even worse set of outrages. The backwoodsmen had little notion of mercy to beaten enemies,
and many of them treated the captured loyalists
with great brutality, even on the march,[2] Colonel
Cleavland himself being one of the offenders.[3]
Those of their friends and relatives who had
fallen into the hands of the tories, or of Cornwallis's regulars, had fared even worse; yet this
cannot palliate their conduct. Campbell himself,
when in a fit of gusty anger, often did things he
must have regretted afterwards; but he was essentially manly, and his soul revolted at the continued
persecution of helpless enemies. He issued a

[1] Campbell's General Orders, October 14th and October 26th.

[2] "Our captors . . . cutting and striking us in a most
savage manner."—*South Carolina Loyalist.*

[3] Allaire's " Dairy," entry of November 1st.

sharp manifesto in reference to the way the prisoners were "slaughtered and disturbed," assuring the troops that if it could not be prevented
by moderate measures, he would put a stop to it
by taking summary vengeance on the offenders.[1]
After this, the prisoners were, on the whole, well
treated. When they met a couple of Continental
officers, the latter were very polite, expressing their
sympathy for their fate in falling into such hands;
for from Washington and Greene down, the Continental troops disliked and distrusted the militia almost as much as the British regulars did the tories.

There was one dark deed of vengeance. It had
come to be common for the victors on both sides to
hang those whom they regarded as the chief offenders among their conquered opponents. As
the different districts were alternately overrun,
the unfortunate inhabitants were compelled to
swear allegiance in succession to Congress and to
king; and then, on whichever side they bore arms,
they were branded as traitors. Moreover, the
different leaders, both British and American, from
Tarleton and Ferguson to Sumter and Marion,
often embodied in their own ranks some of their
prisoners, and these were of course regarded as
deserters by their former comrades. Cornwallis,
seconded by Rawdon, had set the example of
ordering all men found in the rebel ranks after

[1] Campbell's General Orders, October 11th.

having sworn allegiance to the king to be hung; his under-officers executed the command with zeal, and the Americans, of course, retaliated. Ferguson's troops themselves had hung some of their prisoners.[1]

All this was fresh in the minds of the Americans who had just won so decisive a victory. They were accustomed to give full vent to the unbridled fury of their passions; they with difficulty brooked control; they brooded long over their own wrongs, which were many and real, and they were but little impressed by the misdeeds committed in return by their friends. Inflamed by hatred and the thirst for vengeance, they would probably have put to death some of their prisoners in any event; but all doubt was at an end when on their return march they were joined by an officer who had escaped from before Augusta and who brought word that Cruger's victorious loyalists had hung a dozen of the captured patriots.[2] This news settled the doom of some of the tory prisoners. A week after the battle a number of them were tried, and thirty were condemned to death. Nine, including the only tory colonel who had survived the battle, were hung; then Sevier

[1] Allaire's " Diary," entry for August 20th; also see August 2d. He chronicles these hangings with much complacency, but is, of course, shocked at the "infamous" conduct of the Americans when they do likewise.

[2] Shelby MSS.

and Shelby, men of bold, frank nature, could no longer stand the butchery, and peremptorily interfered, saving the remainder.[1] Of the men who were hung, doubtless some were murderers and marauders, who deserved their fate; others, including the unfortunate colonel, were honorable men, executed only because they had taken arms for the cause they deemed right.

Leaving the prisoners in the hands of the lowland militia, the mountaineers returned to their secure fastnesses in the high hill-valleys of the Holston, the Watauga, and the Nolichucky. They had marched well and fought valiantly, and they had gained a great victory; all the little stockaded forts, all the rough log cabins on the scattered clearings, were jubilant over the triumph. From that moment their three leaders were men of renown.[2] The Legislatures of their respective States

[1] *Ibid.*

[2] Thirty years after the battle, when Campbell had long been dead, Shelby and Sevier started a most unfortunate controversy as to his conduct in the battle. They insisted that he had flinched, and that victory was mainly due to them. Doubtless they firmly believed what they said; for, as already stated, the jealousies and rivalries among the backwoods leaders were very strong; but the burden of proof, after thirty years' silence, rested on them, and they failed to make their statements good;—nor was their act a very gracious one. Shelby bore the chief part in the quarrel, Campbell's surviving relatives, of course, defending the dead chieftain. I have carefully examined all the papers in the case, in the Tennessee Historical Society, the Shelby MSS.,

thanked them publicly and voted them swords for
their services.   Campbell, next year, went down
to join Greene's army, did gallant work at Guil-

and the Campbell MSS., besides the files of the *Richmond
Enquirer*, etc.; and it is evident that the accusation was
wholly groundless.

Shelby and Sevier rest their case:

1st, on their memory, thirty years after the event, of some
remarks of Campbell to them in private after the close of the
battle, which they construed as acknowledgments of bad
conduct.   Against these memories of old men it is safe to set
Shelby's explicit testimony, in a letter written six days after
the battle (see *Virginia Argus*, October 26, 1810), to the good
conduct of the "gallant commander" (Campbell).

2d, on the fact that Campbell was seen on a black horse
in the rear during the fighting; but a number of men of his
regiment swore that he had given his black horse to a servant
who sat in the rear, while he himself rode a bay horse in the
battle.   See their affidavits in the *Enquirer*.

3d, on the testimony of one of Shelby's brothers, who said
he saw him in the rear.   This is the only piece of positive
testimony in the case.   Some of Campbell's witnesses (as
Matthew Willoughby) swore that this brother of Shelby was
a man of bad character, engaged at the time in stealing cattle
from both whigs and tories.

4th, on the testimony of a number of soldiers who swore
they did not see Campbell in the latter part of the battle, nor
until some moments after the surrender.   Of course, this
negative testimony is simply valueless; in such a hurly-burly
it would be impossible for the men in each part of the line to
see all the commanders, and Campbell very likely did not
reach the places where these men were until some time after
the surrender.   On the other hand, forty officers and soldiers
of Campbell's, Sevier's, and Shelby's regiments, headed by
General Rutledge, swore that they had seen Campbell
valiantly leading throughout the whole battle, and foremost

ford Court-house, and then died of camp-fever. Sevier and Shelby had long lives before them.

at the surrender. This positive testimony conclusively settles the matter; it outweighs that of Shelby's brother, the only affirmative witness on the other side. But it is a fair question as to whether Campbell or another of Shelby's brothers received De Peyster's sword.

CHAPTER VI

THE HOLSTON SETTLEMENTS TO THE END OF THE REVOLUTION, 1781–83

JOHN SEVIER had no sooner returned from doing his share in defeating foes who were of his own race than he was called on to face another set of enemies, quite as formidable and much more cruel. These were the red warriors, the ancient owners of the soil, who were ever ready to take advantage of any momentary disaster that befell their hereditary and victorious opponents, the invading settlers.

For many years Sevier was the best Indian fighter on the border. He was far more successful than Clark, for instance, inflicting greater loss on his foes and suffering much less himself, though he never had anything like Clark's number of soldiers. His mere name was a word of dread to the Cherokees, the Chickamaugas, and the upper Creeks. His success was due to several causes. He wielded great influence over his own followers, whose love for and trust in "Chucky Jack" were absolutely unbounded; for he possessed in the highest degree the virtues most prized on the frontier. He was open-hearted and hospitable, with winning ways towards all, and combined a cool head with a dauntless heart; he loved a battle for its own sake, and was never so much at his ease as when under fire; he was a first-class marksman, and as good a horseman as was to be found on the border.   In his campaigns against the Indians he adopted the tactics of his foes, and grafted on them some important improvements of his own.   Much of his success was due to his adroit use of scouts or spies. He always chose for these the best woodsmen of the district, men who could endure as much, see as much, and pass through the woods as silently as the red men themselves.   By keeping these scouts well ahead of him, he learned accurately where the war-parties were.   In the attack itself he invariably used mounted riflemen, men skilled in forest warfare, who rode tough little horses, on which they galloped at speed through the forest.   Once in position, they did the actual fighting on foot, sheltering themselves carefully behind the tree-trunks.   He moved with extreme rapidity and attacked with instantaneous suddenness, using ambushes and surprises wherever practicable.[1]   His knowledge of the whereabouts and size of the hostile parties, and the speed of his own movements,

---

[1] The old Tennessee historians, headed by Haywood, base their accounts of the actions on statements made by the pioneers, or some of the pioneers, forty or fifty years after

generally enabled him to attack with the advantage of numbers greatly on his side.   He could then out-flank or partially surround the Indians, while his sudden rush demoralized them; so that, in striking contrast to most other Indian fighters, he inflicted a far greater loss than he received. He never fought a big pitched battle, but, by in-

the event; and they do a great deal of bragging about the prowess of the old Indian fighters.   The latter did most certainly perform mighty deeds; but often in an entirely different way from that generally recorded; for they faced a foe who on his own ground was infinitely more to be dreaded than the best trained European regulars.   Thus Haywood says that after the battle of the Island Flats the whites were so encouraged that thenceforward they never asked concerning their enemies, "How many are they?" but, "Where are they?" Of course, this is a mere piece of barbaric boasting.   If the whites had really acted on any such theory there would have been a constant succession of disasters like that at the Blue Licks.   Sevier's latest biographer, Mr. Kirke, in the *Rearguard of the Revolution*, goes far beyond even the old writers. For instance, on p. 141, he speaks of Sevier's victories being "often" gained over "twenty times his own number" of Indians.   As a matter of fact, one of the proofs of Sevier's skill as a commander is that he almost always fought with the advantage of numbers on his side.   Not a single instance can be produced where either he or any one else during his lifetime gained a victory over twenty times his number of Indians unless the sieges are counted.   It is necessary to keep in mind the limitations under which Haywood did his work, in order to write truthfully; but a debt of gratitude will always be due him for the history he wrote.   Like Marshall's, it is the book of one who himself knew the pioneers, and it has preserved very much of value which would otherwise have been lost.   The same holds true of Ramsey.

cessantly harrying and scattering the different war
bands, he struck such terror to the hearts of the
Indians that he again and again, in a succession of
wars, forced them into truces, and for the moment
freed the settlements from their ravages.   He was
almost the only commander on the frontier who
ever brought an Indian war, of whatever length,
to an end, doing a good deal of damage to his foes
and suffering very little himself.   Still, he never
struck a crushing blow, nor conquered a permanent peace.   He never did anything to equal
Clark's campaigns in the Illinois and against Vincennes, and, of course, he cannot for a moment be
compared to his rival and successor, grim Old
Hickory, the destroyer of the Creeks and the hero
of New Orleans.

When the men of the Holston or upper Tennessee valley settlements reached their homes after
the King's Mountain expedition, they found them
menaced by the Cherokees.   Congress had endeavored in vain to persuade the chiefs of this tribe
to make a treaty of peace, or at least to remain
neutral.   The efforts of the British agents to embroil them with the whites were completely successful; and in November the Otari or Overhill
warriors began making inroads along the frontier.
They did not attack in large bands.   A constant
succession of small parties moved swiftly through
the country, burning cabins, taking scalps, and,

above all, stealing horses.   As the most effectual
way of stopping such inroads, the alarmed and
angered settlers resolved to send a formidable retaliatory expedition against the Overhill towns.[1]
All the Holston settlements both north and south
of the Virginia line joined in sending troops.   By
the first week in December, 1780, seven hundred
mounted riflemen were ready to march, under the
joint leadership of Colonel Arthur Campbell and
of Sevier, the former being the senior officer.   They
were to meet at an appointed place on the French
Broad.

Sevier started first, with between two and three
hundred of his Watauga and Nolichucky followers.
He marched down to the French Broad, but could
hear nothing of Campbell.   He was on the great
war trace of the southern Indians, and his scouts
speedily brought him word that they had exchanged shots with a Cherokee war-party, on its
way to the settlements, and not far distant on
the other side of the river.   He instantly crossed
and made a swift march towards the would-be
marauders, camping on Boyd's Creek.   The scouts
were out by sunrise next morning—December
16th—and speedily found the Indian encampment, which the warriors had just left.   On receipt
of the news, Sevier ordered the scouts to run on,

[1] Campbell MSS.   Letter of Governor Thomas Jefferson,
February 17, 1781.

attack the Indians, and then instantly retreat, so as to draw them into an ambuscade.   Meanwhile, the main body followed cautiously after, the men spread out in a long line, with the wings advanced, the left wing under Major Jesse Walton, the right under Major Jonathan Tipton, while Sevier himself commanded the centre, which advanced along the trail by which the scouts were to retreat. When the Indians were drawn into the middle the two wings were to close in, when the whole party would be killed or captured.

The plan worked well.   The scouts soon came up with the warriors, and, after a moment's firing, ran back, with the Indians in hot pursuit.   Sevier's men lay hid, and when the leading warriors were close up they rose and fired.   Walton's wing closed in promptly; but Tipton was too slow, and the startled Cherokees ran off through the opening he had left, rushed into a swamp impassable for horsemen, and scattered out, each man for himself, being soon beyond pursuit.   Nevertheless, Sevier took thirteen scalps, many weapons, and all their plunder.   In some of their bundles there were proclamations from Sir Henry Clinton and other British commanders.[1]   The Indians were too

[1] Campbell MSS.   Copy of the official report of Colonel Arthur Campbell, January 15, 1781.   The accounts of this battle of Boyd's Creek illustrate well the growth of such an affair under the hands of writers who place confidence in all kinds of tradition, especially if they care more for picturesque-

surprised and panic-struck to offer any serious resistance, and not a man of Sevier's force was even wounded.

Having thus made a very pretty stroke, Sevier returned to the French Broad, where Campbell joined him on the 22d, with four hundred troops. Among them were a large number of Shelby's

ness than for accuracy. The contemporary official report is explicit. There were three hundred whites and seventy Indians. Of the latter thirteen were slain. Campbell's whole report shows a jealousy of Sevier, whom he probably knew well enough was a man of superior ability to himself; but this jealousy appears mainly in the coloring. He does not change any material fact, and there is no reason for questioning the substantial truth of his statements.

Forty years afterward Haywood writes of the affair, trying to tell simply the truth, but obliged to rely mainly on oral tradition. He speaks of Sevier's troops as only two hundred in number; and says twenty-eight Indians were killed. He does not speak of the number of the Indians, but from the way he describes Sevier's troops as encircling them he evidently knew that the white men were more numerous than their foes. His mistake as to the number of Indian dead is easily explicable. The official report gives twenty-nine as the number killed in the entire campaign, and Haywood, as in the Island Flats battle, simply puts the total of several skirmishes into one.

Thirty years later comes Ramsey. He relies on traditions that have grown more circumstantial and less accurate. He gives two accounts of what he calls "one of the best fought battles in the border war of Tennessee"; one of these accounts is mainly true; the other entirely false; he does not try to reconcile them. He says three whites were wounded, although the official report says that in the whole campaign but one man was killed and two wounded. He reduces

men, under the command of Major Joseph Martin.
The next day the seven hundred horsemen made
a forced march to the Little Tennessee; and, on
the 24th, crossed it unopposed, making a feint at
one ford, while the main body passed rapidly over
another.   The Indians did not have the numbers
to oppose so formidable a body of good fighters,
and only ventured on a little very long-range and
harmless skirmishing with the vanguard.   Divid-
ing into two bodies, the troops destroyed Chota
and the other towns up and down the stream,
finding in them a welcome supply of provisions.

Sevier's force to 170 men, and calls the Indians "a large
body."

Thirty-four years later comes Mr. Kirke, with the *Rear-
Guard of the Revolution*.   Out of his inner consciousness he
evolves the fact that there were "not less than a thousand"
Indians, whom Sevier, at the head of one hundred and
seventy men, vanquishes, after a heroic combat, in which
Sevier and some others perform a variety of purely imaginary
feats.   By diminishing the number of the whites, and increasing that of the Indians, he thus makes the relative force
of the latter about *twenty-five times as great as it really was*,
and converts a clever ambuscade, whereby the whites gave a
smart drubbing to a body of Indians one fourth their own
number, into a Homeric victory over a host six times as
numerous as the conquerors.

This is not a solitary instance; on the contrary, it is typical
of almost all that is gravely set forth as history by a number
of writers on these western border wars, whose books are
filled from cover to cover with just such matter.   Almost all
their statements are partly, and very many are wholly, without foundation.

The next day Martin, with a detachment, fell on
a party of flying Indians, killed one, and captured
seventeen horses loaded with clothing, skins, and
the scanty household furniture of the cabins;
while another detachment destroyed the part of
Chilhowee that was on the nearer side of the river.
On the 26th the rest of Chilhowee was burned,
three Indians killed, and nine captured.   Tipton,
with one hundred and fifty men, was sent to attack another town beyond the river; but, owing
to the fault of their commander,[1] this body failed
to get across.   The Indian woman, Nancy Ward,
who in '76 had given the settlers timely warning
of the intended attack by her tribesmen here
came into camp.   She brought overtures of peace
from the chiefs, but to these Campbell and Sevier
would not listen, as they wished first to demolish
the Hiawassee towns, where the warriors had been
especially hostile.   Accordingly, they marched
thither.   On their way there were a couple of
skirmishes, in which several Indians were killed
and one white man.   The latter, whose name was
Elliot, was buried in the Tellico town, a cabin
being burned down over his grave that the
Indians might not know where it was.   The

[1] His "unmilitary behavior," says Campbell.   Ramsey
makes him one of the (imaginary) wounded at Boyd's Creek
Kirke improves on this by describing him as falling "badly
wounded" just as he was about to move his wing forward,
and ascribes his fall to the failure of the wing to advance.

Indians watched the army from the hills. At one point a warrior was seen stationed on a ridge to beat a drum and give signals to the rest; but the spies of the whites stole on him unawares, and shot him. The Hiawassee towns and all the stores of provisions they contained were destroyed, the work being finished on the last day of the year.

On January 1, 1781, the army broke up into detachments which went home by different routes, some additional towns being destroyed. The Indians never ventured to offer the invaders a pitched battle. Many of the war-parties were absent on the frontier, and, at the very time their own country was being invaded, they committed ravages in Powell's Valley, along the upper Holston, and on the Kentucky road, near Cumberland Gap. The remaining warriors were cowed by Sevier's first success, and were puzzled by the rapidity with which the troops moved; for the mounted riflemen went at speed wherever they wished, and were not encumbered by baggage, each man taking only his blanket and a wallet of parched corn.

All the country of the Overhill Cherokees was laid waste, a thousand cabins were burned and fifty thousand bushels of corn destroyed. Twenty-nine warriors in all were killed, and seventeen women and children captured, not including the family of Nancy Ward, who were treated as friends, not prisoners.   But one white man was killed and two wounded.[1]

In the burnt towns and on the dead warriors were found many letters and proclamations from the British agents and commanders, showing that almost every chief in the nation had been carrying

[1] Campbell MSS.   Arthur Campbell's official report.   The figures of the cabins and corn destroyed are probably exaggerated.   All the Tennessee historians, down to Phelan, are hopelessly in the dark over this campaign.   Haywood actually duplicates it (pp. 63 and 99) recounting it first as occurring in '79, and then with widely changed incidents, as happening in '81—making two expeditions. When he falls into such a tremendous initial error, it is not to be wondered at that the details he gives are very untrustworthy.   Ramsey corrects Haywood as far as the two separate expeditions are concerned, but he makes a number of reckless statements apparently on no better authority than the traditions current among the border people, sixty or seventy years after the event.   These stand on the same foundation with the baseless tale that makes Isaac Shelby take part in the battle of Island Flats.   The Tennessee historians treat Sevier as being the chief commander; but he was certainly under Campbell; the address they sent out to the Indians is signed by Campbell first, Sevier second, and Martin third.   Haywood, followed by Ramsey, says that Sevier marched to the Chickamauga towns, which he destroyed, and then marched down the Coosa to the region of the Cypress Swamps.   But Campbell's official report says that the towns "in the neighborhood of Chickamauga and the Town of Cologn, situated on the sources of the Mobile" were *not* destroyed, nor visited, and he carefully enumerates all the towns that the troops burned and the regions they went through.   They did not go near Chickamauga nor the Coosa.   Unless there is some documentary evidence in favor of the assertions of Haywood and

on a double game; for the letters covered the periods at which they had been treating with the Americans and earnestly professing their friendship for the latter and their determination to be neutral in the contest then waging. As Campbell wrote in his report to the Virginian governor, no people had ever acted with more foolish duplicity.

Before returning, the three commanders, Campbell, Sevier, and Martin, issued an address to the Otari chiefs and warriors, and sent it by one of their captured braves, who was to deliver it to the headmen.[1] The address set forth what the white troops had done, telling the Indians it was a just punishment for their folly and perfidy in consenting to carry out the wishes of the British agents; it warned them shortly to come in and treat for peace lest their country should again be visited, and not only laid waste, but conquered and held

Ramsey, they cannot for a moment be taken against the explicit declaration of the official report.

Mr. Kirke merely follows Ramsey, and adds a few flourishes of his own, such as that at the Chickamauga towns "the blood of the slaughtered cattle dyed red the Tennessee" for some twenty miles, and that "the homes of over forty thousand people were laid in ashes." This last estimate is just about ten times too strong, for the only country visited was that of the Overhill Cherokees, and the outside limit for the population of the devastated territory would be some four thousand souls, or a third of the Cherokee tribe, which all told numbered perhaps twelve thousand people.

[1] Campbell MSS. Issued at Kai-a-tee, January 4, 1781; the copy sent to Governor Jefferson is dated February 28th.

for all time. Some chiefs came in to talk, and
were met at Chota [1]; but though they were anxious for peace they could not restrain the vindictive spirit of the young braves, nor prevent them
from harassing the settlements. Nor could the
white commanders keep the frontiersmen from
themselves settling within the acknowledged
boundaries of the Indian territory. They were
constantly pressing against the lines, and eagerly
burst through at every opening. When the army
marched back from burning the Overhill towns,
they found that adventurous settlers had followed
in its wake, and had already made clearings and
built cabins near all the best springs down to the
French Broad. People of every rank showed
keen desire to encroach on the Indian lands. [2]

The success of this expedition gave much relief
to the border, and was hailed with pleasure
throughout Virginia [3] and North Carolina. Nevertheless, the war continued without a break, bands
of warriors from the middle towns coming to the
help of their disheartened Overhill brethren.
Sevier determined to try one of his swift, sudden

[1] The Tennessee historians all speak of this as a treaty; and
probably a meeting did take place, as described; but it led to
nothing, and no actual treaty was made until some months
later.

[2] Calendar of *Virginia State Papers*, ii.   Letter of Colonel
William Christian to Governor of Virginia, April 10, 1781.

[3] State Department MSS., No. 15, February 25, 1781.

strokes against these new foes. Early in March he rode off at the head of a hundred and fifty picked horsemen, resolute to penetrate the hitherto untrodden wilds that shielded the far-off fastnesses where dwelt the Erati. Nothing shows his daring, adventurous nature more clearly than his starting on such an expedition; and only a man of strong will and much power could have carried it to a successful conclusion. For a hundred and fifty miles he led his horsemen through a mountainous wilderness where there was not so much as a hunter's trail. They wound their way through the deep defiles and among the towering peaks of the Great Smoky Mountains, descending by passes so precipitous that it was with difficulty the men led down them even such surefooted beasts as their hardy hill-horses. At last they burst out of the woods and fell like a thunderbolt on the towns of the Erati, nestling in their high gorges. The Indians were completely taken by surprise; they had never dreamed that they could be attacked in their innermost strongholds, cut off, as they were, from the nearest settlements by vast trackless wastes of woodland and lofty, bald-topped mountain chains. They had warriors enough to overwhelm Sevier's band by sheer force of numbers, but he gave them no time to gather. Falling on their main town he took it by surprise and stormed it, killing thirty warriors and capturing a large number of women and children. Of these, however, he was able to bring in but twenty, who were especially valuable because they could be exchanged for white captives. He burnt two other towns and three small villages, destroying much provision and capturing two hundred horses. He himself had but one man killed and one wounded. Before the startled warriors could gather to attack him he plunged once more into the wilderness, carrying his prisoners and plunder, and driving the captured horses before him; and so swift were his motions that he got back in safety to the settlements.[1] The length of the journey, the absolutely untravelled nature of the country, which no white man, save perhaps an occasional wandering hunter, had ever before traversed, the extreme difficulty of the rout over the wooded, cliff-scarred mountains, and the strength of the Cherokee towns that were to be attacked, all combined to render the feat most difficult. For its successful performance there

[1] *Ibid.* Letters of Colonel William Christian, April 10, 1781; of Joseph Martin, March 1st; and of Arthur Campbell, March 28th. The accounts vary slightly: for instance, Christian gives him one hundred and eighty, Campbell only one hundred and fifty men. One account says he killed thirty, another twenty Indians. Martin, by the way, speaks bitterly of the militia as men "who do duty at times as their inclination leads them." The incident, brilliant enough anyhow, of course grows a little under Ramsey and Haywood; and Mr. Kirke fairly surpasses himself when he comes to it.

was need of courage, hardihood, woodcraft, good judgment, stealth, and great rapidity of motion. It was one of the most brilliant exploits of the border war.

Even after his return, Sevier was kept busy pursuing and defeating small bands of plundering savages. In the early summer he made a quick inroad south of the French Broad. At the head of over a hundred hard riders, he fell suddenly on the camp of a war-party, took a dozen scalps, and scattered the rest of the Indians in every direction. A succession of these blows completely humbled the Cherokees, and they sued for peace; thanks to Sevier's tactics, they had suffered more loss than they had inflicted, an almost unknown thing in these wars with the forest Indians. In mid-summer peace was made by a treaty at the Great Island of the Holston.

During the latter half of the year, when danger from the Indians had temporarily ceased, Sevier and Shelby led down bands of mounted riflemen to assist the American forces in the Carolinas and Georgia. They took an honorable share under Marion in some skirmishes against the British and Hessians [1]; but they did not render any special

[1] Shelby MSS. Of course Shelby paints these skirmishes in very strong colors. Haywood and Ramsey base their accounts purely on his papers. Ramsey and his followers endeavor to prove that the mountain men did excellently in these 1781 campaigns; but the endeavor is futile. They were good for

service, and Greene found he could place no reliance on them for the actual stubborn campaigns that broke the strength of the king's armies. They enlisted for very short periods, and when their time was up promptly returned to their mountains, for they were sure to get homesick and uneasy about their families; and neither the officers nor the soldiers had any proper idea of the value of obedience. Among their own hills and forests, and for their own work, they were literally unequalled; and they were ready enough to swoop down from their strongholds, strike some definite blow, or do some single piece of valiant fighting in the low country, and then fall back as quickly as they had come. But they were not particularly suited for pitched battles in the open, and were quite unfitted to carry on a long campaign.

In one respect, the mountain men deserve great

some one definite stroke, but their shortcomings were manifest the instant a long campaign was attempted; and the comments of the South Carolina historians upon their willingness to leave at unfortunate moments are on the whole just. They behaved somewhat as Stark and the victors at Bennington did when they left the American army before Saratoga; although their conduct was on the whole better than that of Stark's men. They were a brave, hardy, warlike band of irregulars, probably better fighters than any similar force on this continent or elsewhere; but occasional brilliant exceptions must not blind us to the general inefficiency of the Revolutionary militia, and their great inferiority to the Continentals of Washington, Greene, and Wayne. See Appendix C.

credit for their conduct in the Carolinas. As a general thing, they held aloof from the plundering. The frightful character of the civil war between the whigs and tories, and the excesses of the British armies, had utterly demoralized the Southern States; they were cast into a condition of anarchic disorder and the conflicts between the patriots and loyalists degenerated into a bloody scramble for murder and plunder wherein the whigs behaved as badly as ever the tories had done.[1] Men were shot, houses burned, horses stolen, and negroes kidnapped; even the unfortunate freedmen of color were hurried off and sold

[1] In the Clay MSS. there is a letter from Jesse Benton (the father of the great Missouri Senator) to Colonel Thomas Hart, of March 23d, 1783, which gives a glimpse of the way in which the tories were treated even after the British had been driven out; it also shows how soon maltreatment of royalists was turned into general misrule and rioting. The letter runs, in part, as follows:

"I cannot help mentioning to You an Evil which seems intaild upon the upper part of this State, to wit, Mobbs and commotions amongst the People. I shall give you the particulars of the last Work of this kind which lately happened, & which is not yet settled; Plunder being the first cause. The Scoundrels, under the cloak of great Whigs cannot bear the thought of paying the unfortunate Wretches whom Fame and ill will call Tories (though many of them perhaps honest, industrious and useful men) for plundered property; but on the other Hand think they together with their Wives and Children (who are now beging for Mercy) ought to be punished to the utmost extremity. I am sorry that Col. O Neal and his brother Pete, who have been useful men and whom

into slavery. It was with the utmost difficulty that a few wise and good commanders, earnest lovers of their country, like the gallant General Pickens, were able to put a partial stop to these outrages, and gather a few brave men to help in overcoming the foreign foe. To the honor of

I am in hopes are pretty clear of plundering, should have a hand in Arbitrary measures at this Day when the Civil Laws might take place.

"One Jacob Graves son of John of old Stinking Quarter, went off & was taken with the British Army, escaped from the Guards, came & surrendered himself to Gen'l Butler, about the middle of Last month & went to his Family upon Parole. Col. O Neal being informed of this, armed himself with gun and sword, went to Graves's in a passion, Graves shut the Door, O Neal broke it down, Graves I believe thinking his own Life at stake, took his Brothers Gun which happened to be in the house & shot O Neal through the Breast.

"O Neal has suffered much but is now recovering. This accident has inflamed and set to work those who were afraid of suffering for their unjust and unwarrantable Deeds, the Ignorant honest men are also willing to take part against their Rulers & I don't know when nor where it is to end, but I wish it was over. At the Guilford Feb'y Court Peter O Neal & others armed with clubs in the Face of the Court then sitting and in the Court house too, beat some men called Tories so much that their Lives were despaired of, broke up the Court and finally have stopd the civil Laws in that County. Your old Friend Col. Dunn got out at Window, fled in a Fright, took cold and died immediately. Rowan County Court I am told was also broke up.

"If O Neal should die I fear that a number of the unhappy wretches called Tories will be Murdered, and that a man disposed to do justice dare not interfere, indeed the times seem to imitate the commencement of the Regulators."

the troops under Sevier and Shelby, be it said that they took little part in these misdeeds. There were doubtless some men among them who shared in all the evil of that turbulent time; but most of these frontier riflemen, though poor and ignorant, were sincerely patriotic; they marched to fight the oppressor, to drive out the stranger, not to ill-treat their own friends and countrymen.

Towards the end of these campaigns, which marked the close of the Revolutionary struggle, Shelby was sent to the North Carolina Legislature, where he served for a couple of terms. Then, when peace was formally declared, he removed to Kentucky, where he lived ever afterwards. Sevier stayed in his home on the Nolichucky, to be thenceforth, while his life lasted, the leader in peace and war of his beloved mountaineers.

Early in 1782, fresh difficulties arose with the Indians. In the war just ended the Cherokees themselves had been chiefly to blame. The whites were now in their turn the aggressors, the trouble being, as usual, that they encroached on lands secured to the red men by solemn treaty. The Watauga settlements had been kept compact by the presence of the neighboring Indians. They had grown steadily but slowly. They extended their domain slightly after every treaty, such treaty being usually though not always the sequel to a successful war; but they never gained any

large stretch of territory at once. Had it not
been for the presence of the hostile tribes they
would have scattered far and wide over the
country, and could not have formed any government.

The preceding spring (1781) the land office had
been closed, not to be opened until after peace
with Great Britain was definitely declared, the
utter demoralization of the government bringing
the work to a standstill. The rage for land speculation, however, which had continued even in the
stormiest days of the Revolution, grew tenfold in
strength after Yorktown, when peace at no distant
day was assured. The wealthy land speculators
of the seaboard counties made agreements of
various sorts with the more prominent frontier
leaders in the effort to secure large tracts of good
country. The system of surveying was much
better than in Kentucky, but it was still by no
means perfect, as each man placed his plot wherever he chose, first describing the boundary marks
rather vaguely, and leaving an illiterate old hunter
to run the lines. Moreover, the intending settler
frequently absented himself for several months, or
was temporarily chased away by the Indians,
while the official record books were most imperfect.
In consequence, many conflicts ensued. The
frontiersmen settled on any spot of good land they
saw fit, and clung to it with defiant tenacity,

whether or not it afterwards proved to be on a tract previously granted to some land company or rich private individual who had never been a hundred miles from the seacoast. Public officials went into these speculations. Thus Major Joseph Martin, while an Indian agent, tried to speculate in Cherokee lands.[1] Of course, the officer's public influence was speedily destroyed when he once undertook such operations; he could no longer do justice to outsiders. Occasionally, the falseness of his position made him unjust to the Indians; more often it forced him into league with the latter, and made him hostile to the borderers.[2]

Before the end of the Revolution, the trouble between the actual settlers and the land speculators became so great that a small subsidiary civil war was threatened. The rough riflemen resolutely declined to leave their clearings, while the titular owners appealed to the authority of the loose land laws, and wished them to be backed up by the armed force of the State.[3]

The government of North Carolina was far too weak to turn out the frontiersmen in favor of the speculators to whom the land had been granted, —often by fraudulent means, or at least for a

[1] See *Virginia State Papers*, iii., 560.

[2] This is a chief reason why the reports of the Indian agents are so often bitterly hostile towards those of their own color.

[3] See in Durrett MSS. " Papers relating to Isaac Shelby " ; letter of John Taylor to Isaac Shelby, June 8, 1782.

ridiculously small sum of money. Still less could
it prevent its unruly subjects from trespassing on
the Indian country, or protect them if they were
themselves threatened by the savages. It could
not do justice as between its own citizens, and it
was quite incompetent to preserve the peace between them and outsiders.[1]   The borderers were
left to work out their own salvation.

By the beginning of 1782, settlements were being
made south of the French Broad. This alarmed
and irritated the Indians, and they sent repeated
remonstrances to Major Martin, who was Indian
agent, and also to the governor of North Carolina.
The latter wrote Sevier, directing him to drive off
the intruding settlers, and pull down their cabins.
Sevier did not obey. He took purely the frontier
view of the question, and he had no intention of
harassing his own staunch adherents for the sake
of the savages whom he had so often fought.
Nevertheless, the Cherokees always liked him per-
sonally, for he was as open-handed and free-
hearted to them as to every one else, and treated
them to the best he had whenever they came to
his house. He had much justification for his refusal, too, in the fact that the Indians themselves
were always committing outrages. When the
Americans reconquered the Southern States many
tories fled to the Cherokee towns, and incited the

[1] Calendar of *Virginia State Papers*, vol. iii., p. 213.

savages to hostility; and the outlying settlements of the borderers were being burned and plundered by members of the very tribes whose chiefs were at the same time writing to the governor to complain of the white encroachments.[1]

When, in April, the Cherokees held a friendly talk with Evan Shelby they admitted that the tories among them and their own evil-disposed young men committed ravages on the whites, but asserted that most of them greatly desired peace, for they were weak and distressed, and had shrunk much in numbers.[2] The trouble was that when they were so absolutely unable to control their own bad characters, it was inevitable that they should become embroiled with the whites.

The worst members of each race committed crimes against the other, and not only did the retaliation often fall on the innocent, but, unfortunately, even the good men were apt to make common cause with the criminals of their own color. Thus in July the Chickamaugas sent in a talk for peace; but at that very time a band of their young braves made a foray into Powell's Valley, killing two settlers and driving off some stock. They were pursued, one of their number killed, and most of the stock retaken. In the same month, on the other hand, two friendly Indians, who had a canoe laden with peltry, were

murdered on the Holston by a couple of white
ruffians, who then attempted to sell the furs.
They were discovered, and the furs taken from
them; but to their disgrace be it said, the people
round about would not suffer the criminals to be
brought to justice.[1]

The mutual outrages continued throughout the
summer, and in September they came to a head.
The great majority of the Otari of the Overhill
towns were still desirous of peace, and after a
council of their headmen the chief Old Tassel, of
the town of Chota, sent on their behalf a strong
appeal to the governors of both Virginia and North
Carolina. The document is written with such
dignity, and yet in a tone of such curious pathos,
that it is worth giving in full, as putting in
strongest possible form the Indian side of the
case, and as a sample of the best of these Indian
"talks."

"A talk to Colonel Joseph Martin, by the Old
Tassell, in Chota, the 25th of September, 1782, in
favour of the whole nation. For His Excellency,
the Governor of North Carolina. Present, all the
chiefs of the friendly towns and a number of young
men.

"Brother: I am now going to speak to you. I
hope you will listen to me. A string. I intended
to come this fall and see you, but there was such

[1] *Ibid.*, pp. 213, 248.

confusion in our country, I thought it best for me
to stay at home and send my Talks by our friend
Colonel Martin, who promised to deliver them safe
to you.   We are a poor distressed people, that is
in great trouble, and we hope our elder brother will
take pity on us and do us justice.   Your people
from Nolichucky are daily pushing us out of our
lands.   We have no place to hunt on.   Your people have built houses within one day's walk of our
towns.   We don't want to quarrel with our elder
brother; we, therefore, hope our elder brother will
not take our lands from us, that the Great Man
above gave us.   He made you and he made us; we
are all his children, and we hope our elder brother
will take pity on us, and not take our lands from
us that our father gave us, because he is stronger
than we are.   We are the first people that ever
lived on this land; it is ours, and why will our
elder brother take it from us?   It is true, some
time past, the people over the great water persuaded some of our young men to do some mischief to our elder brother, which our principal men
were sorry for.   But you our elder brothers come
to our towns and took satisfaction, and then sent
for us to come and treat with you, which we did.
Then our elder brother promised to have the line
run between us agreeable to the first treaty, and
all that should be found over the line should be
moved off.   But it is not done yet.   We have

done nothing to offend our elder brother since the last treaty, and why should our elder brother want to quarrel with us? We have sent to the Governor of Virginia on the same subject. We hope that between you both, you will take pity on your younger brother, and send Col. Sevier, who is a good man, to have all your people moved off our land. I should say a great deal more, but our friend, Colonel Martin, knows all our grievances, and he can inform you. A string." [1]

The speech is interesting, because it shows that the Indians both liked and respected Sevier, their most redoubtable foe; and because it acknowledges that in the previous war the Cherokees themselves had been the wrong-doers. Even Old Tassel had been implicated in the treacherous conduct of the chiefs at that period; but he generally acted very well, and belonged with the large number of his tribesmen who, for no fault of their own, were shamefully misused by the whites.

The white intruders were not removed. No immediate collision followed on this account; but when Old Tassel's talk was forwarded to the governor, small parties of Chickamaugas, assisted by young braves from among the Creeks and Erati, had already begun to commit ravages on the out-

[1] Ramsey, 271. The "strings" of wampum were used to mark periods and to indicate, and act as reminders of, special points in the speech.

lying settlements. Two weeks before Old Tassel
spoke, on the 11th of September, a family of whites
was butchered on Moccasin Creek. The neighbors
gathered, pursued the Indians, and recaptured the
survivors.[1] Other outrages followed throughout
the month. Sevier as usual came to the rescue of
the angered settlers. He gathered a couple of
hundred mounted riflemen, and made one of his
swift retaliatory inroads. His men were simply
volunteers, for there was no money in the country
treasury with which to pay them or provide them
with food and provisions; it was their own quarrel,
and they furnished their own services free, each
bringing his horse, rifle, ammunition, blanket, and
wallet of parched corn. Naturally, such troops
made war purely according to their own ideas, and
cared nothing whatever for the commands of those
governmental bodies who were theoretically their
superiors. They were poor men, staunch patriots,
who had suffered much and done all they could
during the Revolution[2]; now, when threatened by
the savages, they were left to protect themselves,
and they did it in their own way. Sevier led his
force down through the Overhill towns, doing
their people no injury and holding a peace-talk
with them. They gave him a half-breed, John
Watts, afterwards one of their chiefs, as guide;
and he marched quickly against some of the

[1] Calendar of *Virginia State Papers*, vol. iii., p. 317.   [2] *Ibid*.

Chickamauga towns, where he destroyed the cabins and provision hoards. Afterwards, he penetrated to the Coosa, where he burned one or two Creek villages. The inhabitants fled from the towns before he could reach them; and his own motions were so rapid that they could never gather in force strong enough to assail him.[1] Very few In-

[1] The authority for this expedition is Haywood (p. 106); Ramsey simply alters one or two unimportant details. Haywood commits so many blunders concerning the early Indian wars that it is only safe to regard his accounts as true in outline; and even for this outline it is to be wished we had additional authority. Mr. Kirke, in the *Rear-Guard*, p. 313, puts in an account of a battle on Lookout Mountain, wherein Sevier and his two hundred men defeat "five hundred tories and savages." He does not even hint at his authority for this, unless in a sentence of the preface where he says: "A large part of my material I have derived from what may be termed 'original sources'—old settlers." Of course the statement of an old settler is worthless when it relates to an alleged important event which took place 105 years before, and yet escaped the notice of all contemporary and subsequent historians. In plain truth, unless Mr. Kirke can produce something like contemporary—or approximately contemporary—documentary evidence for this mythical battle, it must be set down as pure invention. It is with real reluctance that I speak thus of Mr. Kirke's books. He has done good service in popularizing the study of early western history, and especially in calling attention to the wonderful careers of Sevier and Robertson. Had he laid no claim to historic accuracy I should have been tempted to let his books pass unnoticed; but in the preface to his *John Sevier* he especially asserts that his writings "may be safely accepted as authentic history." On first reading his book I was surprised and pleased at the information it contained; when I

dians were killed, and apparently none of Sevier's people; a tory, an ex-British sergeant, then living with an Indian squaw, was among the slain.

This foray brought but a short relief to the settlements. On Christmas day three men were killed on the Clinch; and it was so unusual a season for the war-parties to be abroad that the attack caused widespread alarm.[1] Early in the spring of 1783 the ravages began again.[2] Some time before, General Wayne had addressed the Creeks and Choctaws, reproaching them with the aid they had given the British, and threatening them with a bloody chastisement if they would not keep the peace.[3] A threat from Mad Anthony meant something, and the Indians paid at least momentary heed. Georgia enjoyed a short respite, which, as usual, the more reckless borderers strove to bring to an end by encroaching on the Indian lands, while the State authorities, on the other hand, did their best to stop not only such encroachments, but also all travelling and hunting in the Indian country, and especially the

came to study the subject I was still more surprised and much less pleased at discovering such wholesale inaccuracy—to be perfectly just, I should be obliged to use a stronger term. Even a popular history ought to pay at least some little regard to truth.

[1] Calendar of *Virginia State Papers*, vol. iii., p. 424.

[2] *Ibid.*, p. 479.

[3] State Department MSS. Letters of Washington, No. 152, vol. xi., February 1, 1782.

marking of trees. This last operation, as Governor Lyman Hall remarked in his proclamation, gave "Great Offence to the Indians," [1] who thoroughly understood that the surveys indicated the approaching confiscation of their territory.

Towards the end of 1783 a definite peace was concluded with the Chickasaws, who ever afterwards remained friendly, [2] but the Creeks, while amusing the Georgians by pretending to treat, let their parties of young braves find an outlet for their energies by assailing the Holston and Cumberland settlements. [3] The North Carolina Legislature, becoming impatient, passed a law summarily appropriating certain lands that were claimed by the unfortunate Cherokees. The troubled peace was continually threatened by the actions either of ungovernable frontiersmen or of bloodthirsty and vindictive Indians. [4] Small parties of scouts were incessantly employed in patrolling the southern border.

Nevertheless, all pressing danger from the Indians was over. The Holston settlements throve lustily. Wagon-roads were made, leading into both Virginia and North Carolina. Settlers thronged into the country, the roads were well travelled, and the clearings became very numer-

[1] *Gazette of the State of Georgia*, July 10, 1783.
[2] *Virginia State Papers*, vol. iii., p. 548.
[3] *Ibid.*, p. 532.   [4] *Ibid.*, p. 560.

ous.   The villages began to feel safe without stockades, save those on the extreme border, which were
still built in the usual frontier style.   The scattering log school-houses and meeting-houses increased steadily in numbers, and in 1783,
Methodism, destined to become the leading and
typical creed of the West, first gained a foothold
along the Holston, with a congregation of seventy-
six members.[1]

These people of the upper Tennessee valleys
long continued one in interest as in blood.
Whether they lived north or south of the Virginia or North Carolina boundary, they were more
closely united to one another than they were to
the seaboard governments of which they formed
part.   Their history is not generally studied as a
whole, because one portion of their territory continued part of Virginia, while the remainder was
cut off from North Carolina as the nucleus of a
separate State.   But in the time of their importance, in the first formative period of the young
West, all these Holston settlements must be
treated together, or else their real place in our
history will be totally misunderstood.[2]

[1] *History of Methodism in Tennessee*, John B. M'Ferrin
(Nashville, 1873), i., 26.

[2] Nothing gives a more fragmentary and twisted view of
our history than to treat it purely by States; this is the reason that a State history is generally of so little importance
when taken by itself.   On the other hand, it is of course true

The two towns of Abingdon and Jonesboro, respectively north and south of the line, were the centres of activity. In Jonesboro the log courthouse, with its clapboard roof, was abandoned, and in its place a twenty-four-foot-square building of hewn logs was put up; it had a shingled roof and plank floors, and contained a justice's bench, a lawyers' and clerk's bar, and a sheriff's box to sit in. The county of Washington was now further subdivided, its southwest portion being erected into the county of Greene, so that there were three counties of North Carolina west of the mountains. The court of the new county consisted of several justices, who appointed their own clerk, sheriff, attorney for the State, entry-taker, surveyor, and registrar. They appropriated money to pay for the use of the log-house where they held sessions, laid a tax of a shilling specie on every hundred pounds for the purpose of erecting public buildings, laid out roads, issued licenses to build mills, and bench warrants to take suspected persons.[1]

Abingdon was a typical little frontier town of

that the fundamental features in our history can only be shown by giving proper prominence to the individual State life.

[1] Ramsey, 277. The North Carolina Legislature, in 1783, passed an act giving Henderson two hundred thousand acres, and appointed Joseph Martin Indian agent, arranged for a treaty with the Cherokees, and provided that any good men should be allowed to trade with the Indians.

the class that immediately succeeded the stockaded hamlets. A public square had been laid
out, round which, and down the straggling main
street, the few buildings were scattered; all were
of logs, from the court-house and small jail down.
There were three or four taverns. The two best
were respectively houses of entertainment for
those who were fond of their brandy, and for the
temperate. There were a blacksmith shop and a
couple of stores.[1] The traders brought their
goods from Alexandria, Baltimore, or even Philadelphia, and made a handsome profit. The lower
taverns were scenes of drunken frolic, often ending
in free fights. There was no constable, and the
sheriff, when called to quell a disturbance, summoned as a posse those of the bystanders whom he
deemed friendly to the cause of law and order.
There were many strangers passing through; and
the better class of these were welcome at the rambling log-houses of the neighboring backwoods
gentry, who often themselves rode into the taverns
to learn from the travellers what was happening in
the great world beyond the mountains. Court-
day was a great occasion; all the neighborhood
flocked in to gossip, lounge, race horses, and fight.
Of course, in such gatherings there were always

[1] One was "kept by two Irishmen named Daniel and
Manasses Freil" (*sic;* the names look very much more German than Irish).

certain privileged characters. At Abingdon, these were to be found in the persons of a hunter named Edward Callahan, and his wife Sukey. As regularly as court-day came round they appeared, Sukey driving a cart laden with pies, cakes, and drinkables, while Edward, whose rolls of furs and deer-hides were also in the cart, stalked at its tail on foot, in full hunter's dress, with rifle, powder-horn, and bullet-bag, while his fine, well-taught hunting-dog followed at his heels. Sukey would halt in the middle of the street, make an awning for herself and begin business, while Edward strolled off to see about selling his peltries. Sukey never would take out a license, and so was often in trouble for selling liquor. The judges were strict in proceeding against offenders—and even stricter against the unfortunate tories—but they had a humorous liking for Sukey, which was shared by the various grand juries. By means of some excuse or other she was always let off, and in return showed great gratitude to such of her benefactors as came near her mountain cabin.[1]

Court-day was apt to close with much hard drinking; for the backwoodsmen of every degree dearly loved whisky.

[1] Campbell MSS.; an account of the "Town of Abingdon," by David Campbell, who "first saw it in 1782."

CHAPTER VII

ROBERTSON FOUNDS THE CUMBERLAND SETTLE-MENT, 1779–1780

ROBERTSON had no share in the glory of King's Mountain, and no part in the subsequent career of the men who won it; for at the time he was doing his allotted work, a work of at least equal importance, in a different field. The year before the mountaineers faced Ferguson, the man who had done more than any one in founding the settlements from which the victors came, had once more gone into the wilderness to build a new and even more typical frontier commonwealth, the westernmost of any yet founded by the backwoodsmen.

Robertson had been for ten years a leader among the Holston and Watauga people. He had at different times played the foremost part in organizing the civil government and in repelling outside attack. He had been particularly successful in his dealings with the Indians, and by his missions to them had managed to keep the peace unbroken on more than one occasion when a war would have been disastrous to the whites.

He was prosperous and successful in his private affairs; nevertheless, in 1779, the restless craving for change and adventure surged so strongly in his breast that it once more drove him forth to wander in the forest. In the true border temper, he determined to abandon the home he had made, and to seek out a new one hundreds of miles farther in the heart of the hunting-grounds of the red warriors.

The point pitched upon was the beautiful country lying along the great bend of the Cumberland. Many adventurous settlers were anxious to accompany Robertson, and, like him, to take their wives and children with them into the new land. It was agreed that a small party of explorers should go first in the early spring to plant corn, that the families might have it to eat when they followed in the fall.

The spot was already well known to hunters. Who had first visited it, cannot be said; though tradition has kept the names of several among the many who at times halted there while on their wanderings.[1]   Old Kasper Mansker and others

[1] One Stone or Stoner, perhaps Boon's old associate, is the first whose name is given in the books. But in both Kentucky and Tennessee it is idle to try to find out exactly who the first explorers were. They were unlettered woodsmen; it is only by chance that some of their names have been kept and others lost; the point to be remembered is that many hunters were wandering over the land at the same time, that they

had made hunting trips thither for ten years past; and they had sometimes met the creole trappers from the Illinois. When Mansker first went to the Bluffs,[1] in 1769, the buffaloes were more numerous than he had ever seen them before; the ground literally shook under the gallop of the mighty herds, they crowded in dense throngs round the licks, and the forest resounded with their grunting bellows. He and other woodsmen came back there off and on, hunting and trapping, and living in huts made of buffalo-hides; just such huts as the hunters dwelt in on the Little Missouri and Powder rivers as late as 1883, except that the plainsmen generally made dug-outs in the sides of the buttes and used the hides only for the roofs and fronts. So the place was well known, and the reports of the hunters had made many settlers eager to visit it, though as yet no regular path led thither. In 1778, the first permanent settler arrived, in the person of a hunter named Spencer, who spent the following winter entirely alone in this remote wilderness, living in a hollow sycamore-tree. Spencer was a giant in his day, a man huge in body and limb, all whose life had been

drifted to many different places, and that now and then an accident preserved the name of some hunter and of some place he visited.

[1] The locality where Nashborough was built, was sometimes spoken of as the Bluffs, and sometimes as the French Lick.

spent in the wilderness.   He came to the bend of
the Cumberland from Kentucky in the early spring,
being in search of good land on which to settle.
Other hunters were with him, and they stayed
some time.   A creole trapper from the Wabash
was then living in a cabin on the south side of the
river.   He did not meet the new-comers; but one
day he saw the huge moccasin tracks of Spencer,
and on the following morning the party passed
close by his cabin in chase of a wounded buffalo,
halloing and shouting as they dashed through the
underwood.   Whether he thought them Indians,
or whether, as is more likely, he shared the fear
and dislike felt by most of the creoles for the
American backwoodsmen, cannot be said; but
certainly he left his cabin, swam the river, and,
plunging into the forest, straightway fled to his
kinsfolk on the banks of the Wabash.   Spencer
was soon left by his companions; though one of
them stayed with him a short time, helping him
to plant a field of corn.   Then this man, too,
wished to return.   He had lost his hunting-knife;
so Spencer went with him to the barrens of Kentucky, put him on the right path, and, breaking
his own knife, gave his departing friend a piece of
the metal.   The undaunted old hunter himself
returned to the banks of the Cumberland, and so-
journed throughout the fall and winter in the
neighborhood of the little clearing on which he

had raised the corn crop; a strange, huge, solitary man, self-reliant, unflinching, cut off from all his fellows by endless leagues of shadowy forest. Thus he dwelt alone in the vast dim wastes, wandering whithersoever he listed through the depths of the melancholy and wintry woods, sleeping by his camp-fire or in the hollow tree-trunk, ever ready to do battle against brute or human foe—a stark and sombre harbinger of the oncoming civilization.

Spencer's figure, seen through the mists that shrouds early western history, is striking and picturesque in itself; yet its chief interest lies in the fact that he was but a type of many other men whose lives were no less lonely and dangerous. He had no qualities to make him a leader when settlements sprang up around him. To the end of his days he remained a solitary hunter and Indian fighter, spurning restraint and comfort, and seeking the strong excitement of danger to give zest to his life. Even in the time of the greatest peril from the savages he would not stay shut up in the forts, but continued his roving, wandering life, trusting to his own quick senses, wonderful strength, and iron nerves. He even continued to lie out at night, kindling a fire, and then lying down to sleep far from it.[1]

[1] *Southwestern Monthly*, Nashville, 1852, vol. ii.   General Hall's " Narrative."

Early in the year 1779, a leader of men came to
the place where the old hunter had roamed and
killed game; and with the new-comer came those
who were to possess the land.   Robertson left
the Watauga settlements soon after the spring
opened,[1] with eight companions, one of a them
negro.   He followed Boon's trace,—the Wilderness Road,—through Cumberland Gap, and across
the Cumberland River.   Then he struck off southwest through the wilderness, lightening his labor
by taking the broad, well-beaten buffalo trails
whenever they led in his direction; they were very
distinct near the pools and springs, and especially
going to and from the licks.   The adventurers
reached the bend of the Cumberland without mis-
hap, and fixed on the neighborhood of the Bluffs,
the ground near the French Lick, as that best
suited for their purpose; and they planted a field
of corn on the site of the future forted village of

[1] It is very difficult to reconcile the dates of these early
movements; even the contemporary documents are often a
little vague, while Haywood, Ramsey, and Putnam are frequently months out of the way.   Apparently, Robertson
stayed as commissioner in Chota until February or March,
1779, when he gave warning of the intended raid of the
Chickamaugas, and immediately afterwards came back to
the settlements and started out for the Cumberland, before
Shelby left on his Chickamauga expedition.   But it is possible that he had left Chota before, and that another man
was there as commissioner at the time of the Chickamauga
raid which was followed by Shelby's counter-stroke.

Nashborough. A few days after their arrival they were joined by another batch of hunter-settlers, who had come out under the leadership of Kasper Mansker.

As soon as the corn was planted and cabins put up, most of the intending settlers returned to their old homes to bring out their families, leaving three of their number "to keep the buffaloes out of the corn." [1] Robertson himself first went north through the wilderness to see George Rogers Clark in Illinois, to purchase cabin-rights from him. This act gives an insight into at least some of the motives that influenced the adventurers. Doubtless, they were impelled largely by sheer restlessness and love of change and excitement, [2] and these motives would probably have induced them to act as they did, even had there been no others. But another and most powerful spring of action was the desire to gain land—not merely land for settlement, but land for speculative purposes. Wild land was then so abundant that the quantity literally seemed inexhaustible; and it was absolutely valueless until settled. Our forefathers may well be pardoned for failing to see that it was of more importance to have it owned

[1] Haywood, 83.

[2] Phelan, p. 111, fails to do justice to these motives, while very properly insisting on what earlier historians ignored, the intense desire for land speculation.

in small lots by actual settlers than to have it
filled up quickly under a system of huge grants to
individuals or corporations.   Many wise and good
men honestly believed that they would benefit the
country at the same time that they enriched themselves by acquiring vast tracts of virgin wilderness, and then proceeding to people them.   There
was a rage for land speculation and land companies of every kind.   The private correspondence
of almost all the public men of the period, from
Washington, Madison, and Gouverneur Morris
down, is full of the subject.   Innumerable people
of position and influence dreamed of acquiring un-
told wealth in this manner.   Almost every man of
note was actually or potentially a land speculator;
and in turn almost every prominent pioneer, from
Clark and Boon to Shelby and Robertson, was
either himself one of the speculators or an agent
for those who were.   Many people did not understand the laws on the subject, or hoped to evade
them; and the hope was as strong in the breast of
the hunter who made a "tomahawk claim," by
blazing a few trees, and sold it for a small sum, to
a new-comer, as in that of the well-to-do schemer,
who bought an Indian title for a song, and then
got what he could from all outsiders who came in
to dwell on the land.

This speculative spirit was a powerful stimulus
to the settlement not only of Kentucky, but of

middle Tennessee. Henderson's claim included the Cumberland country, and when North Carolina annulled his rights, she promised him a large but indefinitely located piece of land in their place. He tried to undersell the State in the land market, and undoubtedly his offers had been among the main causes that induced Robertson and his associates to go to the Cumberland when they did. But at the time it was uncertain whether Cumberland lay in Virginia or North Carolina, as the line was not run by the surveyors until the following spring; and Robertson went up to see Clark, because it was rumored that the latter had the disposal of Virginia "cabin-rights," under which each man could, for a small sum, purchase a thousand acres, on condition of building a cabin and raising a crop. However, as it turned out, he might have spared himself the journey, for the settlement proved to be well within the Carolina boundary.

In the fall very many men came out to the new settlement, guided thither by Robertson and Mansker; the former persuading a number who were bound to Kentucky to go to the Cumberland instead. Among them were two or three of the Long Hunters, whose wanderings had done so much to make the country known. Robertson's special partner was a man named John Donelson. The latter went by water and took a large party of immigrants, including all the women and children, down the Tennessee, and thence up the Ohio and Cumberland to the Bluffs or French Lick.[1] Among them were Robertson's entire family, and Donelson's daughter Rachel, the future wife of Andrew Jackson, who missed by so narrow a margin being mistress of the White House. Robertson, meanwhile, was to lead the rest of the men by land, so that they should get there first and make ready for the coming of their families.

Robertson's party started in the fall, being both preceded and followed by other companies of settlers, some of whom were accompanied by their wives and children. Cold weather of extraordinary severity set in during November; for this was the famous "hard winter" of '79–80, during which the Kentucky settlers suffered so much. They were not molested by Indians, and reached the Bluffs about Christmas. The river was frozen solid, and they all crossed the ice in a body; when in mid-stream the ice jarred, and—judging from the report—the jar or crack must have gone miles up and down the stream; but the ice only settled a little and did not break. By January 1st, there were over two hundred people scattered on both

[1] The plan was that Robertson should meet this party at the Muscle Shoals, and that they should go from thence overland; but, owing to the severity of the winter, Robertson could not get to the Shoals.

sides of the river. In Robertson's company was a man named John Rains, who brought with him twenty-one horned cattle and seventeen horses; the only cattle and horses which any of the immigrants succeeded in bringing to the Cumberland. But he was not the only man who had made the attempt. One of the immigrants who went in Donelson's flotilla, Daniel Dunham by name, offered his brother John, who went by land, £100 to drive along his horses and cattle. John accepted, and tried his best to fulfil his share of the bargain; but he was seemingly neither a very expert woodsman nor yet a good stock hand. There is no form of labor more arduous and dispiriting than driving unruly and unbroken stock along a faint forest or mountain trail, especially in bad weather; and this the would-be drover speedily found out. The animals would not follow the trail; they incessantly broke away from it, got lost, scattered in the brush, and stampeded at night. Finally, the unfortunate John, being, as he expressed it, nearly driven "mad by the drove," abandoned them all in the wilderness.[1]

The settlers who came by water passed through much greater peril and hardship. By a stroke of good fortune the journal kept by Donelson, the

[1] MSS. on "Dunham Pioneers," in Nashville Historical Society. Daniel, a veteran stockman, was very angry when he heard what had happened.

leader of the expedition, has been preserved.[1]   As with all the other recorded wanderings and explorations of these backwoods adventurers, it must be remembered that while this trip was remarkable in itself, it is especially noteworthy because, out of many such, it is the only one of which we have a full account.   The adventures that befell Donelson's company differed in degree, but not in kind, from those that befell the many similar flotillas that followed or preceded him.   From the time that settlers first came to the upper Tennessee valley occasional hardy hunters had floated down the stream in pirogues, or hollowed out treetrunks.   Before the Revolution a few restless emigrants had adopted this method of reaching Natchez; some of them made the long and perilous trip in safety, others were killed by the Chickamaugas or else foundered in the whirlpools or on the shoals.   The spring before Donelson started, a party of men, women, and children, in forty canoes or pirogues, went down the Tennessee to settle in the newly conquered Illinois country,

[1] Original MS. "Journal of Voyage Intended by God's Permission in the Good Boat *Adventure* from Fort Patrick Henry of Holston River to the French Salt Springs on Cumberland River, Kept by John Donelson."   An abstract, with some traditional statements interwoven, is given by Haywood; the journal itself, with some inaccuracies, and the name of the writer misspelt by Ramsey; and in much better and fuller shape by A. N. Putnam in his *History of Middle Tennessee*. I follow the original, in the Nashville Historical Society.

and skirmished with the Cherokees on their way.[1]

Donelson's flotilla, after being joined by a number of other boats, especially at the mouth of the Clinch, consisted of some thirty craft, all told— flat-boats, dug-outs, and canoes. There were probably two or three hundred people, perhaps many more, in the company; among them, as the

[1] State Department MSS., No. 51, vol. ii., p. 45

"JAMES COLBERT TO CHAS. STUART.

"CHICKASAW NATION, May 25, 1779.

"SIR,—I was this day informed that there is forty large Cannoes loaded with men women and children passed by here down the Cherokee River who on their way down they took a Dellaway Indian prisoner & kept him till they found out what Nation he was of—they told him they had come from Long Island and were on their way to Illinois with an intent to settle—Sir I have some reason to think they are a party of Rebels My reason is this after they let the Dellaway Indian at liberty they met with some Cherokees whom they endeavoured to decoy, but finding they would not be decoyed they fired on them but they all made their escape with the Loss of their arms and ammunition and one fellow wounded, who arrived yesterday. The Dellaway informs me that Lieut. Governor Hamilton is defeated and himself taken prisoner," etc.

It is curious that none of the Tennessee annalists have noticed the departure of this expedition; very, very few of the deeds and wanderings of the old frontiersmen have been recorded; and in consequence historians are apt to regard these few as being exceptional, instead of typical. Donelson was merely one of a hundred leaders of flotillas that went down the western rivers at this time.

journal records, "James Robertson's lady and children," the latter to the number of five. The chief boat, the flag-ship of the flotilla, was the *Adventure*, a great scow, in which there were over thirty men, besides the families of some of them.

They embarked at Holston, Long Island, on December 22d, but falling water and heavy frosts detained them two months, and the voyage did not really begin until they left Cloud Creek on February 27, 1780. The first ten days were uneventful. The *Adventure* spent an afternoon and night on a shoal, until the water fortunately rose and, all the men getting out, the clumsy scow was floated off. Another boat was driven on the point of an island and sunk, her crew being nearly drowned; whereupon the rest of the flotilla put to shore, the sunken boat was raised and bailed out, and most of her cargo recovered. At one landing-place a man went out to hunt, and got lost, not being taken up again for three days, though "many guns were fired to fetch him in," and the four-pounder on the *Adventure* was discharged for the same purpose. A negro became "much frosted in his feet and legs, of which he died." Where the river was wide a strong wind and high sea forced the whole flotilla to lay to, for the sake of the smaller craft. This happened on March 7th, just before coming to the uppermost Chickamauga town; and that night the wife of one

Ephraim Peyton, who had himself gone with Robertson overland, was delivered of a child. She was in a boat whose owner was named Jonathan Jennings.

The next morning they soon came to an Indian village on the south shore. The Indians made signs of friendliness, and two men started toward them in a canoe which the *Adventure* had in tow, while the flotilla drew up on the opposite side of the river. But a half-breed and some Indians jumping into a pirogue, paddled out to meet the two messengers and advised them to return to their comrades, which they did. Several canoes then came off from the shore to the flotilla. The Indians who were in them seemed friendly and were pleased with the presents they received; but while these were being distributed the whites saw a number of other canoes putting off, loaded with armed warriors, painted black and red. The half-breed instantly told the Indians round about to paddle to the shore, and warned the whites to push off at once, at the same time giving them some instructions about the river. The armed Indians went down along the shore for some time as if to intercept them; but at last they were seemingly left behind.

In a short time another Indian village was reached, where the warriors tried in vain to lure the whites ashore; and as the boats were hugging the opposite bank, they were suddenly fired at by a party in ambush, and one man slain.   Immediately afterwards a much more serious tragedy occurred.   There was with the flotilla a boat containing twenty-eight men, women, and children, among whom the small-pox had broken out.   To guard against infection, it was agreed that it should keep well in the rear; being warned each night by the sound of a horn when it was time to go into camp.

As this forlorn boat-load of unfortunates came along, far behind the others, the Indians, seeing their defenceless position, sallied out in their canoes and butchered or captured all who were aboard. Their cries were distinctly heard by the rearmost of the other craft, who could not stem the current and come to their rescue.   But a dreadful retribution fell on the Indians; for they were infected with the disease of their victims, and for some months virulent small-pox raged among many of the bands of Creeks and Cherokees.   When stricken by the disease, the savages first went into the sweat-houses, and when heated to madness, plunged into the cool streams, and so perished in multitudes.

When the boats entered the Narrows they had lost sight of the Indians on shore, and thought they had left them behind.   A man, who was in a canoe, had gone aboard one of the larger boats

with his family, for the sake of safety while passing through the rough water. His canoe was
towed alongside, and in the rapids it was over-
turned, and the cargo lost. The rest of the company, pitying his distress over the loss of all his
worldly goods, landed, to see if they could not help
him recover some of his property. Just as they
got out on the shore to walk back, the Indians suddenly appeared almost over them, on the high cliffs
opposite, and began to fire, causing a hurried retreat to the boats. For some distance the Indians lined the bluffs, firing from the heights
into the boats below. Yet only four people were
wounded, and they not dangerously. One of
them was a girl named Nancy Gower. When, by
the sudden onslaught of the Indians, the crew of
the boat in which she was, were thrown into dismay, she took the helm and steered, exposed to
the fire of the savages. A ball went through the
upper part of one of her thighs, but she neither
flinched nor uttered any cry; and it was not known
that she was wounded until, after the danger was
past, her mother saw the blood soaking through
her clothes. She recovered, married one of the
frontiersmen, and lived for fifty years afterwards,
long enough to see all the wilderness filled with
flourishing and populous States.

One of the clumsy craft, however, did not share
the good fortune that befell the rest, in escaping

with so little loss and damage. Jonathan Jennings's boat, in which was Mrs. Peyton, with her new-born baby, struck on a rock at the upper end of the whirl, the swift current rendering it impossible for the others to go to his assistance; and they drifted by, leaving him to his fate. The Indians soon turned their whole attention to him, and from the bluffs opened a most galling fire upon the disabled boat. He returned it as well as he could, keeping them somewhat in check, for he was a most excellent marksman. At the same time he directed his two negroes, a man and woman, his nearly grown son, and a young man who was with him, to lighten the boat by throwing his goods into the river. Before this was done, the negro men, the son, and the other young man most basely jumped into the river, and swam ashore. It is satisfactory to record that at least two of the three dastards met the fate they deserved. The negro was killed in the water, and the other two captured, one of them being afterwards burned at the stake, while the other, it is said, was ultimately released. Meanwhile, Mrs. Jennings, assisted by the negro woman and Mrs. Peyton, actually succeeded in shoving the lightened boat off the rock, though their clothes were cut in many places by the bullets; and they rapidly drifted out of danger. The poor little baby was killed in the hurry and confusion; but its mother, not eighteen hours from child-bed, in spite of the cold, wet, and exertion, kept in good health. Sailing by night as well as day, they caught up with the rest of the flotilla before dawn on the second morning afterwards, the men being roused from their watch-fires by the cries of "help poor Jennings," as the wretched and worn-out survivors in the disabled boat caught the first glimpse of the lights on shore.

Having successfully run the gauntlet of the Chickamauga banditti, the flotilla was not again molested by the Indians, save once when the boats that drifted near shore were fired on by a roving war-party, and five men wounded. They ran over the great Muscle Shoals in about three hours without accident, though the boats scraped on the bottom here and there. The swift, broken water surged into high waves, and roared through the piles of driftwood that covered the points of the small islands, round which the current ran in every direction; and those among the men who were unused to river-work were much relieved when they found themselves in safety. One night, after the fires had been kindled, the tired travellers were alarmed by the barking of the dogs. Fearing that Indians were nearby, they hastily got into the boats and crossed to camp on the opposite shore. In the morning two of them returned to pick up some things that had been left; they found that the alarm had been false, for the utensils that had been overlooked in the confusion were undisturbed, and a negro who had been left behind in the hurry was still sleeping quietly by the camp-fires.

On the 20th of the month they reached the Ohio. Some of the boats then left for Natchez, and others for the Illinois country; while the remainder turned their prows up-stream, to stem the rapid current—a task for which they were but ill suited. The work was very hard, the provisions were nearly gone, and the crews were almost worn out by hunger and fatigue. On the 24th, they entered the mouth of the Cumberland. The *Adventure*, the heaviest of all the craft, got much help from a small square-sail that was set in the bow.

Two days afterward, the hungry party killed some buffalo, and feasted on the lean meat, and the next day they shot a swan "which was very delicious," as Donelson recorded. Their meal was exhausted and they could make no more bread; but buffalo were plenty, and they hunted them steadily for their meat; and they also made what some of them called "Shawnee salad" from a kind of green herb that grew in the bottoms.

On the last day of the month they met Colonel Richard Henderson, who had just come out and was running the line between Virginia and North Carolina. The crews were so exhausted that the progress of the boats became very slow, and it was not until April 24th that they reached the

Big Salt Lick, and found Robertson awaiting them. The long, toilsome, and perilous voyage had been brought to a safe end.

There were then probably nearly five hundred settlers on the Cumberland, one half of them being able-bodied men in the prime of life.[1] The central station, the capital of the little community, was that at the Bluffs, where Robertson built a little stockaded hamlet and called it Nashborough[2]; it was of the usual type of small frontier forted town. Other stations were scattered along both sides of the river; some were stockades, others merely blockhouses, with the yard and garden enclosed by stout palings. As with all similar border forts or stations, these were sometimes called by the name of the founder; more rarely, they were named with reference to some natural object, such as the river, ford, or hill by which they were, or commemorated some deed, or the name of a man the frontiersmen held in honor; and, occasionally, they afforded true instances of clan settlement and clan nomenclature, several kindred families of the same name building a village which grew to be called

[1] Two hundred and fifty-six names are subscribed to the compact of government; and in addition there were the women, children, the few slaves, and such men as did not sign.

[2] After A. Nash; he was the Governor of North Carolina; where he did all he could on the patriot side. See Gates MSS., September 7, 1780.

after them. Among these Cumberland stations
was Mansker's (usually called Kasper's or Gasper's
—he was not particular how his name was spelled),
Stone River, Bledsoe's, Freeland's, Eaton's,
Clover-Bottom, and Fort Union.

As the country where they had settled belonged
to no tribe of Indians, some of the people thought
they would not be molested, and, being eager to
take up the best lands, scattered out to live on
separate claims. Robertson warned them that
they would soon suffer from the savages; and his
words speedily came true—whereupon the outlying cabins were deserted and all gathered within
the stockades. In April, roving parties of Delawares, Chickasaws, and Choctaws began to harass
the settlement. As in Kentucky, so on the banks
of the Cumberland, the Indians were the first to
begin the conflict. The lands on which the whites
settled were uninhabited, and were claimed as
hunting-grounds by many hostile tribes; so that
it is certain that no one tribe had any real title to
them.

True to their customs and traditions, and to
their race-capacity for self-rule, the settlers determined forthwith to organize some kind of government under which justice might be done among
themselves, and protection afforded against outside attack. Not only had the Indians begun
their ravages, but turbulent and disorderly whites

were also causing trouble. Robertson, who had
been so largely instrumental in founding the Watauga settlement, and giving it laws, naturally
took the lead in organizing this, the second community which he had caused to spring up in the
wilderness. He summoned a meeting of delegates
from the various stations, to be held at Nashborough [1]; Henderson being foremost in advo-
cating the adoption of the plan.

In fact, Henderson, the treaty-maker and land-
speculator, whose purchase first gave the whites
clear color of title to the valleys of the Kentucky
and Cumberland, played somewhat the same part,
though on a smaller scale, in the settlement made
by Robertson as in that made by Boon. He and
the Virginian commissioner Walker, had surveyed
the boundary line and found that the Cumberland
settlements were well to the south of it. He then
claimed the soil as his under the Cherokee deed
and disposed of it to the settlers who contracted
to pay ten dollars a thousand acres. This was but
a fraction of the State price, so the settlers were
all eager to hold under Henderson's deed; one of
the causes of their coming out had been the chance
of getting land so cheap. But Henderson's claim

---

[1] It is to Putnam that we owe the publication of the compact of government, and the full details of the methods and
proceedings by which it was organized and carried on. See
History of Middle Tennessee, pp. 84–103.

was annulled by the legislature, and the satisfaction-piece of two hundred thousand acres allotted him was laid off elsewhere; so his contracts with the settlers came to nothing, and they eventually got title in the usual way from North Carolina. They suffered no loss in the matter, for they had merely given Henderson promises to pay when his title was made good.

The settlers, by their representatives, met together at Nashborough, and on May 1, 1780, entered into articles of agreement or a compact of government. It was doubtless drawn up by Robertson, with perhaps the help of Henderson, and was modelled upon what may be called the "constitution" of Watauga, with some hints from that of Transylvania.[1] The settlers ratified the deeds of their delegates on May 13th, when they signed the articles, binding themselves to obey them to the number of 256 men. The signers practically guaranteed one another their rights in the land, and their personal security against wrong-doers;

[1] Phelan, the first historian who really grasped what this movement meant, and to what it was due, gives rather too much weight to the part Henderson played. Henderson certainly at this time did not aspire to form a new State on the Cumberland; the compact especially provided for the speedy admission of Cumberland as a county of North Carolina. The marked difference between the Transylvania and the Cumberland "constitutions," and the close agreement of the latter with the Watauga articles, assuredly point to Robertson as the chief author.

those who did not sign were treated as having no
rights whatever—a proper and necessary measure as it was essential that the naturally lawless
elements should be forced to acknowledge some
kind of authority.

The compact provided that the affairs of the
community should be administered by a Court or
Committee of twelve Judges, Triers, or General
Arbitrators, to be elected in the different stations
by vote of all the freemen in them who were over
twenty-one years of age.   Three of the Triers were
to come from Nashborough, two from Mansker's,
two from Bledsoe's, and one from each of five other
named stations.[1]   Whenever the freemen of any
station were dissatisfied with their Triers, they
could at once call a new election, at which others
might be chosen in their stead.   The Triers had
no salaries, but the Clerk of the Court was allowed
some very small fees, just enough to pay for the
pens, ink, and paper, all of them scarce commodities.[2]   The Court had jurisdiction in all cases
of conflict over land titles, a land office being

[1] Putnam speaks of these men as "notables"; apparently
they called themselves as above.   Putnam's book contains
much very valuable information; but it is written in most
curious style and he interlards it with outside matter; much
that he puts in quotation marks is apparently his own
material.   It is difficult to make out whether his "tribunal
of notables" is his own expression or a quotation, but apparently it is the former.

[2] Haywood, 126.

established and an entry-taker appointed. Over
half of the compact was devoted to the rules of the
land office. The Court, acting by a majority of its
members, was to have jurisdiction for the recovery
of debt or damages, and to be allowed to tax costs.
Three Triers were competent to make a Court to
decide a case where the debt or damage was a
hundred dollars or less, and there was no appeal
from their decision. For a larger sum an appeal
lay to the whole Court. The Court appointed
whomsoever it pleased to see decisions executed.
It had power to punish all offences against the
peace of the community, all misdemeanors and
criminal acts, provided only that its decisions did
not go so far as to affect the life of the criminal.
If the misdeed of the accused was such as to be
dangerous to the State, or one "for which the benefit of clergy was taken away by law," he was to be
bound and sent under guard to some place where
he could be legally dealt with. The Court levied
fines, payable in money or provisions, entered up
judgments and awarded executions, and granted
letters of administration upon estates of deceased
persons, and took bonds "payable to the chairman
of the Committee." The expenses were to be paid
proportionately by the various settlers. It was
provided, in view of the Indian incursions, that
the militia officers elected at the various stations
should have power to call out the militia when

they deemed it necessary to repel or pursue the enemy. They were also given power to fine such men as disobeyed them, and to impress horses, if need be; if damaged, the horses were to be paid for by the people of the station in the proportion the Court might direct. It was expressly declared that the compact was designed as a "temporary method of restraining the licentious," that the settlement did not desire to be exempt from the ratable share of the expense for the Revolutionary War, and earnestly asked that North Carolina would immediately make it part of the State, erecting it into a county. Robertson was elected chairman of the Court and colonel of the militia, being thus made both civil and military commandant of the settlement. In common with other Triers, he undertook the solemnization of marriages; and these were always held legal, which was fortunate, as it was a young and vigorous community, of which the members were much given to early wedlock.

Thus a little commonwealth, a self-governing state, was created. It was an absolute democracy, the majority of freemen of full age in each stockade having power in every respect, and being able not only to elect, but to dismiss their delegates at any moment. Their own good sense and a feeling of fair play could be depended upon to protect the rights of the minority, especially as a minority of such men would certainly not tolerate anything even remotely resembling tyranny. They had formed a representative government in which the legislative and judicial functions were not separated, and were even to a large extent combined with the executive. They had proceeded in an eminently practical manner, having modelled their system on what was to them the familiar governmental unit of the county with its county court and county militia officers. They made the changes that their peculiar position required, grafting the elective and representative systems on the one they adopted, and, of course, enlarging the scope of the Court's action. Their compact was thus in some sort an unconscious reproduction of the laws and customs of the old-time court-leet, profoundly modified to suit the peculiar needs of backwoods life, the intensely democratic temper of the pioneers, and, above all, the military necessities of their existence. They had certain theories of liberty and justice; but they were too shrewd and hard-headed to try to build up a government on an entirely new foundation when they had, ready to hand, materials with which they were familiar. They knew by experience the workings of the county system; all they did was to alter the immediate channel from which the Court drew its powers, and to adapt the representation to the needs of a community where constant warfare obliged the settlers to gather in little groups, which served as natural units.

When the settlers first came to the country they found no Indians living in it, no signs of cultivation or cleared lands, and nothing to show that for ages past it had been inhabited. It was a vast plain, covered with woods and canebrakes, through which the wild herds had beaten out broad trails. The only open places were the licks, sometimes as large as corn-fields, where the hoofs of the game had trodden the ground bare of vegetation, and channelled its surface with winding seams and gullies. It is even doubtful if the spot of bare ground which Mansker called an "old field" or sometimes a "Chickasaw old field" was not merely one of these licks. Buffalo, deer, and bear abounded; elk, wolves, and panthers were plentiful.

Yet there were many signs that in long by-gone times a numerous population had dwelt in the land. Round every spring were many graves, built in a peculiar way, and covered eight or ten inches deep by mould. In some places there were earth-covered foundations of ancient walls and embankments that enclosed spaces of eight or ten acres. The Indians knew as little as the whites [1]

[1] Haywood. At present it is believed that the mound-builders were Indians. Haywood is the authority for the early Indian wars of the Cumberland settlement, Putnam supplying some information.

about these long-vanished mound-builders, and were utterly ignorant of the race to which they had belonged.

For some months the whites who first arrived dwelt in peace. But in the spring, hunting- and war-parties from various tribes began to harass the settlers. Unquestionably, the savages felt jealous of the white hunters, who were killing and driving away the game, precisely as they all felt jealous of one another, and for the same reason. The Chickasaws, in particular, were much irritated by the fort Clark had built at Iron Bank, on the Mississippi. But the most powerful motive for the attacks was doubtless simply the desire for scalps and plunder. They gathered from different quarters to assail the colonists, just as the wild beasts gathered to prey on the tame herds.

The Indians began to commit murders, kill the stock, and drive off the horses in April, and their ravages continued unceasingly throughout the year. Among the slain was a son of Robertson, and also the unfortunate Jonathan Jennings, the man who had suffered such loss when his boat was passing the whirl of the Tennessee River. The settlers were shot as they worked on their clearings, gathered the corn crops, or ventured outside the walls of the stockades. Hunters were killed as they stooped to drink at the springs, or lay in wait at the licks. They were lured up to the

Indians by imitations of the gobbling of a turkey
or the cries of wild beasts. They were regularly
stalked as they still-hunted the game, or were
ambushed as they returned with their horses laden
with meat. The inhabitants of one station were
all either killed or captured. Robertson led pursuing parties after one or two of the bands, and
recovered some plunder; and once or twice small
marauding parties were met and scattered, with
some loss, by the hunters. But, on the whole,
very little could be done at first to parry or revenge the strokes of the Indians.[1]

Horses and cattle had been brought into the new
settlement in some number during the year; but
the savages killed or drove off most of them,
shooting the hogs and horned stock, and stealing
the riding animals. The loss of the milch cows
in particular, was severely felt by the women.

---

[1] Putnam, p. 107, talks as if the settlers were utterly unused to Indian warfare, saying that until the first murder
occurred, in this spring, "few, if any" of them had ever gazed
on the victim of scalping-knife and tomahawk. This is a
curiously absurd statement. Many of the settlers were
veteran Indian fighters. Almost all of them had been born
and brought up on the frontier, amid a succession of Indian
wars. It is, unfortunately, exceedingly difficult in Putnam's
book to distinguish the really valuable authentic information it contains from the interwoven tissue of matter written
solely to suit his theory of dramatic effect. He puts in, with
equal gravity, the "Articles of Agreement" and purely fictitious conversations, jokes, and the like. (See pp. 126, 144,
and *passim*.)

Moreover, there were heavy freshets, flooding the low bottoms on which the corn had been planted, and destroying most of the crop.

These accumulated disasters wrought the greatest discouragement among the settlers. Many left the country, and most of the remainder, when midsummer was past, began to urge that they should all go back in a body to the old settlements. The panic became very great. One by one the stockades were deserted, until finally all the settlers who remained were gathered in Nashborough and Freeland's.[1] The Cumberland country would have been abandoned to the Indians, had Robertson not shown himself to be exactly the man for whom the crisis called.

Robertson was not a dashing, brilliant Indian fighter and popular frontier leader, like Sevier. He had rather the qualities of Boon, with the difference that he was less a wandering hunter and explorer, and better fitted to be head of a settled community. He was far-seeing, tranquil, resolute, unshaken by misfortune and disaster; a most trustworthy man, with a certain severe fortitude of temper. All people naturally turned to him in time of panic, when the ordinarily bold and daring became cowed and confused. The straits

[1] By some accounts, there were also a few settlers left in Eaton's Station; and Mansker's was rarely entirely deserted for any length of time.

to which the settlers were reduced, and their wild clamor for immediate flight, the danger from the Indians, the death of his own son, all combined failed to make him waver one instant in his purpose. He strongly urged on the settlers the danger of flight through the wilderness. He did not attempt to make light of the perils that confronted them if they remained, but he asked them to ponder well if the beauty and fertility of the land did not warrant some risk being run to hold it, now that it was won. They were at last in a fair country, fitted for the homes of their children. Now was the time to keep it. If they abandoned it they would lose all the advantages they had gained, and would be forced to suffer the like losses and privations if they ever wished to retake possession of it or of any similar tract of land. He, at least, would not turn back, but would stay to the bitter end.

His words and his steadfast bearing gave heart to the settlers, and they no longer thought of flight. As their corn had failed them they got their food from the woods. Some gathered quantities of walnuts, hickory-nuts, and shellbarks, and the hunters wrought havoc among the vast herds of game. During the early winter one party of twenty men that went up Caney Fork on a short trip killed one hundred and five bears, seventy-five buffaloes, and eighty-seven deer, and brought the flesh and hides back to the stockades in canoes; so that through the winter there was no lack of jerked and smoke-dried meat.

The hunters were very accurate marksmen; game was plenty, and not shy, and so they got up close and rarely wasted a shot. Moreover, their small-bore rifles took very little powder—in fact, the need of excessive economy in the use of ammunition when on their long hunting trips was one of the chief reasons for the use of small bores. They therefore used comparatively little ammunition. Nevertheless, by the beginning of winter both powder and bullets began to fail. In this emergency Robertson again came to the front to rescue the settlement he had founded and preserved. He was accustomed to making long, solitary journeys through the forest, unmindful of the Indians; he had been one of the first to come from North Carolina to Watauga; he had repeatedly been on perilous missions to the Cherokees; he had the previous year gone north to the Illinois country to meet Clark. He now announced that he would himself go to Kentucky and bring back the needed ammunition; and at once set forth on his journey, across the long stretches of snow-powdered barrens, and desolate, Indian-haunted woodland.

CHAPTER VIII

THE CUMBERLAND SETTLEMENTS TO THE CLOSE OF THE REVOLUTION, 1781–1783

ROBERTSON passed unharmed through the wilderness to Kentucky. There he procured plenty of powder, and without delay set out on his return journey to the Cumberland. As before, he travelled alone through the frozen woods, trusting solely to his own sharp senses for his safety.

In the evening of January 15, 1781, he reached Freeland's station, and was joyfully received by the inmates. They supped late, and then sat up for some time, talking over many matters. When they went to bed all were tired, and neglected to take the usual precautions against surprise; moreover, at that season they did not fear molestation. They slept heavily, none keeping watch. Robertson alone was wakeful and suspicious; and even during his light slumbers his keen and long-trained senses were on the alert.

At midnight all was still. The moon shone brightly down on the square blockhouses and stockaded yard of the lonely little frontier fort; its rays lit up the clearing, and by contrast darkened the black shadow of the surrounding forest. None of the sleepers within the log-walls dreamed of danger. Yet their peril was imminent. An Indian war band was lurking near by, and was on the point of making an effort to carry Freeland's station by an attack in the darkness. In the dead of the night the attempt was made. One by one the warriors left the protection of the tangled wood-growth, slipped silently across the open space, and crouched under the heavy timber pickets of the palisades, until all had gathered together. Though the gate was fastened with a strong bar and chain, the dextrous savages finally contrived to open it.

In so doing they made a slight noise, which caught Robertson's quick ear, as he lay on his buffalo-hide pallet. Jumping up, he saw the gate open, and dusky figures gliding into the yard with stealthy swiftness. At his cry of "Indians," and the report of his piece, the settlers sprang up, every man grasping the loaded arm by which he slept. From each log cabin the rifles cracked and flashed; and, though the Indians were actually in the yard, they had no cover, and the sudden and unexpected resistance caused them to hurry out much faster than they had come in. Robertson shot one of their number, and they in return killed a white man who sprang out-of-doors at the first alarm. When they were driven out, the gate was closed after them; but they fired through the loopholes, especially into one of the blockhouses where the chinks had not been filled with mud, as in the others. They thus killed a negro, and wounded one or two other men; yet they were soon driven off. Robertson's return had been at a most opportune moment. As so often before and afterwards, he had saved the settlement from destruction.

Other bands of Indians joined the war-party, and they continued to hover about the stations, daily inflicting loss and damage on the settlers. They burned down the cabins and fences, drove off the stock, and killed the hunters, the women, and children who ventured outside the walls, and the men who had gone back to their deserted stockades.[1]

---

[1] Haywood says they burned "immense quantities of corn"; as Putnam points out, the settlers could have had very little corn to burn. Haywood is the best authority for the Indian fighting in the Cumberland district during '80, '81, and '82. Putnam supplies some details learned from Mrs. Robertson in her old age. The accounts are derived mainly from the statements of old settlers; but the Robertsons seem always to have kept papers, which served to check off the oral statements. For all the important facts there is good authority. The annals are filled with name after name of men who were killed by the Indians. The dates, and even the names, may be misplaced in many of these instances; but this is really a matter of no consequence, for their only interest is to show the nature of the harassing Indian warfare, and the kind of adventure then common.

On the second day of April another effort was made by a formidable war-party to get possession of one of the two remaining stations—Freeland's and Nashborough—and thus, at a stroke, drive the whites from the Cumberland district. This time Nashborough was the point aimed at.

A large body [1] of Cherokees approached the fort in the night, lying hid in the bushes, divided into two parties. In the morning three of them came near, fired at the fort, and ran off toward where the smaller party lay ambushed, in a thicket through which ran a little "branch." Instantly twenty men mounted their horses and galloped after the decoys. As they overtook the fugitives they saw the Indians hid in the creek-bottom, and dismounted to fight, turning their horses loose. A smart interchange of shots followed, the whites having, if anything, rather the best of it, when the other and larger body of Indians rose from their hiding-place, in a clump of cedars, and running down, formed between the combatants and the fort, intending to run into the latter, mixed with the fleeing riflemen. The only chance of the hemmed-in whites was to turn and try to force their way back through their far more numerous foes. This was a desperate ven-

[1] How large, it is impossible to say. One or two recent accounts make wild guesses, calling it 1000; but this is sheer nonsense ; it is more likely to have been 100.

ture, for their pieces were all discharged, and there was no time to reload them; but they were helped by two unexpected circumstances. Their horses had taken flight at the firing, and ran off towards the fort, passing to one side of the inter-vening line of Indians; and many of the latter, eager for such booty, ran off to catch them. Meanwhile, the remaining men in the fort saw what had happened, and made ready for defence, while all the women likewise snatched up guns or axes, and stood by loopholes and gate. The dogs in the fort were also taking a keen interest in what was going on. They were stout, powerful animals, some being hounds and others watch-dogs, but all accustomed to contests with wild beasts; and by instinct and training they mortally hated Indians. Seeing the line of savages drawn up between the fort and their masters, they promptly sallied out and made a most furious onset upon their astonished foes. Taking advantage of this most opportune diversion, the whites ran through the lines and got into the fort, the Indians being completely occupied in defending themselves from the dogs. Five of the whites were killed, and they carried two wounded men into the fort. An-other man, when almost in safety, was shot, and fell with a broken thigh; but he had reloaded his gun as he ran, and he killed his assailant as the latter ran up to scalp him. The people from the

fort then, by firing their rifles, kept his foes at bay
until he could be rescued; and he soon recovered
from his hurt.   Yet another man was overtaken
almost under the walls, the Indian punching him
in the shoulder with the gun as he pulled the
trigger; but the gun snapped, and a hunter ran
out of the fort and shot the Indian.   The gates
were closed, and the whites all ready; so the Indians abandoned their effort and drew off.   They
had taken five scalps and a number of horses; but
they had failed in their main object, and the whites
had taken two scalps, besides killing and wounding others of the red men, who were carried off by
their comrades.

After the failure of this attempt, the Indians did
not, for some years, make any formidable attack
on any of the larger stations.   Though the most
dangerous of all foes on their own ground, their
extreme caution, and dislike of suffering punishment prevented them from ever making really determined efforts to carry a fort openly by storm;
moreover, these stockades were really very de-
fensible against men unprovided with artillery, and
there is no reason for supposing that any troops
could have carried them by fair charging, without
suffering altogether disproportionate loss.   The
red tribes acted in relation to the Cumberland
settlements exactly as they had previously done
towards those on the Kentucky and Watauga.

They harassed the settlers from the outset; but
they did not wake up to the necessity for a formidable and combined campaign against them
until it was too late for such a campaign to succeed. If, at the first, any one of these communities had been forced to withstand the shock of
such Indian armies as were afterwards brought
against it, it would, of necessity, have been abandoned.

Throughout '81 and '82 the Cumberland settlers
were worried beyond description by a succession
of small war-parties. In the first of these years
they raised no corn; in the second, they made a
few crops on fields they had cleared in 1780. No
man's life was safe for an hour, whether he hunted,
looked up strayed stock, went to the spring for
water, or tilled the fields. If two men were
together, one always watched while the other
worked, ate, or drank; and they sat down back to
back, or, if there were several, in a ring, facing out-
wards, like a covey of quail. The Indians were
especially fond of stealing the horses; the whites
pursued them in bands, and occasionally pitched
battles were fought, with loss on both sides, and
apparently as often resulting in the favor of one
party as of the other. The most expert Indian
fighters naturally became the leaders, being made
colonels and captains of the local militia. The
position and influence of the officers depended

largely on their individual prowess; they were the actual, not titular, leaders of their men.   Old Kasper Mansker, one of the most successful, may be taken as a type of the rest.   He was ultimately made a colonel, and shared in many expeditions; but he always acted as his own scout, and never would let any of his men ride ahead or abreast of him, preferring to trust to his own eyes and ears and knowledge of forest warfare.   The hunters, who were especially exposed to danger, were also the men who inflicted the most loss on the Indians, and, though many more of the settlers than of their foes were slain, yet the tables were often turned on the latter, even by those who seemed their helpless victims.   Thus, once, two lads were watching at a deer-lick, when some Indians came to it; each of the boys chose his man, fired, and then fled homewards; coming back with some men, they found they had killed two Indians, whose scalps they took.

The eagerness of the Indians to get scalps caused them frequently to scalp their victims before life was extinct; and, as a result, there were numerous instances in which the scalped unfortunate, whether man, woman, or child, was rescued and recovered, living many years.   One of these instances is worth giving in the quaint language of the old Tennessee historian, Haywood:

"In the spring of the year 1782 a party of Indians fired upon three persons at French Lick, and broke the arms of John Tucker and Joseph Hendricks, and shot down David Hood, whom they scalped and stamped, as he said, and followed the others towards the fort; the people of the fort came out and repulsed them and saved the wounded men. Supposing the Indians gone, Hood got up softly, wounded and scalped as he was, and began to walk towards the fort on the bluff, when, to his mortification, he saw, standing upon the bank of the creek, a number of Indians, the same who had wounded him before, making sport of his misfortune and mistake. They then fell upon him again, and having given him, in several places, new wounds that were apparently mortal, then left him. He fell into a brush heap in the mow, and next morning was tracked and found by his blood, and was placed as a dead man in one of the out-houses, and was left alone; after some time he recovered, and lived many years."

Many of the settlers were killed, many others left for Kentucky, Illinois, or Natchez, or returned to their old homes among the Alleghanies; and in 1782 the inhabitants, who had steadily dwindled in numbers, became so discouraged that they again mooted the question of abandoning the Cumberland district in a body. Only Robertson's great influence prevented this being done; but by word and example he finally persuaded them to remain.

The following spring brought the news of peace with Great Britain. A large inflow of new settlers began with the new year, and though the Indian hostilities still continued, the Cumberland country throve apace, and by the end of 1783 the old stations had been rebuilt and many new ones founded. Some of the settlers began to live out on their clearings. Rude little corn-mills and "hominy pounders" were built beside some of the streams. The piles of furs and hides that had accumulated in the stockades were sent back to the coast country on pack-horses. After this year there was never any danger that the settlements would be abandoned.

During the two years of petty but disastrous Indian warfare that followed the attack on Freeland's, the harassed and diminishing settlers had been so absorbed in the contest with the outside foe that they had done little towards keeping up their own internal government. When 1783 opened, new settlers began to flock in, the Indian hostilities abated, and commissioners arrived from North Carolina under a strong guard, with the purpose of settling the claim of the various settlers [1] and laying off the bounty lands promised

---

[1] Haywood. Six hundred and forty acres were allowed by pre-emption claim to each family settled before June 1, 1780; after that date they had to make proper entries in the courts. The salt-licks were to be held as public property.

to the Continental troops.[1] It therefore became
necessary that the Committee or Court of Triers
should again be convened, to see that justice was
done as between man and man.

The ten men elected from the different stations
met at Nashborough on January 7th, Robertson
being again made chairman, as well as colonel of
the militia, while a proper clerk and sheriff were
chosen. Each member took a solemn oath to do
equal justice according to the best of his skill and
ability. The number of suits between the settlers
themselves were disposed of. These related to a
variety of subjects. A kettle had been "detained" from Humphrey Hogan; he brought
suit, and it was awarded him, the defendant "and
his mother-in-law" being made to pay the cost of
the suit. A hog case, a horse used in hunting, a
piece of cleared ground, a bed which had not been
made according to contract, the ownership of a
canoe, and of a heifer, a "clevis lent and delayed
to be returned"—such were some of the cases on
which the judges had to decide. There were occasional slander suits; for in a small backwoods
community there is always much jealousy and
bitter gossip. When suit was brought for "cattle
won at cards," the committee promptly dismissed
the claim as illegal; they evidently had clear ideas
as to what was good public policy. A man making

[1] Isaac Shelby was one of these commissioners.

oath that another had threatened his life, the
latter was taken and put under bonds. Another
produced a note-of-hand for the payment of two
good cows, "against John Sadler"; he "proved
his accompt," and procured an attachment against
the estate of "Sd. Sadler." When possible, the
Committee compromised the cases, or advised the
parties to adjust matters between themselves.
The sheriff executed the various decrees in due
form; he arrested the men who refused to pay
heed to the judgments of the Court, and when
necessary took out of their "goods and chattles,
lands and tenements," the damages awarded, and
also the costs and fees. The government was in
the hands of men who were not only law-abiding
themselves, but also resolute to see that the law
was respected by others.

The Committee took cognizance of all affairs
concerning the general welfare of the community.
They ordered roads to be built between the different stations, appointing overseers who had power
to "call out hands to work on the same." Besides the embodiment of all the full-grown men as
militia,—those of each station under their own
captain, lieutenant, and ensign,—a diminutive
force of paid regulars was organized; that is, six
spies were "kept out to discover the motions of
the enemy so long as we shall be able to pay them;
each to receive seventy-five bushels of Indian corn

per month." They were under the direction of
Colonel Robertson, who was head of all the
branches of the government. One of the Committee's regulations followed an economic principle
of doubtful value. Some enterprising individuals, taking advantage of the armed escort accompanying the Carolina commissioners, brought
out casks of liquors. The settlers had drunk nothing but water for many months, and they eagerly
purchased the liquor, the merchants naturally
charging all that the traffic would bear. This
struck the committee as a grievance, and they
forthwith passed a decree that any person bringing in liquor "from foreign ports," before selling
the same, must give bond that they would charge
no more than one silver dollar, or its value in
merchandise, per quart.

Some of the settlers would not enter the asso-
ciation, preferring a condition of absolute freedom from law. The Committee, however, after
waiting a proper time, forced these men in by
simply serving notice that thereafter they would
be treated as beyond the pale of the law—not
entitled to its protection, but amenable to its
penalties. A petition was sent to the North
Carolina Legislature, asking that the protection
of government should be extended to the Cumberland people, and showing that the latter were
loyal and orderly, prompt to suppress sedition and

lawlessness, faithful to the United States, and hostile to its enemies.[1]   To show their good feeling, the Committee made every member of the community, who had not already done so, take the oath of abjuration and fidelity.

Until full governmental protection could be secured the commonwealth was forced to act as a little sovereign state, bent on keeping the peace, and yet on protecting itself against aggression from the surrounding powers, both red and white. It was forced to restrain its own citizens, and to enter into quasi-diplomatic relations with its neighbors.   Thus early this year fifteen men, under one Colbert, left the settlements and went down the river in boats, ostensibly to trade with the Indians, but really to plunder the Spaniards on the Mississippi.   They were joined by some Chickasaws, and at first met with some success in their piratical attacks, not only on the Spanish trading-boats, but on those of the French creoles, and even the Americans, as well.   Finally, they were repulsed in an attempt against the Spaniards at Ozark; some were killed, and the rest scattered.[2] Immediately upon learning of these deeds, the Committee of Triers passed stringent resolutions forbidding all persons trading with the Indians

[1] This whole account is taken from Putnam, who has rendered such inestimable service by preserving these records.

[2] Calendar of *Virginia State Papers*, vol. iii., pp. 469, 527.

until granted a license by the Committee, and until they had furnished ample security for their good behavior. The Committee also wrote a letter to the Spanish Governor at New Orleans, disclaiming all responsibility for the piratical misdeeds of Colbert and his gang, and announcing the measures they had taken to prevent any repetition of the same in the future. They laid aside the sum of twenty pounds to pay the expenses of the messengers who carried this letter to the Virginian "agent" at the Illinois, whence it was forwarded to the Spanish Governor.[1]

One of the most difficult questions with which the Committee had to deal was that of holding a treaty with the Indians. Commissioners came out from Virginia and North Carolina especially to hold such a treaty [2]; but the settlers declined to allow it until they had themselves decided on its advisability. They feared to bring so many savages together, lest they might commit some outrage, or be themselves subjected to such at the hands of one of the many wronged and reckless whites; and they knew that the Indians would expect many presents, while there was very

[1] Putnam, pp. 185, 189, 191.

[2] Donelson, who was one of the men who became discouraged and went to Kentucky, was the Virginian commissioner. Martin was the commissioner from North Carolina. He is sometimes spoken of as if he likewise represented Virginia.

little indeed to give them. Finally, the Committee decided to put the question of treaty or no treaty to the vote of the freemen in the several stations; and by a rather narrow majority it was decided in the affirmative. The Committee then made arrangements for holding the treaty in June some four miles from Nashborough, and strictly prohibited the selling of liquor to the savages. At the appointed time, many chiefs and warriors of the Chickasaws, Cherokees, and even Creeks appeared. There were various sports, such as ball-games and foot-races; and the treaty was brought to a satisfactory conclusion.[1] It did not put a complete stop to the Indian outrages, but it greatly diminished them. The Chickasaws thereafter remained friendly; but, as usual, the Cherokee and Creek chiefs who chose to attend were unable to bind those of their fellows who did not. The whole treaty was, in fact, on both sides, of a merely preliminary nature. The boundaries it arranged were not considered final until confirmed by the treaty of Hopewell a couple of years later.

Robertson meanwhile was delegated by the unanimous vote of the settlers to go to the Assembly of North Carolina, and there petition for the establishment of a regular land office at Nashborough, and in other ways advance the interests

[1] Putnam, 196.

of the settlers.   He was completely successful in
his mission.   The Cumberland settlements were
included in a new county, called Davidson [1]; and
an Inferior Court of Pleas and Common Sessions,
vested by the act with extraordinary powers, was
established at Nashborough.   The four justices
of the new court had all been Triers of the old
Committee, and the scheme of government was
practically not very greatly changed, although
now resting on an indisputably legal basis.   The
Cumberland settlers had for years acted as an
independent, law-abiding, and orderly commonwealth, and the Court of Triers had shown great
firmness and wisdom.   It spoke well for the people
that they had been able to establish such a government, in which the majority ruled, while the
rights of each individual were secured.   Robertson
deserves the chief credit as both civil and military
leader.   The Committee of which he was a member,
had seen that justice was done between man and
man, had provided for defence against the outside
foe, and had striven to prevent any wrongs being
done to neutral or allied powers.   When they became magistrates of a county of North Carolina
they continued to act on the lines they had already

[1] In honor of General William Davidson, a very gallant and
patriotic soldier of North Carolina during the Revolutionary
War.   The county government was established in October,
1783.

marked out. The increase of population had brought an increase of wealth. The settlers were still frontiersmen, clad in buckskin or homespun, with rawhide moccasins, living in log cabins, and sleeping under bearskins on beds made of buffalo-hides; but as soon as they ventured to live on their clearings the ground was better tilled, corn became abundant, and cattle and hogs increased as the game diminished. Nashborough began to look more like an ordinary little border town.[1]

During this year Robertson carried on some correspondence with the Spanish Governor at New Orleans, Don Estevan Miro. This was the beginning of intercourse between the western settlers and the Spanish officers, an intercourse which was absolutely necessary, though it after-wards led to many intrigues and complications. Robertson was obliged to write to Miro not only to disclaim responsibility for the piratical deeds of men like Colbert, but also to protest against the conduct of certain of the Spanish agents among the Creeks and Chickamaugas. No sooner had hostilities ceased with the British than the Span-iards began to incite the savages to take up once more the hatchet they had just dropped,[2] for

[1] The justices built a court-house and jail of hewed logs, the former eighteen feet square, with a lean-to or shed of twelve feet on one side. The contracts for building were let out at vendue to the lowest bidder.

[2] Calendar of *Virginia State Papers*, iii., 358, 608, etc.

Spain already recognized in the restless borderers possible and formidable foes.

Miro, in answering Robertson, assured him that the Spaniards were very friendly to the western settlers, and denied that the Spanish agents were stirring up trouble. He also told him that the harassed Cherokees, weary of ceaseless warfare, had asked permission to settle west of the Mississippi, although they did not carry out their intention. He ended by pressing Robertson and his friends to come down and settle in Spanish territory, guaranteeing them good treatment.[1]

In spite of Miro's fair words, the Spanish agents continued to intrigue against the Americans, and especially against the Cumberland people. Yet there was no open break. The Spanish Governor was felt to be powerful for both good and evil, and at least a possible friend of the settlers. To many of their leaders he showed much favor, and the people as a whole were well impressed by him; and as a compliment to him they ultimately, when the Cumberland counties were separated from those lying to the eastward, united the former under the name of Mero[2] District.

[1] Robertson MSS. As the letter is important, I give it in full in Appendix D.

[2] So spelt; but apparently his true name was Miro.

CHAPTER IX

WHAT THE WESTERNERS HAD DONE DURING THE REVOLUTION, 1783

WHEN the first Continental Congress began its sittings, the only frontiersmen west of the mountains, and beyond the limits of continuous settlement within the old Thirteen Colonies,[1] were the two or three hundred citizens of the little Watauga commonwealth. When peace was declared with Great Britain, the backwoodsmen had spread westward, in groups, almost to the Mississippi, and they had increased in number to some twenty-five thousand souls,[2] of whom a few hundred dwelt in the bend of the Cumberland, while the rest were about equally divided between Kentucky and Holston.

This great westward movement of armed settlers was essentially one of conquest, no less than of

[1] This qualification is put in because there were already a few families on the Monongahela, the head of the Kanawha, and the upper Holston; but they were in close touch with the people behind them.

[2] These figures are simply estimates; but they are based on careful study and comparison, and though they must be some hundreds, and maybe some thousands, out of the way, are quite near enough for practical purposes.

colonization. Thronging in with their wives and children, their cattle, and their few household goods they won and held the land in the teeth of fierce resistance, both from the Indian claimants of the soil and from the representatives of a mighty and arrogant European power. The chain of events by which the winning was achieved is perfect; had any link therein snapped, it is likely that the final result would have been failure. The wide wanderings of Boon and his fellow-hunters made the country known, and awakened in the minds of the frontiersmen a keen desire to possess it. The building of the Watauga commonwealth by Robertson and Sevier gave a base of operations, and furnished a model for similar communities to follow. Lord Dunmore's war made the actual settlement possible, for it cowed the northern Indians, and restrained them from seriously molesting Kentucky during its first and most feeble years. Henderson and Boon made their great treaty with the Cherokees in 1775, and then established a permanent colony far beyond all previous settlements, entering into final possession of the new country. The victory over the Cherokees in 1776 made safe the line of communication along the Wilderness Road, and secured the chance for further expansion. Clark's campaigns gained the Illinois, or northwestern regions. The growth of Kentucky then became very rapid; and in its turn this, and the steady progress of the Watauga settlements, rendered possible Robertson's successful effort to plant a new community still farther west, on the Cumberland.

The backwoodsmen pressed in on the line of least resistance, first taking possession of the debatable hunting-grounds lying between the Algonquins of the North and the Appalachian confederacies of the South. Then they began to encroach on the actual tribal territories. Every step was accompanied by stubborn and bloody fighting with the Indians. The forest tribes were exceedingly formidable opponents; it is not too much to say that they formed a far more serious obstacle to the American advance than would have been offered by an equal number of the best European troops. Their victories over Braddock, Grant, and St. Clair, gained in each case with a smaller force, conclusively proved their superiority, on their own ground, over the best regulars, disciplined and commanded in the ordinary manner. Almost all of the victories, even of the backwoodsmen, were won against inferior numbers of Indians.[1]   The red men were fickle of

[1] That the contrary impression prevails is due to the boastful vanity which the backwoodsmen often shared with the Indians, and to the gross ignorance of the average writer concerning these border wars. Many of the accounts in the popular histories are sheer inventions. Thus, in the *Chronicles of Border Warfare*, by Alex. S. Withers (Clarksburg, Va.,

temper, and large bodies could not be kept together for a long campaign, nor, indeed, for more than one special stroke; the only piece of strategy any of their chiefs showed was Cornstalk's march past Dunmore to attack Lewis; but their tactics and discipline in the battle itself were admirably adapted to the very peculiar conditions of forest warfare. Writers who speak of them as undisciplined, or as any but most redoubtable antagonists, fall into an absurd error. An old Indian fighter, who, at the close of the last century, wrote, from experience, a good book on the subject, summed up the case very justly when he said: "I apprehend that the Indian discipline is as well calculated to answer the purpose in the woods of America as the British discipline is in

1831, p. 301), there is an absolutely fictitious account of a feat of the Kentucky Colonel Scott, who is alleged to have avenged St. Clair's defeat by falling on the victorious Indians while they were drunk, and killing two hundred of them. This story has not even a foundation in fact; there was not so much as a skirmish of the sort described. As Mann Butler—a most painstaking and truthful writer—points out, it is made up out of the whole cloth, thirty years after the event; it is a mere invention to soothe the mortified pride of the whites. Gross exaggeration of the Indian numbers and losses prevails even to this day. Mr. Edmund Kirke, for instance, usually makes the absolute or relative numbers of the Indians from five to twenty-five times as great as they really were. Still, it is hard to blame backwoods writers for such slips in the face of the worse misdeeds of the average historian of the Greek and Roman wars with barbarians.

Flanders; and British discipline in the woods is the way to have men slaughtered, with scarcely any chance of defending themselves." [1]   A comparison of the two victories gained by the backwoodsmen—at the Great Kanawha, over the Indians, and at King's Mountain over Ferguson's British and tories—brings out clearly the formidable fighting capacity of the red men.   At the Kanawha the Americans outnumbered their foes, at King's Mountain they were no more than equal; yet in the former battle they suffered twice the loss they did in the latter, inflicted much less damage in return, and did not gain nearly so decisive a victory.

The Indians were urged on by the British, who furnished them with arms, ammunition, and provisions, and sometimes also with leaders and with bands of auxiliary white troops, French, British, and tories.   It was this that gave to the Revolutionary contest its twofold character, making it on the part of the Americans a struggle for independence in the East, and in the West a war of conquest, or rather a war to establish, on behalf of all our people, the right of entry into the fertile and vacant regions beyond the Alleghanies.   The grievances of the backwoodsmen were not the same as the grievances of the men of the seacoast.

[1] Colonel James Smith, *An Account*, etc., Lexington, Ky., 1799.

The Ohio valley and the other western lands of the
French had been conquered by the British, not
the Americans. Great Britain had succeeded to
the policy as well as the possessions of her prede-
cessor, and, strange to say, had become almost
equally hostile to the colonists of her own stock.
As France had striven for half a century, so England now in her turn strove, to bar out the settlers
of English race from the country beyond the Alleghanies. The British Crown, Parliament, and people were a unit in wishing to keep woodland and
prairie for the sole use of their own merchants, as
regions tenanted only by Indian hunters and
French trappers and traders. They became the
guardians and allies of all the Indian tribes.   On
the other hand, the American backwoodsmen were
resolute in their determination to go in and possess
the land.   The aims of the two sides thus clashed
hopelessly.   Under all temporary and apparent
grounds of quarrel lay this deep-rooted jealousy
and incompatibility of interests.   Beyond the
Alleghanies the Revolution was fundamentally
a struggle between England, bent on restricting
the growth of the English race, and the Americans,
triumphantly determined to acquire the right to
conquer the continent.

Had not the backwoodsmen been successful in
the various phases of the struggle, we would certainly have been cooped up between the sea and

the mountains. If in 1774 and '76 they had been
beaten by the Ohio tribes and the Cherokees, the
border ravaged, and the settlements stopped or
forced back as during what the colonists called
Braddock's War,[1] there is every reason to believe
that the Alleghanies would have become our western frontier. Similarly, if Clark had failed in his
efforts to conquer and hold the Illinois and Vincennes, it is overwhelmingly probable that the
Ohio would have been the boundary between the
Americans and the British. Before the Revolution began, in 1774, the British Parliament had,
by the Quebec Act, declared the country between the Great Lakes and the Ohio to be part
of Canada; and under the provisions of this act
the British officers continued to do as they had
already done—that is, to hold adverse possession
of the land, scornfully heedless of the claims of the
different colonies. The country was *de facto* part
of Canada; the Americans tried to conquer it
exactly as they tried to conquer the rest of Canada;
the only difference was that Clark succeeded,
whereas Arnold and Montgomery failed.

Of course, the conquest by the backwoodsmen
was by no means the sole cause of our acquisition

[1] During this Indian war, covering the period from Braddock's to Grant's defeats, Smith, a good authority, estimates
that the frontiers were laid waste, and population driven back,
over an area nearly three hundred miles long by thirty broad.

of the West. The sufferings and victories of the Westerners would have counted for nothing had it not been for the success of the American arms in the East, and for the skill of our three treaty-makers at Paris—Jay, Adams, and Franklin, but above all the two former, and especially Jay. On the other hand, it was the actual occupation and holding of the country that gave our diplomats their vantage-ground. When the treaty was made, in 1782, the commissioners of the United States represented a people already holding the whole Ohio valley, as well as the Illinois. The circumstances of the treaty were peculiar; but here they need to be touched but briefly, and only so far as they affected the western boundaries. The United States, acting together with France and Spain, had just closed a successful war with England; but when the peace negotiations were begun, they speedily found that their allies were, if anything, more anxious than their enemy to hamper their growth. England, having conceded the grand point of independence, was disposed to be generous, and not to haggle about lesser mat-ters. Spain, on the contrary, was quite as hostile to the new nation as to England. Through her representative, Count Aranda, she predicted the future enormous expansion of the Federal Repub-lic at the expense of Florida, Louisiana, and Mexico, unless it was effectually curbed in its

youth.   The prophecy has been strikingly fulfilled,
and the event has thoroughly justified Spain's
fear; for the major part of the present territory
of the United States was under Spanish dominion
at the close of the Revolutionary War.   Spain,
therefore, proposed to hem in our growth by
giving us the Alleghanies for our western boundary.[1]   France was the ally of America; but as
between America and Spain, she favored the
latter.   Moreover, she wished us to remain weak
enough to be dependent upon her further good
graces.   The French court, therefore, proposed
that the United States should content themselves
with so much of the trans-Alleghany territory as
lay round the headwaters of the Tennessee and
between the Cumberland and Ohio.   This area
contained the bulk of the land that was already
settled [2]; and the proposal showed how important the French court deemed the fact of actual
settlement.

Thus the two allies of America were hostile to
her interests.   The open foe, England, on the
contrary, was anxious to conclude a separate
treaty, so that she might herself be in better
condition to carry on negotiations with France

[1] At the north this boundary was to follow the upper Ohio,
and end towards the foot of Lake Erie.

[2] Excluding only so much of Robertson's settlement as lay
south of the Cumberland, and Clark's conquest.

and Spain; she cared much less to keep the West
than she did to keep Gibraltar, and an agreement
with the United States about the former left her
free to insist on the retention of the latter.   Congress, in a spirit of slavish subserviency, had in-
structed the American commissioners to take no
steps without the knowledge and advice of France.
Franklin was inclined to obey these instructions;
but Jay, supported by Adams, boldly insisted on
disregarding them; and, accordingly, a separate
treaty was negotiated with England.   In settling
the claims to the western territory, much stress
was laid on the old colonial charters; but under-
neath all the verbiage it was practically admitted
that these charters conferred merely inchoate
rights, which became complete only after conquest and settlement.   The States themselves had
already by their actions shown that they admitted this to be the case.   Thus North Carolina,
when by the creation of Washington County—
now the State of Tennessee—she rounded out her
boundaries, specified them as running to the
Mississippi.   As a matter of fact, the royal grant,
under which alone she could claim the land in
question, extended to the Pacific; and the only
difference between her rights to the regions east
and west of the river was that her people were
settling in one, and could not settle in the other.
The same was true of Kentucky, and of the West

generally; if the States could rightfully claim to run to the Mississippi, they could also rightfully claim to run to the Pacific. The colonial charters were all very well as furnishing color of title; but at bottom the American claim rested on the peculiar kind of colonizing conquest so successfully carried on by the backwoodsmen. When the English took New Amsterdam they claimed it under old charters; but they very well knew that their real right was only that of the strong hand. It was precisely so with the Americans and the Ohio valley. They produced old charters to support their title; but in reality it rested on Clark's conquests and above all on the advance of the backwoods settlements.[1]

[1] Mr. R. A. Hinsdale, in his excellent work on the *Old Northwest* (New York, 1888), seems to me to lay too much stress on the weight which our charter-claims gave us, and too little on the right we had acquired by actual possession. The charter-claims were elaborated with the most wearisome prolixity at the time; but so were the English claims to New Amsterdam a century earlier. Conquest gave the true title in each case; the importance of a claim is often in inverse order to the length at which it is set forth in a diplomatic document. The West was gained by: (1) the westward movement of the backwoodsmen during the Revolution; (2) the final success of the Continental armies in the East; (3) the skill of our diplomats at Paris; failure on any one of these three points would have lost us the West.

Mr. Hinsdale seems to think that Clark's conquest prevented the Illinois from being conquered from the British by the Spaniards; but this is very doubtful. The British at Detroit would have been far more likely to have conquered

This view of the case is amply confirmed by a consideration of what was actually acquired under the treaty of peace which closed the Revolutionary struggle. Map-makers down to the present day have almost invariably misrepresented the territorial limits we gained by this treaty. They represent our limits in the West in 1783 as being the Great Lakes, the Mississippi, and the thirty-first parallel of latitude from the Mississippi to the Chattahoochee [1]; but in reality we did not acquire these limits until a dozen years later, by the treaties of Jay and Pinckney. Two points must be kept in mind: first, that during the war our ally, Spain, had conquered from England that portion of the Gulf coast known as West Florida; and, second, that when the treaty was made the United States and Great Britain mutually covenanted to do certain things, some of which were never done. Great Britain agreed to recognize the Lakes as our northern boundary, but, on the

the Spaniards at St. Louis; at any rate, there is small probability that they would have been seriously troubled by the latter. The so-called Spanish conquest of St. Joseph was not a conquest at all, but an unimportant plundering raid.

The peace negotiations are best discussed in John Jay's chapter thereon, in the seventh volume of Winsor's *Narrative and Critical History of North America*. Sparks's account is fundamentally wrong on several points. Bancroft largely follows him, and therefore repeats and shares his errors.

[1] The map in Mr. Hinsdale's book may be given as a late instance.

alleged ground that we did not fulfil certain of
our promises, she declined to fulfil this agreement, and the lake posts remained in her hands
until the Jay treaty was ratified. She likewise
consented to recognize the 31st parallel as our
southern boundary, but, by a secret article,
it was agreed that if by the negotiations she
recovered West Florida, then the boundary
should run about a hundred miles farther north,
ending at the mouth of the Yazoo. The discovery
of this secret article aroused great indignation in
Spain. As a matter of fact, the disputed territory,
the land drained by the Gulf rivers, was not England's to grant, for it had been conquered and was
then held by Spain. Nor was it given up to us
until we acquired it by Pinckney's masterly diplo-
macy. The treaty represented a mere promise,
which in part was not, and in part could not be,
fulfilled. All that it really did was to guarantee
us what we already possessed — that is, the Ohio
valley and the Illinois, which we had settled and
conquered during the years of warfare. Our
boundary lines were in reality left very vague.
On the north, the basin of the Great Lakes remained British; on the south, the lands draining
into the Gulf remained Spanish, or under Spanish
influence. The actual boundaries we acquired can
be roughly stated, in the North, to have followed
the divide between the waters of the lake and the

waters of the Ohio, and, in the South, to have run
across the heads of the Gulf rivers. Had we remained a loose confederation, these boundaries
would more probably have shrunk than advanced;
we did not overleap them until some years after
Washington had become the head of a real, not
merely a titular, nation. The peace of 1783, as
far as our western limits were affected, did nothing
more than secure us undisturbed possession of
lands from which it had proved impossible to oust
us. We were in reality given nothing more than
we had by our own prowess gained; the inference
is strong that we got what we did get only because we had won and held it.

The first duty of the backwoodsmen who thus
conquered the West was to institute civil government. Their efforts to overcome and beat back
'the Indians went hand-in-hand with their efforts
to introduce law and order in the primitive communities they founded; and as exactly as they
relied purely on themselves in withstanding outside foes, so they likewise built up their social
life and their first systems of government with
reference simply to their special needs, and without any outside help or direction. The whole
character of the westward movement, the methods
of warfare, of settlement and government, were
determined by the extreme and defiant individualism of the backwoodsmen, their inborn

independence and self-reliance, and their intensely democratic spirit. The West was won and settled by a number of groups of men, all acting independently of one another, but with a common object, and at about the same time. There was no one controlling spirit ; it was essentially the movement of a whole free people, not of a single master-mind. There were strong and able leaders, who showed themselves fearless soldiers and just law-givers, undaunted by danger, resolute to persevere in the teeth of disaster; but even these leaders are most deeply interesting because they stand foremost among a host of others like them. There were hundreds of hunters and Indian fighters like Mansker, Wetzel, Kenton, and Brady; there were scores of commonwealth founders like Logan, Todd, Floyd, and Harrod; there were many adventurous land-speculators like Henderson; there were even plenty of commanders like Shelby and Campbell. These were all men of mark; some of them exercised a powerful and honorable influence on the course of events in the West. Above them rise four greater figures, fit to be called not merely State or local, but national heroes. Clark, Sevier, Robertson, and Boon are emphatically American worthies. They were men of might in their day, born to sway the minds of others, helpful in shaping the destiny of the continent. Yet of Clark alone can it be said that he did a particular piece of work which without him would have remained undone. Sevier, Robertson, and Boon only hastened, and did more perfectly, a work which would have been done by others had they themselves fallen by the wayside.[1] Important though they are for their own sakes, they are still more important as types of the men who surrounded them.

The individualism of the backwoodsmen, however, was tempered by a sound common sense, and capacity for combination. The first hunters might come alone or in couples, but the actual colonization was done not by individuals, but by groups of individuals. The settlers brought their families and belongings, either on pack-horses along the forest trails, or in scows down the streams; they settled in palisaded villages, and immediately took steps to provide both a civil and military organization. They were men of

[1] Sevier's place would certainly have been taken by some such man as his chief rival, Tipton. Robertson led his colony to the Cumberland but a few days before old Mansker led another; and though without Robertson the settlements would have been temporarily abandoned, they would surely have been reoccupied. If Henderson had not helped Boon found Kentucky, then Hart or some other of Henderson's associates would doubtless have done so; and if Boon had been lacking, his place would probably have been taken by some such man as Logan. The loss of these men would have been very serious, but of no one of them can it be said, as of Clark, that he alone could have done the work he actually did.

facts, not theories; and they showed their usual
hard common sense in making a government.
They did not try to invent a new system; they
simply took that under which they had grown up,
and applied it to their altered conditions.   They
were most familiar with the government of the
county; and therefore they adopted this for the
framework of their little independent, self-governing commonwealths of Watauga, Cumberland, and
Transylvania.[1]

They were also familiar with the representative
system; and accordingly they introduced it into
the new communities, the little forted villages serving as natural units of representation.   They were
already thoroughly democratic, in instinct and principle, and, as a matter of course, they made the
offices elective and gave full play to the majority.
In organizing the militia they kept the old system
of county lieutenants, making them elective, not
appointive; and they organized the men on the
basis of a regiment, the companies representing
territorial divisions, each commanded by its own
officers, who were thus chosen by the fighting men
of the fort or forts in their respective districts.
Thus each of the backwoods commonwealths, dur-

[1] The last of these was the most pretentious and short-lived
and least characteristic of the three, as Henderson made an
abortive effort to graft on it the utterly foreign idea of a
proprietary colony.

ing its short-lived term of absolute freedom, re-
produced as its governmental system that of the
old colonial county, increasing the powers of the
court, and changing the justices into the elective
representatives of an absolute democracy. The
civil head, the chairman of the court or committee,
was also usually the military head, the colonel-
commandant. In fact, the military side of the
organization rapidly became the most conspicuous
and, at least, in certain crises, the most important.
There were always some years of desperate warfare during which the entire strength of the little
commonwealth was drawn on to resist outside
aggression, and during these years the chief func-
tion of government was to provide for the griping
military needs of the community, and the one
pressing duty of its chief was to lead his followers
with valor and wisdom in the struggle with the
stranger.[1]

[1] My friend, Professor Alexander Johnston, of Princeton, is
inclined to regard these frontier county organizations as re-
productions of a very primitive type of government indeed,
deeming that they were formed primarily for war against outsiders, that their military organization was the essential feature, the real reason for their existence. I can hardly accept
this view in its entirety; though fully recognizing the extreme importance of the military side of the little governments, it seems to me that the preservation of order, and
especially the necessity for regulating the disposition of the
land, were quite as powerful factors in impelling the settlers
to act together. It is important to keep in mind the terri-

These little communities were extremely independent in feeling, not only of the Federal Government, but of their parent States, and even of one another. They had won their positions by their own courage and hardihood; very few State troops and hardly a Continental soldier had appeared west of the Alleghanies. They had heartily sympathized with their several mother colonies when they became the United States, and had manfully played their part in the Revolutionary War. Moreover, they were united among themselves by ties of good-will and of services mutually rendered. Kentucky, for instance, had been succored more than once by troops raised among the Watauga Carolinians or the Holston Virginians, and in her turn she had sent needed supplies to the Cumberland. But when the strain of the war was over the separatist spirit asserted itself very strongly. The groups of western settlements not only looked on the Union itself very coldly, but they were also more or less actively hostile to their parent States, and regarded even one another as foreign communities [1]; they considered the

torial organization of the militia companies and regiments: a county and a regiment, a forted village and a company, were usually coextensive.

[1] See in Gardoqui MSS. the letters of George Rogers Clark to Gardoqui, March 15, 1788; and of John Sevier to Gardoqui, September 12, 1788; and in the Robertson MS. the letter of Robertson to McGillivray, August 3, 1788. It is necessary

Confederation as being literally only a lax league of friendship.

Up to the close of the Revolutionary contest the settlers who were building homes and States beyond the Alleghanies formed a homogeneous backwoods population. The woodchoppers, game-hunters, and Indian fighters, who dressed and lived alike, were the typical pioneers. They were a shifting people. In every settlement the tide ebbed and flowed. Some of the new-comers would be beaten in the hard struggle for existence, and would drift back to whence they had come. Of those who succeeded some would take root in the land, and others would move still farther into the wilderness. Thus each generation rolled west-ward, leaving its children at the point where the wave stopped no less than at that where it started. The descendants of the victors of King's Mountain are as likely to be found in the Rockies as in the Alleghanies.

With the close of the war came an enormous increase in the tide of immigration; and many of the new-comers were of a very different stamp from their predecessors. The main current flowed towards Kentucky, and gave an entirely different

to allude to the feeling here; but the separatist and disunion movements did not gather full force until later, and are properly to be considered in connection with post-Revolution-ary events.

character to its population. The two typical figures in Kentucky so far had been Clark and Boon, but after the close of the Revolution both of them sank into unimportance, whereas the careers of Sevier and Robertson had only begun. The disappearance of the two former from active life was partly accidental and partly a resultant of the forces that assimilated Kentucky so much more rapidly than Tennessee to the conditions prevailing in the old States. Kentucky was the best known and the most accessible of the western regions; within her own borders she was now comparatively safe from serious Indian invasion, and the tide of immigration naturally flowed thither. So strong was the current that, within a dozen years, it had completely swamped the original settlers, and had changed Kentucky from a peculiar pioneer and backwoods commonwealth into a State differing no more from Virginia, Pennsylvania, and North Carolina than these differed from one another.

The men who gave the tone to this great flood of new-comers were the gentry from the seacoast country, the planters, the young lawyers, the men of means who had been impoverished by the long-continued and harassing civil war. Straitened in circumstances, desirous of winning back wealth and position, they cast longing eyes towards the beautiful and fertile country beyond the mountains, deeming it a place that afforded unusual opportunities to the man with capital, no less than to him whose sole trust was in his own adventurous energy.

Most of the gentle folks in Virginia and the Carolinas, the men who lived in great roomy houses on their well-stocked and slave-tilled plantations, had been forced to struggle hard to keep their heads above water during the Revolution. They loyally supported the government, with blood and money; and at the same time they endeavored to save some of their property from the general wreck, and to fittingly educate their girls, and those of their boys who were too young to be in the army. The men of this stamp who now prepared to cast in their lot with the new communities formed an exceptionally valuable class of immigrants; they contributed the very qualities of which the raw settlements stood most in need. They had suffered for no fault of their own; fate had gone hard with them. The fathers had been in the Federal or Provincial congresses; the older sons had served in the Continental line or in the militia. The plantations were occasionally overrun by the enemy; and the general disorder had completed their ruin. Nevertheless, the heads of the families had striven to send the younger sons to school or college. For their daughters they did even more; and throughout the contest, even in its darkest hours, they sent them down to receive the final touches of a lady-like education at some one of the State capitals not at the moment in the hands of the enemy—such as Charleston or Philadelphia. There the young ladies were taught dancing and music, for which, as well as for their frocks and "pink cala-manco shoes," their fathers paid enormous sums in depreciated Continental currency.[1]

Even the close of active hostilities, when the British were driven from the Southern States, brought at first but a slight betterment of con-dition to the struggling people. There was no cash in the land, the paper currency was nearly worthless, every one was heavily in debt, and no one was able to collect what was owing to him. There was much mob violence, and a general re-laxation of the bonds of law and order. Even nature turned hostile; a terrible drought shrunk up all the streams until they could not turn the grist-mills, while from the same cause the crops failed almost completely. A hard winter followed, and many cattle and hogs died; so that the well-to-do were brought to the verge of bankruptcy and the poor suffered extreme privations, being forced to go fifty or sixty miles to purchase

[1] Clay MSS. Account of Robert Morris with Miss Eliza-beth Hart, during her residence in Philadelphia in 1780–81. The account is so curious that I give it in full in Appendix E.

small quantities of meal and grain at exorbitant prices.[1]

This distress at home inclined many people of means and ambition to try their fortunes in the West: while another and equally powerful motive was the desire to secure great tracts of virgin lands, for possession or speculation. Many distinguished soldiers had been rewarded by successive warrants for unoccupied land, which they entered wherever they chose, until they could claim thousands upon thousands of acres.[2] Sometimes they sold these warrants to outsiders; but whether they remained in the hands of the original holders or not, they served as a great stimulus to the westward movement, and drew many of the representatives of the wealthiest and most influential families in the parent States to the lands on the farther side of the mountains.

At the close of the Revolution, however, the men from the seacoast region formed but an insignificant portion of the western pioneers. The country beyond the Alleghanies was first won and settled by the backwoodsmen themselves, acting

[1] Clay MSS. Letters of Jesse Benton, 1782 and '83. See Appendix F.

[2] Thus Colonel William Christian, for his services in Braddock's and Dunmore's wars and against the Cherokees, received many warrants; he visited Kentucky to enter them, nine thousand acres in all. See *Life of Caleb Wallace*, by William H. Whitsitt, Louisville, 1888.

under their own leaders, obeying their own desires, and following their own methods. They were a marked and peculiar people. The good and evil traits in their character were such as naturally belonged to a strong, harsh, and homely race, which, with all its shortcomings, was nevertheless bringing a tremendous work to a triumphant conclusion. The backwoodsmen were above all things characteristically American; and it is fitting that the two greatest and most typical of all Americans should have been respectively a sharer and an outcome of their work. Washington himself passed the most important years of his youth heading the westward movement of his people; clad in the traditional dress of the backwoodsmen, in tasselled hunting-shirt and fringed leggings, he led them to battle against the French and Indians, and helped to clear the way for the American advance. The only other man who, in the American roll of honor, stands by the side of Washington was born when the distinctive work of the pioneers had ended; and yet he was bone of their bone and flesh of their flesh; for from the loins of this gaunt frontier folk sprang mighty Abraham Lincoln.

APPENDIX A

TO CHAPTER III

(Haldimand MSS., Series B, vol. cxxiii., p. 302.)

SIR,

My Letter of the 22nd & 23rd of July informed you of the reports brought us of the Enemy's motions at that time which was delivered by the Chiefs of the standing Stone Village & confirmed by Belts & Strings of Wampum in so earnest a manner that could not but gain Credit with us. We had upon this occasion the greatest Body of Indians collected to an advantageous peice of ground near the Picawee Village that have been assembled in this Quarter since the commencement of the War & perhaps may never be in higher spirits to engage the Enemy, when the return of Scouts from the Ohio informed us that the account we had received was false; this disappointment notwithstanding all our endeavours to keep them together occasioned them to disperse in disgust with each other, the inhabitants of this Country who were the most immediately interested in keeping in a Body ware the first that broke off & though we advanced towards the Ohio with upwards of three hundred Hurons & Lake Indians few of the Delawares, Shawanese, or Mingoes followed us.   On our arrival at the Ohio we remain'd still in uncertainty with respect to the Enemys motions, & it was thought best from hence to send Scouts to the Falls & that the main Body should advance into the Enemy's Country and endeavour to lead out a party from some of their Forts by which we might be able to gain some certain Intelligence accordingly we crossed the Ohio and arrived the 18th Inst. at one of the Enemy's settlements—call'd Bryans Station, but the Indians discovering their numbers prevented their coming out and the Lake Indians finding this rush'd up to the Fort and set several out Houses on fire but at too great a distance to touch the Fort the Wind blowing the Contrary way.   the firing continued this day during which time a Party of about twenty of the Enemy approached a part that happened not to be Guarded & about one half of them reached it the rest being drove back by a few Indians who ware near the place, the next morning finding it to no purpose to keep up a fire longer upon the Fort as we were getting men killed, & had already several men wounded which ware to be carried, the Indians determined to retreat & the 20th reached the Blue Licks where we encamp'd near an advantageous Hill and expecting the enemy would pursue determined to wait for

them keeping spies at the Lick who in the morning
of the 21st discovered them & at half past 7
o'clock we engaged them & in a short time totally
defeated them, we ware not much superior to them
in Numbers they being about two hundred picked
men from the settlement of Kentucky. Commanded by the Colonels Todd, Trigg, Boon &
Todd, with the Majors Harlin, and McGary most
of whom fell in the action, from the best inquiry I
could make upon the spot there was upwards of
one hundred & forty killed & taken with near
an hundred rifles several being thrown into a deep
River that ware not recovered. It was said by
the Prisoners that a Colonel Logan was expected
to join them with one hundred men more we
waited upon the ground to-day for him, but seeing
there was not much probability of his coming we
set off & crossed the ohio the second day after the
action. Captain Caldwell & I arrived at this place
last night with a design of sending some assistance
to those who are bring on the wounded people
who are fourteen in number, we had Ten Indians
kill'd with Mr. La Bute of the Indian Department
who by sparing the life of one of the Enemy &
endeavouring to take him Prisoner loss'd his own,
to our disappointment we find no Provisions
brought forward to this place or likely hood of
any for some time, and we have entirely subsisted
since we left this on what we got in the Woods,

and took from the Enemy.   The Prisoners all agree
in their account that there is no talk of an Expedition from that Quarter, nor indeed are they
able without assistance from the Colonies, & that
the Militia of the Country have been employed
during the summer in Building the Fort at the
Falls, & what they call a Row Galley which has
made one trip up the River to the Mouth of the big
Miamis & occasioned that alarm that created us
so much trouble, she carries one six pounder, six
four pounders, & two two pounders & Row's
eighty oars, she had at the big Bone Lick one hundred men but being chiefly draughts from the
Militia many of them left her on different parts of
the River.   One of the Prisoners mentions the
arrival of Boats lately from Fort Pitt & that
Letters has pass'd between the Commanding
officer of that place & Mr. Clark intimating that
preparation is making there for another Expedition into the Indian Country, we have since our
arrival heard some thing of this matter and that
the particulars has been forwarded to you, a Detachment of Rangers with a large party of Delawares, & Shawanese are gone that way who will be
able to discover the truth of this matter.

I am this day favoured with yours of the 6th
Augt. containing the report of Isaac Gians concerning the Cruelties of the Indians.   It is true
they have made sacrifices to their revenge after the

massacre of their women & children some being
known to them to be perpetrators of it, but it was
done in my absence or before I could reach any of
the places to interfere. And I can assure you Sir
that there is not a white person here wanting in
their duty to represent to the Indians in the
strongest terms the highest abhorence of such
conduct as well as the bad consequences that may
attend it to both them & us being contrary to the
rule of carrying on war by Civilized nations, however it is not improbable that Gians may have
exaggerated matters greatly being notoriously
known for a disaffected person and concerned in
sending Prisoners away with Intelligence to the
Enemy at the time Captain Bird came out as
we ware then informed. I flatter myself that I
may by this time have an answer to the Letter
I had the honor of writing to the Commandr. in
Chief on leaving Detroit. Mr. Elliot is to be the
Bearer of this who will be able to give you any
farther information necessary respecting matters
here.

I am with respect Sir your most obedient & Very
Humble Servant

A. McKEE.

SHAWANESE COUNTRY,
    August 28th, 1782.

Major DE PEYSTER.

APPENDIX B

TO CHAPTER III

(Haldimand MSS., Series B, vol. cxxiii., p. 297.)

Extract of a letter from Captain Caldwell, dated at Wakitamiki, August 26, 1782:

"When I last had the pleasure of writing you, I expected to have struck at Wheeling as I was on my march for that place, but was overtaken by a Messenger from the Shawnese, who informed me that the Enemy was on their march for their Country, which obliged me to turn their way, and to my great mortification found the alarm false & that it was owing to a Gondals coming up to the mouth of Licking Creek, and landing some men upon the South side of the Ohio which when the Indians saw supposed it must be Clark.   It would have been a lucky circumstance if they had come on, as I had eleven hundred Indians on the ground, and three hundred within a day's march of me. When the Report was contradicted They mostly left us, many of them had left their Towns no way equipped for War, as they expected as well as myself to fight in a few days, notwithstanding I was determined to pay the Enemy a visit with as many Indians as would follow me: accordingly I crossed the Ohio with three hundred Indians & Rangers, and Marched for Bryants Station on Kentuck, and

surrounded the Fort the 15th in the morning, &
tried to draw 'em out by sending up a small party
to try to take a Prisoner and shew themselves, but
the Indians were in too great a hurry and the
whole shewed too soon—I then saw it was in vain
to wait any longer and so drew nigh the Fort,
burnt 3 Houses which are part of the Fort but
the wind being contrary prevented it having the
desired effect. Killed upwards of 300 Hogs, 150
Head of Cattle, and a number of Sheep, took a
number of Horses, pull'd up and destroy'd their
Potatoes, cut down a great deal of their Corn,
burn't their Hemp and did other considerable
damage—by the Indians exposing themselves too
much we had 5 Killed & 2 Wounded.

"We retreated the 16th and came as far as
Biddle's former Station, when nigh 100 Indians
left me, as they went after their things they left
at the Forks of Licking, and I took the Road by
the blue Licks as it was nigher and the ground
more advantageous in case the Enemy should pursue us—got to the Licks on the 17th and encamped.

"On the 18th in the morning, one of my party
that was watching the Road came in and told me
the Enemy was within a mile of us, upon which I
drew up to fight them—at $\frac{1}{2}$ past seven they advanced in three Divisions in good order, they had
spied some of us and it was the very place they
expected to overtake us.—We had but fired one

Gun till they gave us a Volley and stood to it very well for some time, 'till we rushed in upon them when they broke immediately.—We pursued for about two miles, and as the enemy was mostly on horseback, it was in vain to follow further.

"We killed and took one hundred and Forty six. Amongst the killed is Col. Todd the Commandr Col. Boon, Lt. Col. Trigg, Major Harlin who commanded their Infantry, Major Magara and a number more of their officers. Our loss is Monsr. La Bute killed, he died like a warrior fighting Arm to Arm, six Indians Killed and ten wounded—The Indians behaved extremely well, and no people could behave better than both Officers & men in general—The Indians I had with me were the Wyandots and Lake Indians—The Wyandots furnished me with what provisions I wanted, and behaved extremely well."

APPENDIX C

TO CHAPTER VI

It has been so habitual among American writers to praise all the deeds, good, bad, and indifferent, of our Revolutionary ancestors, and to belittle and make light of what we have recently done, that most men seem not to know that the Union and Confederate troops in the Civil War fought far more stubbornly and skilfully than did their forefathers at the time of the Revolution. It is impossible to estimate too highly the devoted patriotism and statesmanship of the founders of our national life; and however high we rank Washington, I am confident that we err, if anything, in not ranking him high enough, for on the whole the world has never seen a man deserving to be placed above him; but we certainly have overestimated the actual fighting qualities of the Revolutionary troops, and have never laid enough stress on the folly and jealousy with which the States behaved during the contest. In 1776, the Americans were still in the gristle; and the feats of arms they then performed do not bear comparison with what they did in the prime of their lusty youth, eighty or ninety years later. The Continentals who had been long drilled by Washington and Greene were most excellent troops; but they never had a chance to show at their best, because they were always mixed in with a mass of poor soldiers, either militia or just-enlisted regulars.

The resolute determination of the Americans to win, their trust in the justice of their cause, their refusal to be cast down by defeat, the success with which they overran and conquered the West at the very time they were struggling for life or

death in the East, the heroic grandeur of their
great leader—for all this they deserve full credit.
But the militia who formed the bulk of the Revolutionary armies did not generally fight well.
Sometimes, as at Bunker's Hill and King's Mountain, they did excellently, and they did better, as
a rule, than similar European bodies—than the
Spanish and Portuguese peasants in 1807–12, for
instance.   At that time it was believed that the
American militia could not fight at all; this was
a mistake, and the British paid dearly for making
it; but the opposite belief, that militia could be
generally depended upon, led to quite as bad
blunders, and the politicians of the Jeffersonian
school who encouraged the idea made us in our
turn pay dearly for our folly in after years, as at
Bladensburg and along the Niagara frontier in
1812.   The Revolutionary War proved that hastily
gathered militia, justly angered and strung to
high purpose, could sometimes whip regulars, a
feat then deemed impossible; but it lacked very
much of proving that they would usually do this.
Moreover, even the stalwart fighters who followed Clark and Sevier, and who did most important and valorous service, cannot point to any
one such desperate deed of fierce courage as that
of the doomed Texans under Bowie and Davy
Crockett in the Alamo.

A very slight comparison of the losses suffered in

the battles of the Revolution with those suffered in the battles of the Civil War is sufficient to show the superiority of the soldiers who fought in the latter (and a comparison of the tactics and other features of the conflicts will make the fact even clearer). No Revolutionary regiment or brigade suffered such a loss as befell the 1st Minnesota at Gettysburg, where it lost 215 out of 263 men, 82 per cent.; the 9th Illinois at Shiloh, where it lost 366 out of 578 men, 63 per cent.; the 1st Maine at Petersburg, which lost 632 out of 950 men, 67 per cent.; or Caldwell's brigade of New York, New Hampshire, and Pennsylvania troops, which, in Hancock's attack at Fredericksburg, lost 949 out of 1947 men, 48 per cent.; or, turning to the Southern soldiers, such a loss as that of the 1st Texans at Antietam, when 186 out of 226 men fell, 82 per cent.; or of the 26th North Carolina, which, at Gettysburg, lost 588 out of 820 men, 72 per cent.; or the 8th Tennessee, at Murfreesboro, which lost 306 out of 444 men, or 68 per cent.; or Garnett's brigade of Virginians, which, in Pickett's charge, lost 941 men out of 1427, or 65 per cent.

There were over a hundred regiments, and not a few brigades, in the Union and Confederate armies, each of which in some one action suffered losses averaging as heavy as the above. The Revolutionary armies cannot show such a roll of honor as this. Still, it is hardly fair to judge them by this comparison, for the Civil War saw the most bloody and desperate fighting that has occurred of late years. None of the European contests since the close of the Napoleonic struggles can be compared to it. Thus, the Light Brigade at Balaclava lost only 37 per cent., or 247 men out of 673, while the Guards at Inkermann lost but 45 per cent., or 594 out of 1331; and the heaviest German losses in the Franco-Prussian war were but 49 and 46 per cent., occurring, respectively, to the Third Westphalian Regiment at Mars-le-Tours, and the Garde-Schutzen battalion at Metz.

These figures are taken from *Regimental Losses in the American Civil War*, by Colonel William F. Fox, Albany, 1881; the loss in each instance includes few or no prisoners save in the cases of Garnett's brigade and of the Third Westphalian Regiment.

APPENDIX D

TO CHAPTER VIII

(From the Robertson MSS., vol. i., letter of Don Miro.)

New Orleans, the 20th April, 1783.

Sir,

I received yours of 29th January last, & am highly pleased in seeing the good intentions of the People of that District, & knowing the falsehood of the report we have heard they are willing to attack their Province. You ought to make the same account of the news you had that the Indians have been excited in their Province against you, since I wrote quite the contrary at different times to Alexander McGillevray to induce him to make peace, & lastly he answered me that he gave his word to the Governor of North Carolina that the Creeks would not trouble again those settlements: notwithstanding after the letter received from you, and other from Brigadier general Daniel Smith Esqr I will write to him engaging him to be not more troublesome to you.

I have not any connection with Cheroquis & Marcuten, but as they go now & then to Illinois I will give advice to that Commander to induce them to be quiet: in respect to the former in the month of May of last year they asked the permission of settling them selves on the west side of the Mississippi River which is granted & they act accordingly, you plainly see you are quite free from their incursions

I will give the Passeport you ask for your son-in-law, & I will be highly pleased with his coming down to setle in this Province & much more if you, & your family should come along with him, since I can assure you that you will find here your welfare, without being either molested on religious matters or paying any duty & under the circumstances of finding allwais market for your crops which makes every one of the planters settled at Natchez or elsewhere to improve every day, much more so than if they were to purchase the Lands, as they are granted gratis

I wish to be usefull to you being with regard sir
Your most obt. hl. servant
(Dupte.)   ESTEVAN MIRO.
Colonel JAMES ROBERTSON, Esqr.

The duplicity of the Spaniards is well illustrated by the fact that the Gardoqui MSS. give clear proof that they were assisting the Creeks with arms and ammunition at the very time Miro was writing these letters. See the Gardoqui MSS., *passim*, especially Miro's letter of June 28, 1786.

APPENDIX E

TO CHAPTER IX

Account of Robert Morris with Miss Betsey Hart,

Dr.   MISS HARTE   IN ACCOUNT

[Oldest daughter of Colonel Thomas Hart.

			Continental			Exchange	Specie		
1780 Aug.	29	To cash paid for a Pair of Shoes for you......	£64	2	6	at 60 for 1	£ 1	1	4½
		To a Chest of Sugar delivered Mrs. Brodeau & Porterage..........	1107	15		Do	18	9	3
		To two ps Sheeting Delivered Ditto.........	1116	10		Do	18	12	0
		To Cash paid Wm. McDugall's Bill for one & a half Quarters Tuition at Dancing.......	223	10		Do	3	12	6
		Paid E. Denaugheys Bill for washing Done for you................	95	12	6	Do	1	11	10½
Dec.	6	To Ditto paid Hannah Estys Bill for making Frocks for you...... £257 10/ Paid D Denaugheys Bill for Washg... £125.12.6	383	2	6	at 75 for 1	5	2	2
	29	To Ditto paid for pair of Pink Calemancoi Shoes for you.............	78	15	0	Do	1	1	0
1781 Feb.	3	To Ditto paid B. Victor your music master for one Quarter Tuition of Music............	506	5	0	75 for 1	6	15	0
		To the following Articles delivered Mrs. Brodeau on your Accot. One Firkin of Butter one Box of Candles & a Box of Soap Amounting p Account to...........	629	1	2	Do	8	7	9
		To cash paid Mrs. Brodeau in full of her Accot. to October last against you..........	3856	17	6	Do	51	8	6
							£115	3	5
		Allowed for Depreciation...............					57	13	7
							£172	17	0

Philadelphia, 1780–81. From the Clay MSS.

CURRENT WITH   ROBERT MORRIS   Cr.

She married Dr. Richard Pendell.]

	Con-tinental	Exchg	Specie

Received Philad. April 7th 1781 the One hundred and Seventy two Pounds 17/ State Specie being in full the amount of the annexed account for Robt. Morris

£172. 17. State Specie   J. SWANNICK

APPENDIX F

In the Clay MSS. the letters of Jesse Benton to Colonel Hart, of December 4, 1782, and March 22, 1783, paint vividly the general distress in the Carolinas. They are taken up mostly with accounts of bad debts and of endeavors to proceed against various debtors; they also touch on other subjects.

In the first, of December 4, 1782, Benton writes: "It seems the powers above are combined against us this year. Such a Drouth was never known here [in the upper Carolinas] before; Corn sells from the stack at 4 & 5/ p. Bushel, Wheat 6 & 8/, Rye the same, Oats 3/6 &c &c . . . I have not had Water to keep the Grist Mill Fuling Mill and Oyl Mill at Work before this Week . . . Johny Rice has gone to Kentucky with his goods to buy Furs, but before he went we talked of your debts and he did not like to be concerned, saying he should gain ill will for no profit; However I will immediately enforce the Law to recover your Debts . . . the Lands which You had of me would sell as soon as any but this hard year makes many settlers and few buyers. I have heard nothing more of Major Haywoods desire of purchasing & all I ever heard upon the subject was from his son-in-law who now appears very sick of his late purchase of Elegant Buildings.

. . . Your Brother Capt. Nat Hart, our worthy
and respectable Friend, I doubt is cut off by the
Savages at the time and in the manner as first
represented, to wit, that he went out to hunt his
horses in the month of July or August it is supposed the Indians in Ambuscade between Boons-
boro and Knockbuckle, intended to take him
Prisoner, but killd his horse and at the same time
broke his Thigh, that the savages finding their
Prisoner with his Thigh broken was under the
necessity of putting him to Death by shooting
him through the Heart at so small a Distance as
to Powder burn his Flesh. He was Tomahawkd,
scalped & lay two Days before he was found and
buried. This Account has come by difrent hands
& confirmd to Col. Henderson by a Letter from an
intimate Friend of his at Kentuck."

This last bit of information is sandwiched in
between lamentations over bad debts, concerning
which the writer manifested considerably more
emotion than over the rather startling fate of
Captain Hart.

The second letter contains an account of the
"trafficking off" of a wagon and fine pair of
Pennsylvania horses, the news that a debt had
been partially liquidated by the payment of sixty
pound's worth of rum and sugar, which in turn
went to pay workmen, and continues: "The common people are and will be much distressed for

want of Bread. I have often heard talk of
Famine, but never thought of seeing any thing so
much like it as the present times in this part of
the Country.   Three fourths of the Inhabitants of
this country are obliged to purchase their Bread
at 50 & 60 miles distance at the common price of
16/ and upwards per barrel. The winter has been
very hard upon the live stock & I am convinced
that abundance of Hogs and Cattle will die this
Spring for want of Food. . . . Cash is now
scarcer here than it ever was before. . . . I
have been industrious to get the Mills in good repair and have succeeded well, but have rcd. very
little benefit from them yet owing entirely to the
general failure of a Crop.   We have done no Mer-
chant work in the Grist Mill, & she only supplies
my Family and workmen with Bread.   Rye, the
people are glad to eat.   Flaxseed the cattle have
chiefly eaten though I have got as much of that
article as made 180 Gallons of Oyl at 4/ per bushel.
The Oyl is in great demand; I expect two dollars
p. Gallon for it at Halifax or Edenton, & perhaps a
better price. We were very late in beginning with
the Fulling Business; for want of water. . . .
[there are many] Mobbs and commotions among
the People."

END OF VOLUME III